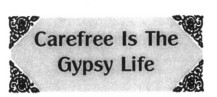

Carefree Is The
Gypsy Life

Carefree Is The Gypsy Life

Aaron Braude

PENTLAND PRESS, INC.
ENGLAND • USA • SCOTLAND

PUBLISHED BY PENTLAND PRESS, INC.
5124 Bur Oak Circle, Raleigh, North Carolina 27612
United States of America
919-782-0281

ISBN 1-57197-049-5
Library of Congress Catalog Card Number 96-71765

Printed in the United States of America

Contents

Acknowledgments

My gratitude and heartfelt thanks to Dorothy, my wife, who was by my side during this entire time; who guided me and kept the stress level within bounds during periods of panic. She devoted endless hours typing this manuscript without one slight whisper of complaint.

To Clover Linton, a jewel, who motivated me to write this journal, critiqued it, constantly kept my morale from slipping into despair with kind words and judicious advice. Without these two lovely ladies this book would have never happened.

To Beverly and Bruce Gladstone for technical and literary help. To Mary Caridi for determinedly typing the manuscript on computer disks, through sickness and health; and for minor grammatical and spelling corrections. To Jack Kennedy for his generosity in making his high tech equipment available. To Jerome Orloff, for his patience and steadfastness in teaching me how to use my Word Processor. And to Mandy Biazo for so much help and advice in many areas.

Introduction

Sometime in late 1978, my wife, Dorothy, and I got the wild idea of taking a trip to Europe. Because of our age (I was sixty-eight, Dorothy sixty seven) and because of our limited financial resources, we decided we would make it a big one. We felt it would be our only extensive trip, as we could afford no other. Our previous trips—mostly camping—had been in the United States, Canada, and Mexico. We had also visited Hawaii and Cuba.

So, after many days of serious discussion, painstaking planning, and carefully counting our cash, the die was cast, our fate sealed, and come hell or high water, we definitely decided to make this a year long vacation; a once-in-a-lifetime event.

Our plan was to purchase, locally, a small, diesel-fueled Volkswagen car and pick it up in Brussels, Belgium, after first spending a month in Great Britain without a car. We both felt apprehensive about driving in Britain on the opposite side of the roads. This isn't true of the rest of Europe.

Now that we made the decision to make this trip, we visited several European countries' tourist offices, located in Los Angeles and San Francisco. We wrote for literature to those offices we couldn't visit and got every pertinent bit of information available from travel agents. We received maps and tour books from the Auto Club, and bought Frommer's book, *Europe on $15 a Day* (remember, this was 1979). However, it was closer to fifteen dollars an hour (not really). Our daughter-in-law gave us the *Harvard Youth Travel Book* and an excellent book of maps of Europe.

We then spent hours and days planning our trip, giving serious consideration to the weather in each country to make sure we'd be in the
right place at the right time of the year. This was indeed quite a pro-
ject, as we planned to be entirely on our own.

The only exception to being completely on our own was in the
USSR. There, if you don't go with an organized tour, but plan to go on
your own or drive your own car, you must prepare an itinerary of the
cities you wish to visit, the date on which you will arrive in each city,
the length of stay in each city, and the type of accommodations you
desire. This itinerary must be arranged in the US prior to your visit,
through a travel agent who deals with Intourist, the Soviet State Travel
Agency in Moscow. Our San Francisco travel agent submitted our itinerary—over which I had spent hour upon hour preparing—to Intourist.
Intourist would then return it to our agent either approved as submitted or modified.

Our itinerary was accepted by Intourist, with one major change.
Our plans called for us to camp in the USSR for a month. We request-
ed a ten-day stay in Moscow. For whatever reason, Intourist granted us
only five days. However, our travel agent was Russian, born in China.
Her parents had fled the revolution. She was a real sharp lady. She
arranged a five-day stay in a campground in Moscow, then one night
in a hotel in Suzdal, not far from Moscow; then, back to the same
campground in Moscow for an additional five days! This, Intourist
accepted.

All we had to do now was pay in advance for all our accommodations while there. Our accommodations in the campground turned out
to be furnished cabins that averaged about sixteen dollars a night—a
bit steep, we thought. We had no idea what these cabins would be
like. Nevertheless, our stay in the Soviet Union was all set.

In all the other countries we planned to visit, we intended to travel completely uninhibited—and totally uninformed about what we might
expect. Since we planned to spend a whole year in Europe, our inten-
tions were to camp wherever possible and to travel as cheaply as possible.

Fortunately, we have a very dear friend who has traveled considerably in Europe. On one trip, he and his wife camped for thirteen
months. His advice to us was to go to Bed and Breakfast (B&B) establishments wherever such accommodations would be available. He dis-

couraged camping. He insisted that at our age, and given the not-too-pleasant camping conditions in much of Europe in the summer, it would be more pleasant and comfortable for us to go to B&Bs, despite the fact that it would cost us more money. Of all the advice we received from other travelers, his was the soundest, and ultimately proved to be extremely exciting and rewarding.

Next came the packing; trying to calculate what and how much to bring for all four seasons. Needless to say, we packed enough for four seasons for four years! We could have made back some of our expenses by selling our surplus clothes. As a matter of fact, in the USSR we were offered $150 (in rubles) for Levi jeans—the one item neither of us possessed.

I must also disclose additional information. Most of the events you'll read about happened during our 1979 trip. However, we experienced events and "fairy tales" of a similar nature during our second six-month trip in 1984; I have added several of these. You also may wonder why I mentioned that our trip in 1979 lasted just six months, and that we made another six-month trip in 1984. This is explained near the end of this journal.

The many experiences, unusual events, and memorable happenings will live with us forever! What happened to us seemed more like a fairy tale than true life experiences.

All of these events have been excerpted from extensive, detailed logs that I kept on our two trips.

Carefree is the Gypsy's Life

It was Monday, 2 April 1979, a warm day in Los Angeles, when Dorothy and I took off from the airport into uncharted waters (for us) for a year of adventure, visiting much of Western and Eastern Europe, completely on our own.

The fun began as off we went into the wild blue yonder via Freddy Laker's cheapie airlines, British-based and no longer in existence.

I would be less than honest if I didn't say we were a bit tense and apprehensive about traveling completely by ourselves, especially in the (then) socialist countries. We had no idea what to expect, and no one to give us any advice or hints about what it would be like touring Eastern Europe. It came as a real shock when Dorothy told me, after we got back home, that she honestly feared we'd never come back. She was that frightened!

The long flight to Gatwick Airport in London and lack of sleep made us both groggy, but we managed to schlep all our luggage and hop aboard the shuttle train that would take us to Victoria Station. We settled down in one of the compartments, in which there was another passenger, a rather attractive young woman. She had a pack on her back and appeared somewhat disheveled. She kept searching through her pack and the several pockets in her jacket, shirt, and elsewhere for her train ticket, cigarettes, matches, or whatever, and appeared to be flustered. I turned to her and said, "You seem to be having a bit of trouble." This started a conversation among us, and we soon became very friendly. As so often happens when strangers meet, especially confined as we three were in a train compartment, the conversation followed that usual pattern of inquiry, such as, "Where are you going?", "How long will you stay?", and other questions about family, employment, hobbies, and non-controversial subjects of a not-too-personal nature.

Thus we found out that Brigitte was a nineteen-year-old Swedish citizen, lived in a suburb of Stockholm with an older sister, mother, and father, and was going to college in Dallas, Texas. This explained her ability with the English language.

About us, she learned our ages, that we lived in a small country town in north-central California, had two children and five grandchildren, were retired, that this was the first day of our first trip to Europe, and that we intended to visit Sweden during our year of traveling.

When we were discussing Sweden, I mentioned that in our travel books there were practically no listings of modestly-priced accommodations in Stockholm. Immediately, Brigitte replied, "No problem, you can stay with my parents!" She continued, "My father speaks English and loves to talk with Americans." Well, you can believe me, Dorothy and I were absolutely flabbergasted. Here was a nineteen-year-old girl offering to put us up in her parents' home after knowing us less than half an hour, and her parents not knowing us at all. Besides, she obviously hadn't consulted with them previously as to whether we would be welcome. This was unheard of!

Moments later, for whatever reason, I mentioned that we were Jewish. Brigitte, very animated, replied, "My father is Jewish also! My mother is French."

Soon, we drew near Victoria Station where we were to part company. Again, the customary procedure, in such instances, is to exchange addresses before saying good-bye, which we did.

For our part, we pretty much dismissed the idea of staying at her home. We figured Brigitte's offer was merely a spontaneous, friendly gesture on the part of a teen-aged girl; we weren't about to impose ourselves on her parents. It would be too embarrassing if they refused us. We would leave to chance where we would stay in Stockholm, and worry about it when we got there. After all, except for our month in the USSR, where our accommodations were prearranged, we would be faced with finding reasonable places to stay no matter where we were. With no previous experience in this matter, we would have to rely on the Frommer and Harvard travel books we brought along, the little "i"

(signifying tourist information offices in most countries), our wits, and trust to luck.

After bidding Brigitte adieu at Victoria Station, we went to the Tourist Bureau office and for a fee of 1.20 pounds they located a small B&B for us. The British pound, incidentally, was valued at two US dollars. The B&B where we were to stay was eight pounds, or sixteen dollars—not bad. This hotel was far from elegant, but adequate.

At this point let me say, as I said before, that we were traveling on a tight budget. We calculated that we should be able to get by on one thousand dollars a month. This would include all our expenditures except our round trip flight from the US, our car insurance, and a couple of items related to the car purchase. So sixteen dollars a night for a place to stay and breakfast seemed reasonable enough.

Breakfast in these B&Bs in England was pretty standard, we found. They consisted of overcooked eggs, undercooked bacon, and hard, dry toast. Sometimes, there were corn flakes and milk available.

Another feature of these B&Bs was that they all were two or three stories high, with no elevators and narrow stair wells. This was quite a burden and annoyance for me since I had to carry most of our luggage. It was quite obvious that this wouldn't do. After some inquiring we found out about a storage company near Victoria Station. We proceeded to put half of our luggage in storage for a month. Now the world looked brighter!

After storing our surplus luggage, then consulting Frommer's book, we found an upscale B&B for nine pounds (eighteen dollars). Like so many others we later discovered, it was owned by Iranian people who called themselves Persians, and it was operated by several members of the family.

London, it appeared, was host to many foreigners. We surmised that most of them were British citizens from Africa, the Middle-East, and the Far East—all races, colors, and creeds. And from our limited experiences, nearly all of them spoke English. The fact that so many of these people spoke English solved a minor problem for us—a rather strange problem.

Being total strangers trying to find our way around in a city as large as London, with its confusing street system, we were forced to ask directions quite often. We invariably would ask someone who looked "English" (i.e. Caucasian) for the information we sought. Much to our

chagrin, and at times embarrassment, we would have difficulty understanding the reply.

One time, we asked a non-Caucasian person and were pleasantly
surprised to find we could understand him better. We discovered that
their rapid speech and unfamiliar dialects made many British people
hard to understand. Indians, Jamaicans, Africans, etc., had a slower
rhythm and were easier to understand. From then on, while in Britain,
they were the people we asked for information.

We spent the next couple of days running down to the Polish and
East German Embassies in order to get our visas to enter these countries. We planned to drive our car, but follow a tour bus for a seven-
day tour of East Germany, staying at the same hotels and eating at the
same restaurants as the tourists on the bus. The travel agent discouraged this and said that for a little more money we should drive to
East Berlin, leave our car there, and go with the other tourists on the
bus. This made sense, so we made these arrangements. At the Polish
embassy we had no problem getting visas.

As a result of all this activity, we did little sightseeing. On our third
day in London, we set out to "do the town." We walked and gawked;
rode the double-deck buses and the "tube," trying to see as much of
London as we could on this, our first day of sightseeing.

At lunch time we popped into a pub, the "Crown and Scepter," for
bangers and beer, a standard meal in most pubs. For most of our stay
in Britain, we ate in pubs. The food in this pub was quite good and
fairly adequate; it was fun to eat there and we loved its name. It sounded very romantic, and in a sense historical. We found this true of so
many of the pubs we patronized all over Britain.

At the "Crown and Scepter," it was fairly crowded, but we managed
to find a seat and ordered lunch. Seated next to us was a couple in
their mid-to-late twenties. It must have been obvious to them that we
were Americans—probably because of our speech—so they opened a
conversation with us. Their names were Jonas and Eva. They both
spoke good, understandable English.

As it turned out, they were Swedish and on their honeymoon,
though she was about six-months pregnant! Again, there was the
usual "tourist talk" as when we met Brigitte. We outlined our planned
travel route, telling them that after picking up our car in Brussels, we
would be heading north through Holland, Denmark, Norway, and

Sweden. Jonas then said, "If you go via the main route from Oslo, Norway to Stockholm you will pass close by where Eva and I live, so please drop in and spend some time with us!" Eva also insisted we visit them.

Dorothy and I looked at each other in complete astonishment. We both thought that the Swedes are either trusting, super-friendly people or they are naive and somewhat provincial if they all react to strangers the way Eva, Jonas, and Brigitte reacted toward us. In both instances we'd known each other less than an hour! Before parting, we did the usual—exchanged names, addresses, and phone numbers, and said our good-byes.

As with Brigitte, we never really intended to stay with Eva and Jonas. Nevertheless, Dorothy and I were both thrilled at the reception we'd gotten from these kids, especially considering we were two generations apart in age! What did they find in common with us to react to us as they did? The Swedes must just be great people.

Before we left on our trip, a very good friend and neighbor of ours told us that when we got to London we should absolutely contact his brother, Tony, who lives there. Our friend, Peter, said that he would alert Tony that we would contact him when we arrived in London.

When we were settled in our second B&B, we called Tony and he invited us to his home for dinner. On the evening of the dinner, our host came for us in his car. He and his wife live in a lovely home, nicely and comfortably furnished. The ambiance was conducive to relaxing, which we did, over hors d'oeuvres, drinks, and small talk.

Soon dinner was served and it was most enjoyable, especially after nearly a week of delicatessen dinners and inexpensive restaurants. Our hostess was certainly a good cook and we were enjoying to the fullest the delicious food and the delightful conversation.

In the course of our conversation, we discovered that our host had previously served for the State Department in the USSR. Since we were to drive a diesel-fueled car in Russia, we had him print the word "diesel" on a small card for us. We wanted to be absolutely certain that when we were in the USSR we wouldn't get fouled up (literally and figuratively) by getting the wrong fuel.

It soon was time to depart and our host drove us back to our B&B. This evening with these folks was quite unexpected, but most gratifying.

Time slipped by like greased lightning and our first week in London was history. Looking back, it was during that first week that we were faced with a stark realization—the one-thousand-dollar-a-month budget we'd planned to live within was shot to Hell! The costs of our B&Bs were pretty much within the budget, but our food costs were much greater than we anticipated. And we didn't anticipate the bus, tube, and tram, fares to be so frequent and so great.

One expense that we didn't take into consideration was the fee for using the public toilets! There was definite gender discrimination in the charge for their use. The men could almost always use them free. But women always had to pay. Here is where we discovered our budget plans "went down the toilet!" Well, we weren't going to panic—after all, it was only one week. It wasn't fair to base our financial situation on the first week.

At this point we decided to put our Britrail Passes to use. These passes can be purchased only outside of Great Britain. We purchased two-week passes. By doing this we saved some money; because we were seniors, we were allowed first-class accommodations on all the trains.

With the help of our guide books, maps, and the tourist information services at the depots, we could plan day trips, wherein we could go, see, do, and return to our home base the same day; or we could plan overnight or longer trips, such as our excursions to St. Ives in Cornwell, North Wales, Scotland (mainly Edinburgh), Inverness, and other places in Great Britain too far for day trips.

Our trip to Scotland was a bit of an experience. We took the night train with sleeper accommodations. These were two tiny adjoining rooms, efficiently equipped with a "potty" and everything. Almost like a doll house on wheels!

We didn't get much sleep—too many stops, and we weren't accustomed to the shake, rattle, and roll of the train, the noise of the wheels on the tracks, and the constant whistle blowing. Still, it was fun.

Shortly before our train arrived in Edinburgh, we went through the usual procedure of consulting our guide books; we located a B&B not far from the train depot. A phone call confirmed that accommodations were available, so we hightailed it to our destination.

When we reached the B&B's street, we were quite surprised to see two long blocks consisting of rather fine looking two- and three-story wood frame houses, several of which displayed B&B signs.

Upon entering our B&B, we were immediately struck by the rich, newly-painted interior of the house. The living room and dining room areas had high embossed and decorated ceilings, as did our bedroom, which was quite spacious. There was a metered heater, but no towels. We had to rent them.

Our hosts, Mr. & Mrs. Shannon, greeted us quite formally. This was unusual, but nice. Curiosity got the better of us and we asked about the many middle-class houses on these couple of blocks and the fact that several were B&Bs. Mr. Shannon explained that these homes were formerly owned by upper-management of the coal mining industry that was closed several years back. They were later sold to people like the Shannons, and subsequently many became B&Bs.

Soon the sun went down, and since the weather in Scotland is mostly cold, cloudy, rainy, and windy, you can be sure we fed the meter heater plenty. What a voracious appetite it had!

The next morning, fresh and frisky, we came down for breakfast. The room sparkled and the dining area was truly elegant. It was quite a pleasant surprise to be greeted by Mr. Shannon, who was formally dressed in dark trousers, white shirt and tie, a white jacket, and a neatly folded towel draped over his arm. He looked like the head waiter at the Ritz! We loved it.

Now, I had an acquaintance, an older man—this was back in the '30s—who was born and bred in Scotland. He quite often would tell me fascinating stories of Scotland and also recite poems, ditties, and short tales, mostly risqué, which he attributed to the famous Scottish poet Bobbie Burns. In the course of our many conversations, he told me about eating haggis, a typical ethnic dish that was commonly eaten at breakfast by the Scots. He described it as a sort of porridge. But, he said, "one really had to acquire a taste for it." His vague description was a bit on the negative side. Yet somehow, the conversation about haggis always stuck in my mind.

Back to Mr. Shannon and our breakfast. No sooner did we sit down to the table than I recalled haggis, and I asked Mr. Shannon if he would serve us some. He quickly replied, "Oh no, I'm sure you would not like it." He was quite adamant in his refusal.

My curiosity about haggis was decidedly aroused. Months later, after we returned home, I remembered the incident with Mr. Shannon and looked up "haggis" in the dictionary. This is what I found: Haggis: A Scottish dish made of the lungs, heart, etc., of a sheep or calf, mixed with suet, seasoning, and oatmeal and boiled in the animal's stomach!

After reading this, I could easily understand Mr. Shannon's reluctance to serve us haggis. To assuage us, he served us Scottish oat cakes, a sort of cookie that didn't taste too bad, but was a bit bland and had the texture of cardboard! However, we were served quite good breakfasts and greatly enjoyed our stay with the Shannons: another entry in our book of memories.

After breakfast, we took off to tour the city. Edinburgh is a fascinating city, especially the walk down the Royal Mile. Walking the Royal Mile, so-called because it links the castle with the palace of Holyrood House, the residence of the Queen when she is in Edinburgh, is treading through the history of ancient Scotland. We certainly hated to leave it, but we wanted to see Inverness and Loch Ness, just to say hello to the "Monster."

Loch Ness is twenty-four miles long and averages about a mile in breadth. I was standing on the shore of Loch Ness when I excitedly yelled to Dorothy, "Come quick, I see the Monster!" She dashed over immediately, peered into the lake, and said, "You nut, that's your reflection in the lake!" Unfortunately, our train passes were running out, so we had to leave Scotland and head back to London, but not without a visit to North Wales.

I might mention that while we were in Inverness we were watching television in the B&B. Much to our dismay, we saw scenes of many people enjoying beautiful sunny weather and frolicking on the beaches in Southern England! We had nothing but fairly miserable weather all the time we were in England. Then, just as soon as we left (continuing, as I said, to suffer lousy weather), Southern Englanders enjoyed this splendid summer weather—a rarity, we were told, because a common saying in England is, "Summer was on Thursday last July!"

It was train time again, and time to say good-bye to Scotland. We were greatly impressed with this country, especially Edinburgh, with its enchanting ancient castles, sparkling clean streets, and all its history and culture. But on we must go.

One rather unpleasant episode that forever stays with us was our B&B in the town of Crewe. On our way back to London from Scotland, we got off the train at Crewe to make train connections for North Wales. It was getting a bit late and in the train depot we spotted a circular, advertising a B&B within walking distance for only sixteen dollars. We hurried to this hotel and got settled. Much to our dismay, this place was a disaster.

It was located in a rather run-down section of the town. The street was dirty and littered, the building was old and shabby, and it stunk. We called it "the sewer." How happy we were to leave this dump the next morning. Like they say, "you can't win them all."

When we decided to go to North Wales, our destination was the city of Bangor. We soon struck up a conversation with a Welsh couple seated in our compartment on the train. They suggested we go to Anglesey Island instead. We accepted their suggestion and mentioned that we would be seeking a B&B, as we intended to spend the night there.

At Anglesey Island we all disembarked. These folks told us that their son was to meet them in his car and perhaps he could take us to a B&B—a very friendly gesture. We all piled into their rather small car, loaded with people and luggage, and before long we were deposited at a pretty little cottage surrounded by gorgeous flower gardens.

A nice lady welcomed us and soon we were safely ensconced in a cute, cozy, comfortable room. However, there were two rather unusual features in this B&B. One was that in order to get heat into the room—and the nights are cold—we again had to "feed" a heater meter which cost about twenty-five cents per half hour. The other was that, in order to go to the toilet, we had to walk down a flight of stairs, through the kitchen, out the back door, and through the yard to a separate room, a small, neat, and very clean bathroom with a flush toilet!

This posed a problem for us (at our age) because, as we sheepishly explained to our hostess, "we both would certainly have to go potty more than once a night." "No problem," she said. She reached under our bed and withdrew an old-fashioned porcelain chamber pot and said, "Be my guest." How about that!

Because Dorothy and I both had colds, we went to our room early, after dining in a cute, small, and busy pub where a young Welshman fawned over us because we were Americans, which was slightly embarrassing.

In our room we read, played gin rummy, and fed the heater meter to keep warm. Later, our landlady brought us hot tea and cookies. The next day we'd say "so long" to Anglesey Island, the birthplace of Owen Tudor, founder of the House of Tudor. Our stay there was short, but sweet. After fond farewells, we left for the depot to catch our train to Oxford.

One last tiny stroke of good fortune was that a nice young man, who was also staying there, offered to drive us to the depot. This was one small, sweet touch to add a little frosting to the cake.

The last few days in London were spent on more sightseeing in the city and a couple of one-day train trips outside of London. Thus we consumed nearly a month in visiting much of Great Britain. It was a month of nasty, wet, and cold weather. But it was also a month of seeing marvelous sights, famous and fabulous villages, churches, homes, castles, government buildings, fantastic museums, art galleries, and historical places. Above all, we met wonderful people of all races, creeds, and colors. This was truly a memorable month for us, and time went swiftly by.

What surprised us most was that, recalling all we had done and seen and all the places we had visited, we felt we had just a bare taste of knowing Great Britain. How we wished we could have spent at least another month there.

Headin' North

On the morning of the first of May, we bade good-bye to our Iranian B&B host and his family and boarded the train for the chalk cliffs of Dover. There we boarded a large ferry boat for Ostende, Belgium, and took the train from Ostende to Brussels.

In our haste to catch this last train, we got into a first-class car by mistake (we had second-class tickets). The conductor chased us off at the next stop and we had to run, dragging our luggage behind us, to board a second-class car before the train pulled away. Just as in England, it rained all day and into the night. It was coming down pretty hard when we arrived in Brussels at 7:15 P.M.

We perused our travel books and located a B&B, but had to take a taxi to get there. The taxi driver charged us about nine dollars over the fare. After a month in England dealing in pounds, it was a bit difficult and confusing trying to figure out Belgian francs, which were worth about three cents. That cost us.

The next day, we picked up our van, a Volkswagon Dasher. We felt greatly relieved that now, for the first time, we were no longer dependent on public transportation. It was especially good to know that we no longer would be burdened with so much luggage to drag around.

Our B&B was in a small hotel and was nothing to rave about. It had no heat, and the two nights we spent there were quite cold. The breakfasts also were very meager—just bread, butter, jelly, and coffee. We had been spoiled by the abundant breakfasts in Britain. Also, the cost per night was more than in England. Add to this an 18 percent charge to exchange money, and it's easy to see why we fell out of love with Belgium.

With all due respect, though, we had to admit that the country was lovely. The cities were very clean. Brussels in particular was nice. Throughout the city there were beautifully landscaped parks and gardens, lots of statues and many very old, fascinating houses and other buildings.

This city was especially exciting for me because almost fifty years ago to the day, as a young lad, I and a buddy, a couple of years older than me, sailed out of Galveston, Texas as sailors on a tramp freighter. I was a deck-boy, my buddy an ordinary seaman. One of our ports of call was Antwerp. One day, while in Antwerp, another sailor and I went to Brussels to sightsee. Now it was 1979, and Dorothy and I were treading the same areas and seeing many of the same sights I saw in 1929. It was thrilling.

After our month in Britain and just three days in Belgium—where everything cost more—Dorothy and I had to seriously re-evaluate our budget. It was only too obvious, much to our dismay, that our plan to get by on one thousand dollars a month wouldn't do. We then decided to boost our spending limit to twelve hundred dollars a month. We weren't sure that twelve hundred dollars a month would even do. Traveling as we were, on our first trip of this kind, there were many incidental expenses we didn't anticipate. The charge to exchange money was one of them. The 18 percent charge here in Belgium was especially hard to take. In this respect, it was fortunate that we weren't spending much time in this country.

On 4 May, we left Belgium behind and crossed the border into Holland with the rain and cold still following us. How we longed for some warmth and sunshine. Amsterdam was our destination, but the sky darkened and opened up with a heavy downpour, so we decided to look for a B&B. We consulted our guide books and found a B&B listed in Harlem, which was nearby. Making a call to this B&B was difficult for us. A young woman was standing nearby, so Dorothy asked her if she would kindly make the call. She very graciously assented, only to be told by the hostess that the B&B was full. She recommended a friend of hers who lived in the small town of Hoofddorp. Our intermediary called this person and found she had a room available. So, after profusely thanking our assistant and getting the address to this B&B, we headed for Hoofddorp, which was even closer than Harlem.

However, finding this B&B was a challenge. It seemed as though the street names in Hoofddorp changed nearly every block. After having to ask several people, we finally found the place. Our trouble in finding it was due to the fact that it was located on a street just one block long and few people knew of it. Much to our joy, the clouds dissipated and we finally had the sun and warmth we so longed for.

Our hostess and her neighbor were awaiting us on the sidewalk. This neighbor lady spoke English and our hostess couldn't, so she acted as an interpreter. She explained to us that this was the first time our hostess had ever attempted to accommodate B&B guests, and she was a bit nervous about it.

This B&B, a private home, was located in a lovely, clean, well-kept, working-class neighborhood and simply looked and felt friendly. Our hostess and her husband were probably in their mid-thirties, had two young daughters aged five and seven, a cat, a parrot, and a turtle. Our room, as usual, was on the second floor, quite spacious, very clean and orderly, and was heated by a free (!) heater, which, soon after we got settled, I proceeded to foul up. The husband fixed it.

The morning breakfasts were quite a pleasant surprise. Each morning, we were served soft boiled eggs, ham, cheese, bread, butter, two kinds of jelly, and lots of good hot coffee. What a treat.

Holland, like Belgium, is a small country and it was quite easy to get around. We were able to see many sights and visit many places of interest.

This part of Europe was experiencing unseasonably cold weather and spring was later than usual. As a result, the fabulous flowers Holland is famous for were just popping out. Still, we were blessed with seeing many beautiful gardens and farms with many flowers coming into bloom, especially tulips. What was really extraordinary was the sight of a large billboard made completely with fresh flowers!

Once we left England, we discovered that for the rest of Europe, English was not the native tongue, although many did speak English even in the socialist countries. Therefore, for those who could not speak English, we resorted to speaking Yiddish, which is a sort of bastardized German. German was commonly spoken in many countries.

This fact enabled us to barely communicate with many, many people. Such was the case with our Dutch hostess, and it sufficed.

We were faced with the problem of having to do laundry. We asked our hostess where we could find a do-it-yourself laundry. She told us to just leave it on our bed and she'd take care of it. We did so and left for a day of sightseeing—walking and gawking. When we returned in the evening, there on the bed was our laundry, sparkling clean and folded as though we had just purchased it, and no charge.

Due to the inclement weather, we rarely went out nights. Mostly, we would keep company with our hostess. With a few words of English, our not-quite-fluent Yiddish, and much gesticulating, we spent nice, comfortable, relaxed evenings with them over powdered coffee and cookies. Who needs formal, indifferent tourist hotels?

With heavy hearts, we left Hoofddorp, Holland and Mr. and Mrs. Van Wyngaarden, heading through West Germany toward the Scandinavian countries. Our stay with the sweet family in Hoofddorp was such a pleasure. The friendliness of our hostess, the peace and quiet of the neighborhood, the serenity of the small town, and the beauty of this part of Holland made it difficult for us to say *tot ziens* (good-bye).

The West German border was quite near and we had no trouble crossing it. Once in West Germany we drove on the autobahns, comparable to our freeways in California, with a couple of exceptions. First, the autobahns are not for the weak at heart. The native drivers tailgate at ninety miles per hour and more! If you drive slower than ninety miles per hour in the fast lane your life isn't worth a dime! This was an experience. Second, there are rest stops, some quite elaborate, about every five miles. Some contained restaurants, small shops, etc.

As it was approaching dusk, we got off the autobahn and drove along the parallel secondary road. These roads, although much slower, go through lots of small towns and even smaller villages. Our guess was that we could find less expensive accommodations and more available B&Bs along these roads. Our assumption proved correct, and from that day on, this was the pattern we followed.

Just south of Hamburg, on a side road, we spotted a *gasthaus*, which is comparable to an inn—a combination beer parlor and small hotel. The room we checked into was quite large, with twin beds. Instead of blankets, we each had a thick, fluffy, light feather quilt, called a duvet. There was a bottom sheet, but the feather quilt was stuffed into a sort of pocket that resembled two sheets sewn together with a large hole in the top sheet in which the feather tick was stuffed. This acted as our top sheet and also protected the feather quilt. This was a very practical arrangement except when the night was warm. Then the feather quilt was too warm and we either slept on top or threw it on the floor. As our trip progressed, we realized that this sort of bedding arrangement was quite common in the B&Bs we stayed in, especially in Western Europe. They were hung out of a window every morning!

Since there were no restaurants close by, we had dinner in the beer parlor. We ate a plain, simple German meal. It was quite good, plentiful, and rather inexpensive—a great combination!

As usual, we bedded down fairly early, but soon the beer drinkers started to arrive. As the night progressed, so did the noise level of the drinkers and by midnight they were in all their glory. The hall was filled with loud talk, song, and laughter. Though it kept us awake, we were enjoying the gaiety and *gemutlichkeit* of the beer guzzlers.

Fruhstuch (breakfast) the next morning was quite elaborate, consisting of an egg, cheese, cold cuts, three kinds of bread, butter, jelly, and lots of delicious coffee—quite a treat. German bread is great.

Another pattern that seemed to prevail—and again mostly in Western Europe—was the way we were served eggs. In nearly every instance, our egg was served in the shell so we didn't know whether it was soft or hard boiled. We soon discovered that in nearly every case it was neither. It was in between. Invariably, when we cracked it, it would run, making it a bit messy to eat. It became a game with us trying to guess the degree of hardness so we could figure out how to eat it!

After this luscious breakfast, we packed our bags and headed for Denmark. One of our guide books said the west coast of Denmark was quite scenic, so, gypsies that we were, off we went in that direction. However we were a bit disappointed as the going was slow and not very scenic at all. We decided to stop at Ribe, Denmark's oldest city.

Just before we got to Ribe we spotted a small motel. We hadn't seen any signs indicating a B&B, so we stopped to check it out. In Ribe, we stopped at a small hotel, only to discover that the cost for one night was nearly double the motel price, so we purchased some goodies for our dinner and went back to the Motel Rovli to rent a room for the night.

This room was equipped with a tiny kitchenette that had a single burner hot plate. Because we were traveling by car, we had purchased some basic kitchen utensils, anticipating eating some meals in our room. When we had purchased the food in Ribe, we indulged ourselves in some Danish pastry. After settling in, Dorothy prepared dinner, a very tasty cold plate. We finished it off with the Danish pastry and tea.

What a treat! From then on we never passed a Danish bakery without purchasing pastry. What the alcoholic said about whisky, "It's all good, only some is better than others," is what Dorothy and I said about Danish pastry. We concluded that it's all made with pure cream and butter plus whatever!

This motel was unusual in that, besides the cost of the room, we had to rent the linen. Also, we slept in narrow bunk beds. I was in the upper. Nevertheless, we really enjoyed our one night stand at the Rovli Motel. The next morning, we awoke to a bright, sunny day—the day before had been one of the best days we'd had weatherwise—and Dot made a light breakfast (coffee) on the single burner.

Copenhagen was the next stop for us. It took us two days to get there, because we had to take a ferry boat from the Jutland Peninsula to the Isle of Zealand. The ferry boat ride was only fifty minutes long and was not enjoyable as the weather was windy and nasty.

By referring to our guide books, we selected a B&B owned by a Mrs. P.—her last name was obviously Italian—in a suburb of Copenhagen called Klampenborg. Our book said the hostess spoke very good English. We spotted a phone, managed to use it to get in touch with the lady (her English was good), and got directions.

We were near a confluence of freeways and it wasn't long after we took off that we got hopelessly lost.

To locate her home, we suffered the usual complications: getting lost and having to ask directions from several people before we found it. This was a traumatic experience which, with very few exceptions, haunted us throughout our entire trip. This was especially true in the larger cities. Fortunately for us, in Western Europe we rarely failed to find an English speaking person to assist us.

It was a very pleasant feeling when we drove up to Mrs. P's old, but attractive large house, completely surrounded by enchanting gardens of exquisite flowers and shrubs. This was a good omen. We sensed we'd like it here. Mrs. P. greeted us at the door and invited us in. She was a rather tall, stately, handsome woman, and appeared to be in her late fifties. She did not look Italian.

When we entered her house we were amazed at the many magnificent knickknacks scattered throughout the main room. It was obvious to us, who aren't knowledgeable about such things, that many of the objets d'art were expensive, and some appeared to be genuine antiques. They were displayed in somewhat reckless abandon, due perhaps to the fact that they were so many and so varied.

There were two rooms available to guests in the main portion of the house, but both were occupied. However, the basement area was huge and well-kept and had a nice room, which was available to us. In addition to this very adequate sleeping room, we had a full bath and, much to our delight, a full kitchen with all the necessary utensils, silverware, and dishes at our complete disposal! Our hunch proved correct. We knew we would like it here.

Besides our accommodations, there were two other rooms. One was apparently kept empty except for some pieces of simple furniture and quite an assortment of books and magazines. The second room, Mrs. P. informed us, was her classroom where she was presently teaching English to a small group. She told us that she spoke six languages fluently and had given Spanish lessons to the Princess of Norway when the princess was a young girl! You can be sure we were quite impressed with our hostess and her home.

Within walking distance of our B&B was quite a large park named Baaken. It was called "the little Tivoli," after the world-renowned Tivoli Gardens in Copenhagen. What made it popular was the large herd of deer that roamed freely throughout the park—quite a sight. There was also a large section for amusement rides and scads of food stalls all over the place. As in nearly all amusement parks, the food was costly. A single ice cream cone was seventy cents—this in 1979! Both in the afternoon and at night there was free outdoor entertainment, mostly high wire acts. They were interesting, and the price was right.

While strolling in the Park, I found a ten cent coin, and about ten minutes later found a hundred kronen bill, the equivalent of about twenty dollars. Yes, we really liked it here!

The next morning, we came up for breakfast. Although Mrs. P. had told us that breakfast was not included in the cost for the room, she would serve us breakfast for an additional charge. The charge was four dollars for us both and was simply a continental breakfast. She was quite frank in admitting that the charge was a bit steep and strongly urged us to make our own breakfasts. "After all," she said, "you have all the equipment you need." For the balance of our stay with her, that's exactly what we did.

At the breakfast table were the two other couples staying here, one couple from Australia and the other from South Africa. In the course of a pleasant conversation they informed us that the European Women's Gymnastic Competition was being held in Copenhagen. This sounded like something we'd be interested in seeing, and we were able to get tickets.

At this stage in our travels, we recognized how difficult it was, especially in larger cities, to drive our car to and from our B&B into the main part of the city when sightseeing within the metropolitan area. Thus, we would just leave our car at "home" and use public transportation. It certainly saved wear and tear on our nerves and cut down on the amount of petty quarreling we would get involved in.

Transportation from Klampenborg to downtown Copenhagen, by tram, was adequate and efficient, so off we went to see the women gymnasts. These were the best in Europe, including Nadia Comaneci, the world's greatest, from Romania and an Olympic gold medal winner. We were surprised to see her miss the bar in one event and fall flat on her back! She appeared to be unhurt and continued performing. It was truly an exciting experience to see her and the others perform. They were so remarkable.

During our stay in Copenhagen, we saw and did about everything most tourists see and do—within the limits of our budget, of course. One of the highlights included visiting the famous Tivoli Gardens. They were absolutely gorgeous, with many floral gardens. There were free concerts and other entertaining events there, including many amusement park rides, with magnificent colored light displays at night and all the other things in the Garden that make it world famous, despite the commercialism. There were even slot machines. We absorbed it all with much joy.

Then came our walk along the canal through Churchill Park to see the famous statue of the "Little Mermaid" resting on a rock in the harbor. We expected her to be much bigger. An amusing way to describe a mermaid is that she is "too much fish to eat and not enough woman to love!"

In the park were many other fine statues, especially the Genion Fountain, which depicts the myth of how the Islands of North Zealand were formed. A canal boat ride and city tour by bus were relaxing, informative, and enlightening. By taking these local tours, we saw things in minutes which would otherwise take us hours if we did it on our own.

And, of course, we visited several museums. All of them contained fascinating displays. Our favorite was the Glyptotek. A special display of most unusual art was perhaps the most beautiful, indescribable work one could imagine. It was an exhibit of pictures of all sizes made with pieces of colored cloth in abstract designs. The creativity expressed in these pictures was awesome! Just looking at them would cause your imagination to run wild. One could visualize innumerable scenes in each picture. Naturally, they were done by a woman.

One day, coming back "home" on the tram, an elderly lady seated near us and hearing us speak apparently recognized us as American tourists and struck up a conversation. In the course of the conversation she asked us where we were staying. We replied, at Mrs. P.'s B&B in Klampenborg. "Oh yes," she said, "I know Mrs. P. Did you know that her Grandfather was the founder of the Carlsburg Brewery? And," she continued, "she was once married to an Italian Count!"

Well, the mystery of her Italian name was solved. We could now account for all the lovely expensive artifacts on display in her home. And the fact that Mrs. P was so refined, intellectual, and yet so down to earth was now explained by her past. We struck it rich here in Klampenborg.

That night, we told Mrs. P. that tomorrow we were going to visit the Carlsburg Brewery. At this point, she told us that her grandfather founded it and that her father was at one time the director of the Glyptotek museum. We in turn disclosed to her our conversation with the lady on the tram, and told her we now knew quite a bit about her—all good, of course.

Right after breakfast, we headed for the brewery and took the interesting tour that ended up in the tasting room—a large beautifully-appointed room where the groups were seated at long, white linen-covered tables and served bottles of Carlsburg beer and bottles of soft drinks—all we wanted.

The irony of beer drinking in Denmark is that also located there is another quite famous brewery, the Tuborg Brewery. Two of the largest in Europe and yet beer was very expensive—$1.30 for a small glass or bottle of beer!

After a few more days in Denmark, gypsies that we were, we packed up to leave for Norway. Our experiences in this lovely country will be another chapter in our book of memories. What we'll remember about Denmark, besides those things already noted, will be how clean and orderly everything was there; our pleasant strolls through the Strogets (pedestrian malls); the many people walking with canes; the amount of drinking and smoking amongst youngsters, mostly boys; the Danish people, friendly yet a bit cool; and above all, Danish pastry—the best in the world!

Entering "Fairy Tale Land"

And away we go, headed for Norway via the west coast of Sweden. Our last stop in Denmark was in Elsinore to visit the Kronborg Castle, built in the late sixteenth century. It was the setting for one of Shakespeare's most famous plays, *Hamlet*. This castle, the principal attraction in Elsinore, intrigued us.

We walked to the castle and joined a tour group. As we approached this gray and dismal edifice, we sensed a repellent aura surrounding it. Once inside, there was a feeling of repulsion that intensified when we toured the underground chambers. This damp, gloomy, forbidding area was where the military and prison guards once had their quarters. When our guide told us that the soldiers had been rationed an alcoholic beverage of sixteen liters a day, we found this hard to believe. Either we heard wrong or the drink had contained a very low content of alcohol, similar to our beer. We also saw huge vats in which they salted meat, game, and fish to preserve them. Even today there was a lingering smell that added to the unpleasant feeling.

Here also were the strange cells that had held the worst of criminals, the most gruesome sight in these unwholesome quarters. The prisoners had been confined to small "V"-shaped cells. Each day they were forced back to the apex of the "V" until there was only room to stand upright. They were held in this position day and night! As a result, the average prisoner rarely lived longer than six weeks. This was a horrifying example of man's inhumanity to man. By this time, I could hardly breathe. I felt as if there was a rope tightening around my throat. Once we exited the castle and were able to breathe fresh air, we could easily understand why the Kronborg Castle was chosen by Shakespeare as the setting for the tragic play, *Hamlet*.

The tour through the castle took less than two hours. Now, we would head north to Oslo, the capital of Norway and its major city. We didn't feel despondent about leaving the castle, as the tragedies of the dungeons and their relationship to *Hamlet* had worked their effect upon us. They left us in a very somber mood. In silence, we headed to the boat dock, which was a short distance away.

To reach Oslo, we first had to go by ferry across the northern tip of the Strait of Kattegat, which flows to Helsingborg, Sweden. It was highly improbable that we could reach Oslo in one day, due to our late start. We carefully checked our map and decided to spend the night in Gothenburg, Sweden. After making this decision, we scanned our two guide books and (from the Harvard book) we selected a small hotel. We found no B&Bs listed in either book. The brief description of this hotel was satisfactory and the price of fifty-four kroner (one kroner equals twenty-three cents) per night was especially attractive. It fit our budget of thirty dollars per day.

Shortly after reaching the dock, the ferry tied up and its jaws opened wide. We scooted in over a metal ramp and entered the bowels of the boat. Our small car was an asset in these circumstances. In our many travels we have become familiar with ferry boats and know that they park the vehicles like sardines in a can. In the larger boats, they often park your car so close to the bulkhead that it is impossible to open the door. Our little Volkswagen allowed some additional space to maneuver.

Once we disembarked, it was a short distance to Helsinborg, and so we headed almost due north to the city of Gothenburg. We drove, now, along the west coast of Sweden following the Skattegat Strait. The sun was shinning, the day was warm, but muggy, and the scenery was delightful. The combination improved our mood, and it kept improving the further we drove. As we traveled, we would often see the roiling waves of the strait on our left. On our right, in the distance, we observed rolling hills covered with forests of deciduous and coniferous trees. Through much of the drive, we crossed turbulent streams and occasionally unruffled rivers. Below the hills were many small farms that grew mainly vegetable crops. Nestled on the farms were small, well-kept cottages with flower beds surrounding the homes. It was mid-May and everything was flourishing. All this beauty put us in an extremely pleasant mood as we neared Gothenburg.

At the outskirts of the city, we located a phone and I called the hotel. I inquired about a room and also got directions. We found the hotel without incident, a lucky break, since both Dorothy and I have trouble following directions. Our first impression of the hotel was not very favorable. It was small, old, and its wooden construction was under repair. The fact that repairs were being made encouraged us, and so we entered. The clerk greeted us and introduced himself. He then showed us our room. It was a plain and simple room, but the guide book had indicated that the price was well within our budget. When I went to pay the clerk for the accommodations, he said, "That will be ninety-seven kroner." I was shocked! The price of the room was over twenty-two dollars! Trying to get by on thirty dollars a day, the price of this room would consume nearly our entire day's expenses. When I mentioned the price listed in the Harvard book to the clerk, he seemed surprised. He replied, "That price hasn't been in effect for several years. Your book is outdated."

We had no choice but to accept the room, as it was getting late and we were weary. Looking back, we recalled that we had experiences like this before, although not as drastic. We realized that the countries we had been to before also had inflation. It would be nearly impossible for our guide books to update the hundreds of places listed. We were a couple of disgruntled gypsies. The gypsy life is not a bed (and breakfast) of roses; so we simply accepted the situation and then tried to forget it.

About half past eight the next morning, we drove to a nearby restaurant and parked our car next to the sidewalk, in a large parking lot. We entered a warm dining area, which was a welcome relief from the cold and wet of the morning. The ambiance stimulated our appetites, so we ordered a full breakfast of orange juice, scrambled eggs, coffee, and all the trimmings. The juice was unexpectedly fresh; the coffee hot, strong, and plentiful. The scrambled eggs were heaped on platters in mounds that looked like miniature haystacks and they had the smell and taste of the country.

Our appetites assuaged, Dorothy surreptitiously took some slices of bread and made egg sandwiches for our lunch. Our rationale was that due to the high cost of food, this would help to keep us within our budget. Later, we discovered that this was a common practice by the less affluent European travelers.

After we had finished eating, we left to get our car. When we reached the parking lot we couldn't find the car! We searched all through the lot to no avail. I began to panic (I panic a lot earlier than Dorothy) and thought that somebody stole our car. A couple of minutes later, a mail carrier came down the sidewalk pushing his little mail cart. I asked him if there was another parking lot, other than the one nearby. I explained our predicament to him, and he asked, "Is your car a green VW?" Amazed, I replied that it was. Then he said, "Well, it's just around the corner." Plainly, he'd passed our car, since I had parked it by the sidewalk. He saw it was a foreign car, and when we (foreigners) asked him about it, he just put "one and two" together (one car and two dumb Americans), and arrived at the correct conclusion. This mix-up occurred because the restaurant was quite large and we exited by a different door than the one we had used to enter.

We left Gothenburg with no regrets. The weather was cold and windy. It felt like we were entering another ice age. Oslo was our destination. We drove to Highway E6 and headed almost due north. The route passed through stands of conifer and birch, along and over several fjords, and through farming areas. Such pleasant conditions certainly take the strain out of driving. It was close to noon when we crossed the border and said good-bye to Sweden and hello to Norway. The drive to Oslo from the border would take slightly more than an hour.

Oslo is a city of about a half million people, and as we neared its outskirts I could feel the tension rising; my body began to stiffen and my hands began to grip the steering wheel tighter. This was a condition I experienced every time we approached a large city.

We knew the name, address, and telephone number of the place where we had selected to stay, but finding it would be another traumatic event. Both Dorothy and I had problems following directions and instructions, but I was much worse than she. I would get nervous and panicky; this happened time and time again.

Nearby we noticed a telephone. Our troubles usually started with trying to use the phone, and we normally had one heck of time in making the connection. It did not seem to matter which one of us would attempt the call—we always had problems. It would take two or three tries which, of course, cost more; or we would prevail upon a stranger to make the call for us. The latter was always the better choice. This time we were lucky. We reached our party on our own. We obtained directions from the woman on the telephone, and here is where our troubles began.

The following is a fictitious example of what could take place no matter which one of us would listen to the directions. We might be told, "Go two kilometers straight ahead, then make a left. Next, go a full block and turn right. Then, go another three and a half kilometers past the electric signal and you will see our place on your right." Then the one who took the directions would repeat it to the other one. Sounds simple, doesn't it? HA! Off we would go two kilometers ahead (remember that we will have to convert the kilometers into miles), then one of us would say, "Did she say turn right or left?" From there on, it's the same old hassle. We would pull over and ask someone for directions. We would repeat this procedure two or three times, maybe even four times! Each time, I begin to panic a little more, until soon we're snapping and snarling at each other. When we finally reach our destination, we're about ready to go for one another's jugular.

In this manner, we finally reached the Bella Vista Hospit. The hospit, much to our surprise, was located in the outskirts of the city. This sparsely settled neighborhood consisted of small stores interspersed amongst modest dwellings. It appeared to be a working-class neighborhood. We preferred this location because there was less traffic and less trouble finding parking places. There was nothing special about the hospit. It was a plain wooden structure, and, considering that we were seeking inexpensive accommodations, we could hardly expect a glamorous edifice. It was not a B&B, but basically a small hotel.

The day was nearly gone when we arrived, due to our getting lost in the usual manner. But when Mrs. Madsen greeted us at the door, our difficulties melted away with her gracious manner. We became "all smiles" and returned her warm greeting. Later, we met her husband, Captain Madsen. He was an old former sea captain, and looked like a character from a Scandinavian sea tale. He was not very tall, but was built sturdily and had a face that was wrinkled and weather-beaten. One could almost visualize him standing on the deck of a ship, the salt spray hitting his face. His eyes were bright blue, and very sharp. He gave the impression that he was constantly looking for other ships, or land on the distant horizon. Yet there was a humorous twinkle in those clear eyes that belied his stern physiognomy.

After the introductions, the Captain showed us to our room. It consisted of two narrow beds and, as in many of the places we'd stayed in since leaving England, the beds had *perenehs* (Russian for the big fluffy quilts). This place also had a small kitchenette and dining area for the use of all the guests. Fortunately for us, the cost was only eighty kroner, which did not include breakfast.

We slept well that night. After washing up the next morning, we went to the small dining room and prepared our breakfast. This room was furnished with a small gas stove, silverware, dishes of all sorts, pots and pans, and four small tables with chairs.

Later, we went sightseeing via bus. Unknown to us, that day, 18 May, was Norway's Constitution Day celebration. Norway enacted its constitution in 1814. Despite the threatening weather, there was a festive atmosphere in all of Oslo. Practically the entire business section of town was closed for the festivities. There were many colorful groups in parades all over town. Youngsters were dressed in what appeared to be native costumes. They marched with such pride and dignity. The adult marchers were dressed in their finest, and the marching bands added a festive touch. Nearly everyone carried a Norwegian flag. Many of the older men walked with canes, more as a symbol than a necessity.

Several marchers and spectators seemed to be under the influence of liquor, including a number of drunken teen-aged boys. On a bus we took, a drunken young man was having an argument with the bus driver. At the next stop, the driver evicted the drunk, but before he could pull away, and while the bus was still moving, the young man physically forced the doors open. He tried to get back into the bus. The bus picked up speed, and the driver reached over and forcefully pushed the young man. Out he fell into the street! It was a sickening sight. Evidently he didn't fall too hard, because he appeared to be unhurt. I guess his inebriated condition spared him somewhat.

Oslo, with its nine hundred years of history, lies at the head of the Oslofjord and, like much of Norway, has snow-capped mountains surrounding it. Heavily forested areas cover much of the mountainsides. It has a large port, and shipping and shipbuilding, fishing, and lumbering are the main industries. The warm waters of the Gulf Stream and the North Atlantic Drift temper Oslo's weather. These waters drift at about three miles an hour from the Gulf of Mexico to the Norwegian coast and enter the Oslofjord. This creates an ice-free port year round.

Many years ago, there was an article in "Ripley's Believe It Or Not" that recounted that at one time, during a severe hurricane, Galveston, Texas was heavily drenched with rain. This caused a coffin in the cemetery to rise out of its burial plot and to float out into the Gulf Stream current. The coffin allegedly floated for days, and finally reached the very village where the Norwegian sailor within the coffin had been born! Quite a story.

Oslo is one of Europe's most expensive cities, to which we could attest after our stay there. The metropolitan area of the city is compact, and this enabled us to see most of the sights, both by bus and by walking. We did a lot of sightseeing. In its recent history, an unprecedented event occurred that attracted worldwide attention. The women of Oslo, during an election in 1971, used a write-in campaign to capture majority control of the municipal government!

In our wanderings, we came upon the City Hall, a rather new, impressive building. The architecture, which we thought to be modern Scandinavian, was exceptionally attractive. As we entered the building, we immediately became aware of the many works of art displayed around a large room. Our first thought was that this was more like a museum than a government building. There were displays of arts and crafts of every description: painting, furniture, murals, chandeliers, and more. All of it was breathtaking and beautifully displayed. One section was significantly outstanding: a collection of gifts presented to Oslo by other countries, cities, and individuals to commemorate the building of the City Hall.

This building was so impressive that we also took a free guided tour of it the next afternoon. A very sweet, middle-aged lady was our guide; she reminded me of my prim and proper eighth grade teacher. She knew a great deal about the objects on display. At the end of the tour, our docent pointed out something very odd. There, on the rear wall, an artist had painted a plain door for no apparent reason. Our guide explained that originally the building plans called for a door to be built into this wall. However, for some reason the builders had left it out. To rectify this error, the artist painted a door on the wall. It looked so real that had our guide not told us about it, we would have assumed that it was real.

Since the cost of our room didn't include breakfast, we got up early to go to market to buy breakfast grub. We came home with two small bags of groceries for "only" twenty dollars! With these prices, we figured we'd have to make some rubber sandwiches that could last a few weeks. Despite the unexpected higher costs, we managed OK, not losing any weight, but sure as heck not gaining any, either. Beer was two dollars and fifty cents a glass!

While reading about Norway in our guide books, the description of the city of Bergen intrigued us. This city is the second largest in Norway. It was founded in 1070 and has a wealth of unusual history. The map showed a hard surfaced road from Oslo, so we decided to make the drive. That evening, we contacted Captain Madsen and spoke to him about driving there. I asked him, "What do you think about our plan?" He replied, "I wouldn't advise it." When I asked him the reason for this, he replied, "It is too dangerous. The weather is bad and this road is too difficult to drive. It is narrow, twisting, and goes through mountainous country." He went on, "I think it is much better that you go by train. You will enjoy it more."

We decided to take the train trip to Bergen, about three hundred kilometers north and a bit west of Oslo. I asked the Captain if he could please arrange a room for us for two nights, the twenty-fifth and the twenty-sixth. I wanted to pay for the additional nights we were to stay at his place when we returned. He took only seventy kroner per night. On the first night, he had charged us eighty. He confided, "Don't tell my wife!" During our conversation, I asked him where I could find a barber shop, as I needed a haircut. He replied, "I'll cut your hair." I figured that he was joking, and immediately forgot about it. Later in the evening, the Captain came to our room to tell us that he'd arranged a place for us to stay in Bergen for eighty kroner per night. Then he turned to me and said, "I'm ready to give you a haircut. Come on downstairs; I won't charge you anything."

While the Captain was cutting my hair (I was seated on an old kitchen chair), I imagined what life would be like to be sailing under Captain Madsen. In the little time I had known him, he had made a strong impression on me. While he was snipping, I was picturing him standing on the deck of a sailing vessel, wearing sea-boots and oilskins. I could see him leaning into a strong wind, the ocean spray misting on his face, and the vessel heeling into the wind. All this time, his sharp, watchful eyes were taking in every aspect of the boat and crew. I imagined that he must have been a stern, resolute master who would not tolerate inefficiency or carelessness from his crew.

Yet, beneath this tough demeanor was a man with a heart and a humanity that came forth at any occasion that demanded it. In answer to my speculation about the Captain's character, I thought, why else would he cut my hair and not accept any payment? Why would he surreptitiously deduct ten kroner from the cost of a night's lodging? Why, also, would he take the time and effort to arrange accommodations for us in Bergen, unless he was the type of man I thought him to be? Soon the Captain was through snipping and clipping, and I was through guessing. Thoroughly satisfied with both events, I left.

Mrs. Madsen was the opposite of the Captain. Where he was congenial and outgoing, she was strictly business. We saw very little of her during our stay, and when we did meet, she was cordial. Our only conversation, aside from formal greetings, related to operating the hospit. She managed the business end of the operation, and also contributed considerable effort to maintaining the physical appearance of the establishment. In appraising them both, I felt that the Captain and Mrs. Madsen made a good team. We felt grateful to benefit from their individual and combined characteristics.

The next few days were spent sightseeing. We thrilled at all the fabulous and unusual, ancient and modern artistic objects that we saw in Oslo. We went to the Defense Museum and learned about Norway's part in World War II. Next, we went to the Akershus Fortress, which dates back to 1300. Finally, we saw Vigeland Park, an indoor and outdoor museum devoted entirely to the statuary of Gustav Vigeland. Words cannot describe the talent and prodigious production of this artist, who started his artistic career at age nine, making wood carvings. You have to see his work to believe it. He devoted forty years to creating 1,650 sculptures, woodcuts, carvings, and thousands of sketches. He created life-sized monolithic figures, mostly in plaster. Each one took about ten months to finish. These plaster statues then took three men thirteen years to reproduce in stone! When you see Vigeland's work, it literally overpowers your senses.

Later we went off to Bygdoy to see Roald Amundsen's ship, *Gjoa*, in which he sailed to the Arctic. Next, came Thor Heyerdahl's famous papyrus boat, *Ra II*, and his balsa wood raft, *Kon-Tiki*. In both these weird seagoing crafts he sailed thousands of miles.

At Oslofjord, we found ancient and modern replicas of Viking boats, and the sailing ship *Fram* which had sailed to both poles. Nearby, the paintings of Edvard Munch, Norway's most renowned expressionist painter, are displayed in the Edvard Munch Museum. We also saw fascinating artistic works from the past. An outstanding example of this was a large wall tapestry which took nearly five years to produce. An obvious factor in Norwegian art is the influence of its history and culture on the artists of the country. They were a people who lived under the conditions of freedom, independence, and peace. This is reflected in their art, which gives it an added dimension. Oslo enthralled us. The most wonderful part of all this was that all the marvelous sights could easily be reached through public transportation.

Now, we prepared for the trip to Bergen. And what a trip it was! The train ride from Oslo to Bergen is a story in itself: three hundred kilometers of sheer beauty. The train went through more than two hundred tunnels, over scores of bridges, and through eighty miles of snowsheds, reaching a height of 4,267 feet! The scenery was a photographer's heaven. Every time I'd get my camera set for a fabulous shot, the train would enter another tunnel. We were constantly admiring the sight of forests, lakes, rivers, waterfalls by the hundreds, and fjords. At one point, we traveled sixty miles across a barren plateau. Looking out we saw nothing but snow as far as the eye could see in any direction! At times the glare off the snow made it difficult to look upon. It was like an ocean of sparkling diamonds.

Dorothy had prepared a lunch to eat on the train. We were getting smart, and were cutting down on our expenses. During the trip, we struck up conversations with other passengers, mostly from the US. At six thirty in the evening, eight and a half hours after we began the trip, we arrived in Bergen.

We stayed in a pension in a large, comfortable room, which was the owner's sitting room during the winter. We took our meals (breakfast not included) at a cafeteria nearby. It dawned on us that we were eating a lot of fish, even when we ate in our room. We ate fish of all descriptions and in all forms: cooked, smoked pickled, fried, and baked. It was all delicious, no matter how the cooks had prepared it. The Scandinavians are copious fish eaters.

We arose the next morning to light rain and a cold, stiff breeze. We dressed, then went in search of a restaurant. Our hotel didn't serve meals and had no accommodations like the Bella Vista to enable us to cook for ourselves. We picked the cafeteria we ate in the previous night. What a relief it was to get out of the cold and to feel the warmth in the dining room. We savored the odors of cooked foods that drifted from the kitchen. This environment stimulated our appetites. We got in line to select our food. Not surprisingly, when we saw the prices, we lost our appetites. Though we expected to pay higher prices for most everything in Bergen, our dinner last night hadn't cost too much. The breakfast prices, however, were outrageous. There was little we could do about it, except to restrict our appetites. We settled for a very meager breakfast that included two cups (not mugs) of coffee each, which cost us five dollars!

So, light of heart and light of stomach, despite the disagreeable weather, we took off on foot to see what Bergen had to offer. The first things that drew our attention were the many brightly colored houses which were built on the slopes of the seven mountains which surround the city. At first glance, they looked like cardboard cutouts, stacked one on top of another. I would guess that because Bergen has lots of rainfall and dreary days, perhaps the citizens painted the houses these colors to add a bright spot to their lives.

We had read that Bergen is a historical city. It was also acclaimed for its cultural and educational facilities. It has many impressive monuments dedicated to its medieval past, a fine university, several scientific institutions, and some fine museums.

Despite the disgusting wet weather that kept following us, Bergen proved interesting. We especially enjoyed walking around the Torget, an open market located on the docks at the head of an ice-free fjord. Many of the stalls sold fish of every kind, size, and species. Other stalls sold fruit, vegetables, lots of flowers, and other items. Two small tomatoes cost us thirty-two cents each! At some stalls, folks sold their handicrafts. Dorothy and I really enjoyed these open markets. Although the merchandise sold there is similar to that sold in open-air markets across Europe, you can always find something new and different to buy. Most of the time, we couldn't resist buying something.

Next came the aquarium, the largest in Northern Europe. The antics of the penguins entertained and delighted us. Finally, we visited the new (one-year-old) Grieg Concert Hall, beautifully situated on a man-made lake. The weather was so nasty that we were getting depressed; especially me—I'm a sun worshiper. So we headed back to our pension and prepared to leave the next day.

The return trip was a bit less exciting, but still very enjoyable. Despite the cost, the trip to Bergen was worthwhile, another page to our book of memories.

Well, the gypsy blood started percolating in our veins, and we prepared to head east to Sweden. It was a bit difficult to say good-bye to Norway. There is so much natural beauty—fjords, rugged mountains, heavy forests, and water everywhere. The marvelous art work, the creativity of its artists, and the progressive political culture that reflects itself in the government and its people, were compelling. On the negative side, we saw much drunkenness, especially among youngsters. This was disturbing to us. The travel books consider Oslo an expensive city for tourists. The price of food, both in the markets and in restaurants, exceeded our budget. We also found the weather disagreeable.

On the morning of 25 May, we arose early, made a light breakfast, packed up our "Vantz" (nickname we gave our VW—yiddish for bedbug), and bought diesel. We bade the Captain and Mrs. Madsen farewell and took off under dark and threatening clouds: when would it ever end? Our route was highway E18 heading nearly due east for Stockholm, Sweden. Despite the minor irritations we found in Norway, we left the country with heavy hearts—and light wallets!

Before long, it started to pour. When we crossed the border into Sweden, the rain came down in buckets. About half past three, we arrived in Orebro, a fair-sized city. Because of the heavy rain, we decided to spend the night here. In a cursory check, we could find no moderately priced inns or B&Bs. Then it dawned on us that Orebro was near the home of Eva and Jonas, the young couple we had met in the London pub. The pub had been crowded, and we four had to sit fairly close together. We were so busy talking, eating, and drinking beer that neither Dorothy nor I observed much about them except that they both were very friendly and open. Before we parted, that London evening, they invited us to visit them on our drive from Oslo to Stockholm. With the nasty weather and the lack of suitable accommodations, Dorothy and I looked at each other and said, "Heck, let's call these kids and see what happens." There was a small general store nearby, and we asked the lady in charge to please call for us. She agreed, and soon got hold of Jonas. At first, he didn't recall who we were. When I told him, he gave me directions to the little town of Falltorp, where they lived, and invited us to stay with them.

So, with light hearts, and some trepidation, off we went. Falltorp was twenty-five miles away, and the further we drove, the better the weather became. The drive was through flat country inundated with lush, prosperous-looking small farms. Much to our amazement and delight, we arrived without getting lost once! It was a record for us. This was the second time. The house that Eva and Jonas were renting was a rather large, old, wood-framed structure, somewhat like you would expect to see in farming country. They kept two bull terriers behind a fence that surrounded the house. The dogs were ugly, but docile, so Dorothy and I went through the gate and rang the bell. Eva and Jonas heartily greeted us. Once inside, they introduced us to Sylvia, Jonas' mother. She was a pretty, young-looking, petite, and neatly-dressed woman. She could have almost passed for Jonas' sister. To our dismay, she acted reserved toward us. She, too, was visiting, and perhaps (we thought) she felt somewhat piqued that we would be intruding on her time with the kids. This, of course, was pure guesswork on our part.

You must believe me when I tell you that we really hadn't intended to accept their offer when we met in London, weeks before. The circumstances when we arrived in Orebro, however, caused us to change our minds.

Jonas and Eva were just ordinary folks. Ordinary in nearly every respect. Eva was obviously pregnant. This would be their first child. She was plainly dressed in maternity clothes. Her hair was medium blonde, straight, and reached her shoulders. Jonas was more animated and outgoing than Eva. He gave us the impression that he was the decision-maker in the family.

We all got settled and soon gathered in the parlor, conversing over a glass of wine. This put all of us at ease. Dorothy and I felt quite comfortable, as Sylvia had now warmed up to us. After a short period of talking and imbibing, we moved to the dinner table and spent considerable time eating, drinking, and conversing. We sat up until nearly midnight enjoying beer, wine, coffee, and pleasant conversation. A genuine feeling of friendship pervaded the surroundings and affected us all. How wonderful for us; we were perfect strangers, and yet they treated us like old friends!

The next morning, it was still raining. Eva, Jonas, Dorothy, and I went *schpatseering* (Yiddish for sightseeing) in the area. We visited a unique twelfth-century wooden stave church and graveyard. These wooden stave structures are not uncommon in Sweden, and the architectural design is unusual. They must be quite durable. The rest of the time, we just wandered around the countryside. By this time, the sky had cleared, and blessed us with clear, cool weather. It was a very welcome change.

Back home, before the trip, we had discussed the problem of finding modest accommodations in Stockholm, our next stop. There were very few listed in our guide books. Sylvia was going home, also, and she lived near Stockholm. Jonas asked us if we would take her to the depot (she was going by train). "Of course," we said. Jonas called a place in Stockholm that might have a room for us and asked for a week's reservation. The owner said he could accommodate us for just two nights, Saturday and Sunday. We were in a quandary. At this point we told Jonas about Brigitte, the young lady we'd also met in London. We told him we were a bit hesitant to accept her generous offer to stay at her parents' home. Jonas replied, "If she invited you, she was sincere. I'll call her." He proceeded to do just that.

Jonas was right; she had meant it. Dorothy then spoke with her and made arrangements to call her when we arrived in Stockholm. The next day was Sunday, Mother's Day. I wanted to pay Jonas for all the long-distance calls, but he refused, saying that he liked to talk on the phone!

Now, by the grace of a wonderful young lady, we were all set for our stay in Stockholm. Saturday night, however was a problem. Sylvia soon solved that. She said, "Look, I have a brother-in-law and sister who own an inn in Malmkoping, near Stockholm. You'll love it. My brother-in-law and sister have quite a reputation for their cooking! Let me call them and see if they have a room available for tonight." This she did, and the answer was "yes." Then she said, "You needn't take me to the depot; I'll just go with you to the inn. They always have a room for me."

We kissed Eva and Jonas *adjo* (good-bye) and thanked them profusely for their hospitality and generosity. We gave them one hundred kroner (one Swedish krone was equal to twenty-three American cents) for the baby soon to come. Realistically, this was a bargain for us. How do you value the kindness of these folks and what value can you place on such an unexpected experience?

The weather remained partially cloudy all day, yet the driving was pleasant. During our conversation, Sylvia told us that she, too, was Jewish. This brought us closer together. At three o'clock, we arrived at the inn and met Sylvia's relatives. We were given a cozy, nicely furnished room.

I must digress for a moment; what I'm about to tell you is related to the coming events. Our daughter, who lives in Los Angeles, and our son, who lives in Omaha, insisted we call them (collect) about once a week. In our latest conversation with our daughter, we had related our budgetary problems and the many times we had eaten inexpensive delicatessen dinners in our room. Our daughter insisted that we eat better and (since she is a gourmand) she insisted that we indulge in authentic ethnic food. She said we shouldn't skimp, and she would send us money!

At the inn, after a light lunch of scrumptious smoked fish, the three of us walked to the Train Museum (which was quite meager), and rode in an old trolley car. We walked a bit more, and then went back to the inn.

After we had freshened up, the three of us went to the dining room. It was a sparkling room, with fine linen tablecloths and linen napkins. The silverware was shiny and bright. The glassware glistened. I remarked to Sylvia, "We would like an authentic Swedish dinner, and price is no object. Would you kindly order for us?" Then we told her about our daughter. She agreed, and the fun and the food began. Our first course was a fish smorgasbord of twelve kinds of smoked and pickled fish. Each was placed in a separate small dish. These dishes were nestled on a conical, circular wire tier of three height levels. Next, the waitress served two kinds of cheese, small bits of bread, radishes, and grapes. Sylvia explained that these tidbits had to be eaten before the rest of the meal, to take away the taste of the fish. Then came the main course: Swedish beef steak with an onion gravy and vegetables. Naturally, we had wine with dinner, and afterwards we drooled over a platter of chocolate wafer candies. We finished the repast with Swedish coffee, hot and strong. In European countries, to our knowledge, you must pay for each separate cup of coffee, and it isn't cheap! However, Sylvia went into the kitchen and brought out the whole pot! After this marvelous meal, Dorothy and I felt stuffed.

Sylvia's relatives had a spacious apartment above the inn, where they lived permanently. Their son and his friends celebrated in a banquet room next to the apartment. Sylvia offered us drinks, either alcoholic or soft drinks, but we couldn't eat or drink another thing. A bit later, her nephew came in and we tried to talk to him; but he couldn't understand us. In fact he was a bit too drunk to converse with us even if he could understand. From a quick glance into the banquet room, we could see that all of his friends were feeling little pain and having a great time.

Just before midnight, the three of us went down to the kitchen. Sylvia's relatives were through cooking, so we could chat a bit. They, too, offered us drinks and again we refused. Although we were together for less than an hour, we felt completely at ease and comfortable with them. They still wore their cooking garb. Both were on the chubby side. They had round, full faces and both wore broad smiles. Their overall appearance, and the meal we had just eaten, confirmed what Sylvia had told us about their cooking. It was surprising to us that they were so amiable after so many hours cooking for so many people. We asked them if they would arrange for our breakfast the next morning, and also if they would please prepare our bill so that we could pay immediately. I expected a pretty big one, but what did it matter? Our daughter was paying. When we were presented with the bill, it was less than I expected. I asked, "Did you include breakfast for tomorrow?" He replied that he had. Then I inquired, "Did you include our room rent and our dinner?" Again he replied that he had. When I totaled it up, I saw that he had deducted one hundred twenty-five kroner—nearly twenty-nine dollars. I was speechless! Seeing the look on my face, he said, "Just send me a card from the USSR; I've never received one from there!" Can you beat that? You can be sure that they were the first people we sent cards to when we arrived in the Soviet Union.

Since we were leaving early the next morning, we bade Sylvia and her relatives our heartfelt thanks and farewells. We turned in about half past midnight. The gods surely smiled on us. Even the weather man blessed us. The events we experienced during these few days were entered in our book of memories in capital letters! Does all this not sound like a fairy tale?

The morning greeted us with a sunny, though breezy day. We packed, and were on our way to Stockholm, not too far distant. The drive was pleasant, especially because of the sunny weather and the good highway. However, one must drive carefully. The highways are three lanes wide, and passing another car can be dangerous. It's a law here that you must drive with your headlights on.

The countryside was rather flat and dotted with small, well-kept farms. All the farms we saw in Scandinavia fit this description. One unusual, yet colorful sight was the acres of land covered solidly with yellow-blossomed plants. We had no idea what they were. To us, it looked like mustard weed.

In the early afternoon, we arrived at the outskirts of Stockholm, and spotted a service station with a garage. We pulled in, and without even trying to use the phone, we collared one of the mechanics and asked him to make the call for us. He was a bit reluctant, but we begged him (politely, of course) and he finally did. He reached Brigitte and he immediately gave me the phone. Brigitte greeted me, then explained that the man who called was a Finn, and Finnish is not like Swedish! We then understood his reluctance to call and had to laugh at ourselves. Brigitte put her father, Oskar, on, and I described where we were. He said, "I know exactly where you are. I'll be there in ten minutes." He spoke excellent English. In ten minutes he arrived. He had no idea what we looked like, and we knew nothing about him. When he got out of the car, it took us only seconds to intuitively recognize each other. We followed him to his house, an old, two-story, wood structure with large lawns, flower gardens, and fruit and shade trees. Since they lived in a working-class neighborhood, we both sensed that we would find quiet and comfort here. Brigitte and her mother greeted us and we settled into Brigitte's own room.

Her father was Jewish and her mother, Mireille, was French. We judged them to be in their mid-fifties. Oskar was a large, husky man with a cherubic and young-looking face. He had twinkling eyes and a ready smile. Mireille's appearance exuded friendliness and warmth. Mireille didn't speak English, but she understood it quite well. We had very little trouble getting along. For us, it was love at first sight!

Mireille and Oskar had one other daughter, Barbara, who was five years older than Brigitte. Although Barbara didn't live at home, we saw her often, after she got off work. Brigitte was pretty, bright as a new penny, and quite worldly for a young lady just nearing twenty. Oskar owned a small radio and television sales and repair shop. Mireille was a dressmaker and worked at home for an exclusive ladies' dress shop. She also made dresses and did alterations for private customers.

Here we had the best of two worlds: emotional and gastronomical. Mireille loved cooking and always prepared gourmet meals. Here's a sampling of life with them: often after coming home from sightseeing, we would have coffee. Swedes are big coffee drinkers. They say, "A good cup of coffee must be as hot as the seven hinges of Hell, and as strong as a woman's love!" Sometimes the four of us had gin and tonic before dinner.

For one dinner, we started with chicken soup and *knaidlach* (dumplings), then chicken, rice, salad, and we finished with the common Western European dessert: cheese and fruit. After Mireille cleared the table, we had coffee, cookies, and candies. On another night, she prepared a dinner of coq au vin with boiled potatoes, homemade biscuits—the works. On yet a different night, she made a fish dish consisting of shrimp and cod in a white sauce with mashed potatoes au gratin. All of her dinners were superb and served with elegant simplicity. To eat home-cooked meals of the gourmet quality of Mireille's preparation was heavenly!

After one of her scrumptious feasts, I was sure that we would never be able to enjoy our past regimen of meager delicatessen dinners. A couple of years after our incredible stay with this family, Mireille began teaching French cooking. It was easy to understand why.

On our first night with this family, we sat up chatting until midnight. On another night, the others went to bed, leaving Oskar and me to sip a drink (also strong coffee) and talk. Many nights we talked about everything and anything. Mostly we discussed politics and the economic situations in both our countries. Oskar was well-informed. His opinions reflected the attitude and values of the progressive politics of Sweden, a Social Democratic country. On these subjects, there was an affinity between us and we enjoyed those late night gab-fests. We were kindred spirits. Still another time, after dinner, a young neighbor couple dropped in for dessert, drinks, coffee, and conversation. We carried on until near midnight. It was such a wonderful feeling for Dorothy and me. It was a real ego trip to be so welcomed and accepted by these people who were so much younger than us.

From the very first, Oskar couldn't wait to show us the highlights of Stockholm. Here's what we saw and did over the next few days: He first took us to Drottingholm Castle, called the "Versailles of Sweden;" a very ornate structure, it is the home of Sweden's king and queen. Next came the city of Uppsala, Sweden's oldest and most famous university and cathedral. He also took us to see the new hospital, the largest in Europe. It was more like a huge factory. We went shopping and gawking in downtown Stockholm. We bought Swedish herring and salmon lox at seventeen dollars a pound. Later, we went into a State liquor store to replenish the liquor supply at home. I was paying for it, so Oskar picked out some wine and a pint of Gordon's Gin. I said, "Oskar, that's not enough gin. Get a larger bottle." He replied, "Oh, it's quite expensive." I thought to myself, how expensive could it be? Gordon's Gin in the US is rather inexpensive. He then took a liter. It was nineteen dollars! This was in 1979.

The Scandinavians are pretty heavy drinkers. In Sweden, if one gets caught driving a car with even a hint of liquor imbibing, they are almost certain to lose their driver's license. As a result, they stock up on liquor for the weekend and drink to their heart's content. Because of this, customers jam the liquor stores near the weekend. In the store, Oskar said to me, "Did you notice something unusual in the store?" When I responded that I had not noticed anything, he said, "Did you notice the armed guard? We don't have them in the banks, but they're always in the liquor stores." Does that tell you something? He never explained why the police were there; we just assumed it was to protect against theft and/or burglary.

The next day was warm and overcast, with a few drops of rain. Dorothy's shoes needed repair, so we left them at a cobbler and then took the tube to Centralen, the business section of Stockholm. We strolled through the expansive and very elaborate underground market. This market stocks everything from a baby rattle to a clap of thunder! While in the market, we bought some Swedish *pirozkis* for lunch.

Pirozkis are like a Jewish *knish* or a Cornish pastie. They were delicious, but not quite as good as the Russian *pirozkis*.

After wandering through the market, we took a boat in the harbor to see the ancient sailing ship, the *Wasa*; what there was of her to see. The government built the *Wasa* in the early seventeenth century. They launched her in 1628. She sailed for about ten minutes, and then sank! The government raised her in 1961—some feat! She is now being restored; a process that will take six or more years to accomplish. We were told that the government will invest quite a lot of money to do this. They acquired the best scientific, nautical, and engineering people they could find. Their job is to restore and preserve the *Wasa* to the condition she was in on the day she was launched. When this job is completed, the *Wasa* will be quite a tourist attraction.

Later that day, we picked up Dorothy's shoes—it cost us eighteen dollars for new soles and heels! We then took off for the small town of Sigtuna. During the drive there, we passed many more fields of densely massed yellow blossoms. Oskar explained that the name of the plant is rape, and that one of its uses is to color margarine. They also use it to make a cooking oil from the seeds. The old town of Sigtuna is on Lake Malaren. It's a quaint, orderly old town with interesting arts and crafts shops. We walked the main street, which is reported to be the oldest one in Sweden and is paved with the original cobblestone-like paving.

In the afternoon, we drove to the Lord Nelson Hotel, where Brigitte was working the night shift, on weekends, as desk clerk. The woman owner of the hotel has a fascination for Lord Nelson, the famous British admiral. The small hotel was designed in the architectural motif of Nelson's period (1750-1800). Each room has its own individual name. The hotel actually resembled a tiny museum. Brigitte also worked as a substitute teacher at a primary school, and when she returned from work that day, we took a leisurely walk.

The next morning, we drove Brigitte to school; she was teaching the fifth grade. She invited us to speak to her class. They had been studying English. We hadn't anticipated this request, so we were not at all prepared for it. We asked Brigitte how long to talk, and she thought about thirty minutes would be fine. So what does one say to ten-year-old Swedish kids who barely understand English? Aha! Of course! What would foreign children like to hear from Americans, especially those who live in California? Why, the nearly universal topic that would interest them: Disneyland! My guess was correct. I spoke to them about Disneyland, in words that I hoped they would understand. Dorothy told them about the area near where we live in the foothills of mountains as high as forty-five hundred meters. She spoke of our home, where we live on two hectares in a wooded area. She said we had a big garden, an orchard, and flowers. She recounted that we had two cats, ten chickens, and that deer often come into our yard. Well, our thirty-minute talk stretched into eighty minutes, and we held the children's attention the whole time. We could see that they were fascinated. Later, Brigitte told us the kids loved it! Again this was a fairy tale experience few tourists would ever have.

Before we knew it, it was Sunday, 3 June, and the last day of our stay with our now dearest friends. We awoke a bit late, had breakfast, then started to pack. As we packed, we both sensed a feeling of sadness, as we realized we were soon coming to the end of a fairy tale. Mireille and Brigitte planned a going-away party for us that day. At two o'clock, the guests began to arrive. Nearly all of them were friends of Brigitte and Barbara, young people about their age. From two until nearly eight, we ate, drank, chatted (nearly all could speak English), and socialized until it was time to say our *hedos* (good-byes) to this friendly gang. What a marvelous way to end this extraordinary experience.

We presented thank-you cards and gift certificates to Mireille, Oskar, and Brigitte. They were speechless! Mireille wept profusely, and Oskar shed a tear or two himself. Copious tears filled Brigitte's eyes; our eyes, too, were damp. Brigitte and Oskar came with us to the dock where we were to board a huge auto ferry bound for Turku, Finland, and then on to Helsinki. Before we boarded, we said our final *hedos* and gave our final hugs and kisses. Thus ended our fantastic, incredible, dream-like week! At this point Oskar presented us with a basket full of homemade goodies, mostly sweets, prepared by Mireille.

After boarding the ferry, we set sail at nine-thirty in the evening. It was still daylight. Dorothy and I began immediately recalling the events of the past eight days. In retrospect, we could not have possibly predicted what lay in store for us. It began when we met a charming young woman on the train from Gatwick airport to downtown London on the first day of our first trip to Europe. How unexpected was the offer she made for us to stay at her parents' home during our visit to Stockholm! And who could have dreamed that we would have had such an unforgettable time with these wonderful, friendly people? We could not have been treated better if we had been royalty.

The most inspiring part of our relationship was that for all the days we were their guests, there was not one iota of friction. There was no hint of conflict or even mild confrontation. It was nothing but sheer pleasure, an indescribable experience. Our fairy godmother was certainly looking out for us. Gypsies never had it so good!

Our boat ride left something to be desired. We were on board for nearly eleven hours and found it difficult to get much sleep in the lounge chairs provided. The trip was most unpleasant.

We passed the thousands of islands in the Swedish Archipelago in the Baltic Sea. It was about eleven o'clock, and just beginning to become dusk. We could easily see and admire the islands, while we indulged in all the goodies that Mireille had provided us with.

At 8:15 A.M., we docked at Turku, and by 8:40 we got our car, cleared customs, and were on our way to Helsinki, Finland, in the last Scandinavian country on our itinerary.

After about two hours of driving through countryside similar to that of the other Scandinavian countries, we arrived at the outskirts of Helsinki. We stopped at a small grocery store and met a man who could speak English. We asked him to call the hospitz, confirm a room for us, and get directions. This he did, and again we got quite lost before finding the place.

This hospitz was similar to our YMCA in the States, in that it had a slight Christian ambiance. It was a rather large structure. Our room was also large and very clean, with separate toilet and shower facilities. There were very few guests, so we had the place pretty much to ourselves. The room cost us seventy-five markka (one markka was twenty-six cents), or about twenty dollars per night.

After resting a while, we drove to the Jean Sibelius Park, where the Finns had erected a monument honoring the great Finnish composer. The design resembled a pipe organ. Whoever created it had a phenomenal imagination. We kept circling around the monument, always finding something different about it.

The trip on the boat the previous night had left us a bit groggy, so we decided to eat a light dinner in our room. We shared a bottle of

Finnish beer, which was not too good, and a bit warm. Shortly after-wards, we went to sleep.

The next morning, we walked to the open market, which for us was always fun, and bought some barbecued chicken and ribs and other groceries (our dinner). Then we went to the American Express office to get some cash, went to some shops, and lastly back to our room to relax and nap. We were very impressed with the Finnish girls. They were all very pretty and nearly all had light blue eyes and beautiful blonde hair.

After this, we decided to take the tram to Finlandia Park. However, in the lobby we met a couple of lads in their mid-twenties and got to talking with them. They suggested that they show us around, using our car.

We offered no objection and one of the boys, who said he had been a race car driver, took the wheel. He was an excellent driver. Both boys were neatly dressed and were going to a theology school, so we had no misgivings about them. They took us to Finlandia Park. It was a nice park along the Baltic coast, with nothing exciting going on except for the chess games being played there. The chess board was approxi-mately ten feet square, painted on a concrete sidewalk, and I judged the chess pieces to be about three feet tall! It was fascinating to watch them play. Next, the boys drove us through old Helsinki, to a very unusual and uniquely-designed cemetery where we saw Gustav Mannerheim's grave. He was the commander of the Finnish army in the 1939-1940 war against the Russians.

One very unusual sight that had us baffled, was seeing signs, per-haps about three feet square, hanging from power poles along the town's streets. One sign had the word "Blackjack" (in English!) and the other had Japanese or Chinese characters on it. We asked what these signs meant and both of the boys seemed hesitant to explain. Dorothy asked, "Are they advertising Blackjack gum, which we have in the United States?" Finally, one of the boys implied that it had to do with sex. Remember, these were theology students and we were old folk, which explained their reluctance. Ultimately, they confided that the signs were advertising condoms. It was hilarious!

We got back to our room at a quarter after nine, very grateful for the boys' assistance and guidance. It was especially helpful to have them take us; driving in Helsinki would have been a real problem for us. The street names are in both Finnish and Swedish, which would have added to our confusion if I had been driving.

These couple of interesting days in Finland wound up our stay in the Scandinavian countries. The next day we would be heading for the USSR. Looking back, there were several common threads that tied the Scandinavian countries together. The topography is similar; each country abounds with lakes, rivers, thick forests, mountains, and fjords. Each country also connects with the sea on one or more sides. All of them have a government that provides its citizens with social amenities that, to a great degree, are just and democratic. None of them places much emphasis, or wealth and resources, on their military. The emphasis of their political philosophy is on peace! The people have a penchant for drinking liquor. This is true in most northern countries. However, their governments are very strict about drinking and driving. Stringent penalties are given to those who do drink and drive. Nearly all of the people we met have a rather reserved demeanor. This is probably due to the long winters, during which they see so little sunshine. Many of the Swedes we met told us that their winters were depressing. There were several features that we recognized in most of the people we met in all four countries: we found them polite, sincere, and friendly, above all.

We added many pages to our book of memories and many photo slides for visual evidence of these memorable events, places, people, and things. During all of our stay in Sweden, and the time spent in Finland, we had good weather, which was a blessing after all the rain and miserable weather we had experienced before. This part of the world is a must for everyone who travels to Europe, especially if traveling by car. The highways are very good, well-marked, and easy to navigate. They traverse through beautiful countryside with a wide variety of natural wonders and, except for the major cities, are devoid of heavy traffic of the sort we Californians experience on our highways. Above all, the people are great! Everyone we met was kind and considerate, especially in Sweden. Without a doubt, these cold countries found a warm spot in our hearts!

Behind the (Late) Iron Curtain

It was morning on 6 June when we bade Helsinki good-bye and, with some minor qualms, headed for the USSR. Despite directions by our two young friends, we once more got hopelessly lost, which cost us considerable time and several miles of backtracking. Eventually, we neared the border of the Soviet Union at Vyborg.

The apprehension we felt was based on several factors. First, we planned to travel in a country much different from the rest of the Western world. We had no idea what to expect.

Secondly, at this period in time, there was considerable antagonism between the US and the USSR. Both countries existed under the tension of the Cold War.

Finally, we had no idea where we had been designated to stay. We knew the cities we had been booked in, but had no knowledge of our accommodations. We knew nothing about what we would find or what we could expect. All the people we knew who had visited the USSR had gone on tours, where nearly everything on the trip was prearranged. They nearly always would be under the care and guidance of an Intourist guide. Finally, we felt apprehensive (as Americans) about how the Soviet citizens would react towards us.

So, with all these concerns and mixed feelings, we pulled into Vyborg and up to the border station. The streets approaching the border, lined on both sides with Russian soldiers, were a bit ominous!

At the border station, the Russians thoroughly searched our luggage, three times. They searched our car inside and out, and had us drive over a pit where they searched underneath the car. After seeing the many soldiers, and going through this search, our apprehension was confirmed.

After all this, and after spending so much time in Western European countries, our first introduction to the Soviet Union was very disappointing. Where these countries were so neat, clean, and orderly, Vyborg was a mild disaster. It was a poor-looking city. We saw many dilapidated buses and trucks, very few passenger cars, and shack-like houses. The whole scene was depressing.

We located the Intourist Bureau office, where a very nice lady welcomed us and sold us petrol coupons (you can't buy petrol with cash, only with coupons) and auto insurance. She also gave us our official itinerary for our entire stay in the Soviet Union. This included the names of all the campgrounds and hotels assigned to us. After going through all the formalities, we proceeded on our way. Our first campground, called Repino, was near Leningrad (now called St. Petersburg). Before we had gone very far, I realized we needed diesel.

We kept our eyes open for a service station. I spotted a sign with the symbol of a gasoline pump on it, but the service station was not on the highway. I noticed a dirt road on my left and saw trucks going in and out, so I assumed it led to the station. I was right. However, we had to drive about two hundred yards through the woods to reach it. What I saw shocked me.

It had been raining. The station wasn't a station, as we know them. It was a large, flat, slightly muddy area, with no paved surface anywhere. I saw about twenty gas pumps, a small, rickety kiosk, and at least thirty trucks waiting for gas. When I saw all those trucks, I was in a state of despair. I figured it would take us an hour to get served! I had no idea which of these many pumps served diesel. I had no choice but to make some effort to get help. All the pumps were self-serve. The trucks were pulling in from all directions, at random, to wherever they could find a pump. I pulled up to the first pump, and approached the driver of the truck. I pulled out the card marked "diesel" in Russian, given to me by our friend's brother in London, and showed it to this driver. What happened next was unbelievable! He immediately started to direct traffic, waving the truck drivers left and right, forwards and backwards until there was a pump standing all alone. He directed me towards it and I got my quota of fuel! The petrol coupons are in units of ten liters each, so you have to be sure you cal-culate your needs quite carefully.

From then on, for our entire month in the USSR, getting fuel was an experience. One time I pulled up to a pump, started to pump, got a few liters, and the pump stopped. A truck driver at a pump close by saw my predicament, pulled the hose from his tank, inserted it in mine, and filled my tank full!

Another incident happened on a Sunday when there were a lot of Russians out driving. We drove to a filling station only to find it closed. We drove several miles to the next one and there was a line waiting for gas nearly two blocks long. We pulled into the line, waited a bit, then Dorothy said, "I'm going out to see what the trouble is." A few minutes passed when I saw her near the head of the line frantically waving for me to drive towards her. When I reached the petrol station, I saw her standing by a pump with no cars. This puzzled me, but it soon became apparent that practically none of the small Russian cars (some are very small) use diesel. Instead, they use low octane gaso-line. Because it was Sunday and there were very few trucks, the diesel pump was available to us. It was a real break.

That first little episode of getting diesel put us in a better frame of mind, and we went merrily on our way. As we drove along, things looked much better. The highways improved, and new ones were being built. We saw many parks, several monuments dedicated to World War II (which the Russians call the Great Patriotic War), lots of billboards with political messages, and lots of folks strolling along the road, old and young. They all waved at us. Apparently, our car indicated to them that we could be foreigners. This was their way of welcoming us.

Driving alone, with little difficulty, we felt relieved. There ahead, we saw a couple of men standing in the middle of the road waving their arms frantically. We had no idea why, as there was nothing else in the road as far as we could see. I came to a stop beside them. Looking at them, I judged they were in their late twenties. Both were very poorly dressed, their boots heavily covered with mud. They both had rather unpleasant appearances and faces to match. They began talking rapid-ly in Russian, almost shouting, and waving their arms wildly. It dawned on me that they wanted a ride. They appeared to be drunk. Needless to say I was somewhat frightened. I had stopped in the middle of the road (there was no traffic), but I decided to pull over to the side of the road. This apparently alarmed them. They evidently thought I was going to pull away. Instantly one of the drunks put his arm through the window and snatched Dorothy's glasses from her face. Now I was really scared. I had no choice but to let them in, muddy boots and all. Once in the car they became less threatening. Dorothy was then given back her glasses. I drove about three miles when they indicated they wanted out.

This was a very unpleasant incident, the first since we arrived in Europe. Since we had some apprehension of the USSR to begin with, this disagreeable event only added more anxiety to our feelings. We hoped fervently that this was not a harbinger of things to come. A short time later, we stopped to clean out all the mud from the back.

After driving over a not-too-well constructed highway, at about five o'clock we arrived at the Repino campground. This main highway was somewhat of a disappointment compared to all the roads we used in Western Europe. So what? Gypsies allegedly take life as it comes!

I parked the car next to a tour bus and we prepared to register at the Intourist office in the campground. Just as we got out of our car, a man (presumably the bus driver) stepped out of the bus. He looked at us quizzically, and then looked over at our car. He appeared to be in his early forties, about medium height, and quite husky. His face was swarthy yet friendly. We nodded greetings to each other. It was obvious he was very curious about our Volkswagon. My immediate reaction, since it was a German car and we had German license plates, was to identify ourselves as Americans. I was concerned about his reaction to us if he thought we were Germans. I said to him, quite firmly, "Americansky!" (This is the way they invariably pronounce it in the movies and on television when speaking to a Russian.) He repeated, "Ho! American," (I don't know whether he said Americansky), then I said, "California." Well, his reaction was a sight to behold. He threw up his arms, his eyes grew as large as saucers, his face broke out in a big grin, and he shouted, "Ho, California!" We immediately knew we were "in."

What we learned, after traveling for months in Europe, was that everyone knew about California. Disneyland and Hollywood, as far as they were concerned, represented California. Our newfound friend just couldn't contain his curiosity over our car. He walked all around it, looked inside, and then pointed to the hood. He then curled his fingers on each hand, hooked them together, and then tugged, with a grimace on his face as though he was using all his strength. It was amazing, but I immediately understood that he wanted to know the strength (horsepower) of the car. I wrote the figure, I believe it was forty-two, in the dust on the hood. He was satisfied. Next, he indicated, again with gestures which I understood, that he wanted to know the speed. I showed him the speedometer. He showed surprise on his face. I assumed he was surprised that the car could go so fast. Although our car wasn't a large car, it had much more power and speed than most of the little Russian cars. This interesting little session over, we bade each other good-bye and parted company.

Dorothy and I then registered. We had no problem with language as there were always Intourist people who spoke several languages. In our four weeks in the USSR, all of the Intourist people were very friendly, accommodating, and helpful.

We were shown to our cabin. It was a double unit with one bathroom in between. Our unit was rather barren with no frills: just two single beds, a small table with an empty bottle for water, and a chair. There was no closet, and no dresser or place to put, or hang, clothes. It was not very attractive. It was basically a large wooden tent with beds and a shared bathroom.

Since we hadn't eaten anything for dinner, we went to what we thought was the restaurant. It turned out to be a rather meager snack bar. Our choices were limited, but there was caviar on crackers, some cold cuts, hard boiled eggs, cold fish on crackers, and cheese. Naturally we tried the caviar. Personally, I don't particularly care for it, judging from the few times I'd eaten it in the past. Dorothy likes it though. We selected some other tidbits (it was a do-it-yourself arrangement) and sat down to indulge. Much to our delight, the black caviar was out of this world! It was nothing like we'd ever eaten in the US.

After our snacks, back to the "wooden tent" we went. I took the empty bottle to get drinking water. We didn't know if the water in the bathroom was potable. I went to the office and asked the Intourist lady (most of the Intourist staff consisted of women) about the water in the bathroom. She said, "You'd better not drink it. Get water from the community kitchen." This was a rather large building equipped with stoves, sinks, tables, chairs, and all the utensils for campers who prepared their own meals.

I went to the kitchen, opened the door, and there, seated at the head of a long table, was our "friend" the bus driver. When he saw me he waved his arms and shouted "California!" I walked over to him and we shook hands. I then glanced at the table, and saw about forty people seated there, mostly women, and most well-past middle age. Nearly all of them looked and dressed like peasants. I could see their tanned and wrinkled faces and their work-worn hands. Everything about them suggested that they labored outdoors, presumably in farming. When I glanced at them, they all looked at me and smiled. They appeared as curious about me as I was about them. They had just finished dinner, and I could see that they had plenty to eat.

Apparently, my "friend" explained me to them. I must have met with their approval. I turned towards my "friend" to address him when another man from the group literally shoved in my hand a water glass about two-thirds full of vodka. He also gave me a slice of an orange. I was in a bit of a quandary about how to handle this situation. From what I'd seen in movies and on television, I thought I was expected to toss the drink down in one gulp! No way. I'm not that kind of a drinker. However, I did manage to polish it off in three gulps, and surprisingly it was quite smooth. Then he instructed me, through gestures, to eat the orange. After this, someone handed me a piece of cheese on a cracker. I thought the welcoming ceremony was over. But no, they wanted me to sit down at the table and join them for dinner!

With hand and facial gestures I indicated that my wife was in the cabin. In turn, they indicated that I should go get her. So I got my bottle of water, went back to our cabin, and said to Dorothy, "Do you want to join a Russian party?" She replied, "Why not?" So back to the kitchen we went.

Now the fun began. Dorothy and I seated ourselves and the Russians began plying us with food and drink; wine and vodka! By again communicating in sign language, we somehow learned that they came from Samarkand, Tashkent, Uzbekistan, and Turkestan, on their vacation, traveling by this bus. After a couple of drinks and some food (it was delicious but we couldn't eat much, since we had just eaten previously), they lustfully sang many Russian folk songs. Dorothy knew an old Russian song she had learned from her father when just a child.

Many of them knew it and we sang with gusto! Even though we didn't know the other songs, we enjoyed the singing. As the evening progressed, we became less inhibited and soon we joined in the dancing. Men and women together, women dancing with women, men dancing with men, and Dorothy and I dancing with anybody. The rafters rang with our singing, dancing, laughing, and shouting. We were having one hilarious time.

Later, a little old Uzbek woman, with a dark round face and slanting eyes, took a pin off her jacket and pinned it on Dorothy. Then a young man, from Tashkent, took his pin off and pinned it on me. We learned, after several days of traveling in the USSR, that Russian people of all ages love to wear pins. Many, mostly men, wore military medals. Some signified a reward for something they had done in civilian life. Often young boys would approach you and want to exchange pins for chewing gum!

Anyway, back to the festivities. We carried on with reckless abandon till well past eleven o'clock. We felt so happy and thrilled with such a wonderful, unexpected happening that we kissed them all good night. When we got back to our cabin, we pinched ourselves to see if what happened this night was really true. It being our first day in the Soviet Union, we said, "If this is the way life is here, then we're taking out citizenship papers!" Tired but happy, we took off the pins that were given us, threw them in a suitcase, undressed, and hit the sack. We never even bothered to look at the pins again until nearly six months later, when we were finally back home.

When unpacking our clothes, Dorothy found the pins, which both of us had forgotten. We recalled the night in the Repino campground when we received the pins. We really had not bothered to look at them very carefully. Now we did. The pin the young man gave me was very unusual. It was a colorful pin of a famous church in Tashkent. The pin the little Uzbek woman pinned on Dorothy—hold your breath—was a Russian pin of Donald Duck! We both howled with laughter. Remember what I said about everyone knowing about Disneyland?

The next day we headed for the beautiful city of Leningrad. Our camp was about twenty-seven miles away. We had to go by bus to the train station. Then the train took us to Finlandsky station, near Lenin Square in Leningrad. Public transportation is very reasonable in

Russia. From the station we walked to the Leningrad Hotel to take a bus tour of the city.

Almost every campground is located near a major city and one of the perks we got was a tour of the city with an English speaking guide, at no cost to us. Because we arrived late, we missed the tour. So we started walking. It was raining hard when we left camp, but fortunately cleared up when we got to the city.

Our first stop was to board the famous cruiser, *Aurora*, anchored in the Neva River. The *Aurora* played a vital part in the 1917 revolution. During a critical period in the revolt, the sailors aboard her mutinied, captured her officers, then turned her big guns on the Winter Palace, home of the tsars and the last refuge of the bourgeois Provisional Government.

On October 26, 1917, a shot was fired from the cruiser, which alerted the revolutionary workers, soldiers, and sailors to storm the Winter Palace and break the back of the Provisional Government, ending the long, terrible rule of the tsars once and for all! Thus a new era in human history was born.

After Lenin's death in 1924, the city was renamed Leningrad in his honor. It was an hour-and-a-half wait in line before we were allowed to board the *Aurora*. We tingled with excitement thinking about the history that was made at that time, and by that ship. It is now a very popular tourist attraction.

From the *Aurora* we walked to the Peter and Paul Cathedral, capped by its magnificent gold spire. The rain had stopped, and the sun came out. The day was bright and sparkling. We stood there enraptured by the beauty of this splendid structure. The rays of the sun were reflected from the spire like a halo of golden threads.

As we stood there gazing in awe at this ethereal sight, we were approached by a tall, nicely-built young man, well-dressed in city clothes. He spoke to us in fairly good English and asked, "You're Jewish, aren't you?" This certainly surprised us. We didn't think this was so obvious. We answered, "Yes." He said, "I am, also." We happened to be standing near one of the many small kiosks in Leningrad that sell snacks and drinks. Dorothy mentioned that she was thirsty. Our new friend then went over to the kiosk and said in English to the lady clerk, "These are my friends, American Imperialists." This was hilarious because we knew that the woman didn't understand a word of English. He then bought Dorothy a fruit drink. We didn't get to talk much, but he implied conditions were not very good there, especially for Jews. He arranged to meet us later at a given spot, at a given time. He never showed up and, truthfully, we weren't disappointed. We really didn't care to have anything to do with dissidents. We preferred to see things on our own, and we wanted to avoid anything that would spoil our visit.

Soon it was time to head back to the campground, but first we wanted to have dinner in town. So we walked back to the lovely dining room in the Leningrad Hotel and ordered dinner.

While in the dining room, a young Finnish couple, sitting in a booth behind us, became quite friendly. The young man behaved as though he had drunk too much liquor. He insisted on buying us Russian colas, several of them. They didn't taste very good.

It was getting late, though it was still very light. We took the train and bus back to our campground. A bit later, we went over to the Intourist office for some information and the Intourist lady invited us for a cup of tea, which we heartily accepted. She took us into a back room, made some hot tea, and brought out some bread and sausage.

We were having a pleasant time when a bit later, a handsome young man, the camp director, came into the room and joined us. He also spoke quite good English. He came in carrying a bag. The lady introduced us. He took off his coat, opened the bag, and brought out a piece of cheese, a loaf of bread, and a bottle of vodka about two-thirds full.

Here we go again! We snacked on the cheese, sausage, and bread. He and I proceeded to polish off the bottle of vodka (the ladies didn't drink). Again the vodka went down smoothly; it was not quite as fiery as the vodka we drink in the US. I discovered later that Russia produces sixty proof vodka. I would guess that this is what most Russians drink, and why it is so easy to take. This unexpected little episode was almost a repeat of last night's affair except for the singing and dancing. As the evening progressed, we all felt very loose and friendly, and had much to talk about. We ate, drank, and gabbed until well past midnight. Before we parted, they gave us some posters depicting the Olympic theme. The Olympic games would be held in Moscow the following year (1980), and these attractive Russian Olympic posters depicted this major event. Yes, the fairy tales kept piling up, day after day.

The next morning we got up early, so as not to miss the tour. We took the same route as we did the day before. I might mention that the buses we took to the train station were always filled with passengers. In order to put our fare in the coin receptacle, first we had to know how much to pay. This we did by holding out a handful of kopeks. A Russian, recognizing us as foreigners, selected the proper coins and then passed them on to passengers ahead of us who in turn passed them on until it reached the receptacle. Then he or she got the tickets and the process started all over again, in reverse, until the tickets reached us! We also observed that several passengers didn't even bother to pay. It appeared obvious that they weren't cheating. It was merely a practice that appeared acceptable and not unusual!

Our destination was again the Leningrad Hotel. We boarded the bus there and were taken on an hour and a half tour of the highlights of Leningrad. It is indeed a beautiful city. Peter the Great, the tsar who is very much respected and admired by Russians even today, built the city in 1703 as the capital of the Empire. He was very much enamored of, and influenced by, the culture of Western Europe, so he brought outstanding architects and artisans from France and Italy to the city. With the cooperation of famous Russian artists and architects they built many of the splendid buildings that stand today. Each building is a masterpiece of craftsmanship. An hour and a half tour is just a minuscule amount of time to see all that this marvelous city has to offer. It is the cultural and artistic center of the USSR.

The tour ended before noon, so for lunch we braved a *pirozki* restaurant. We had to get in line and select from a couple dozen varieties of fillings. We couldn't dilly-dally in making our selections as the Russian people are a bit impatient; prone to push and shove. Perhaps this is because they have to do so much queuing up for so many things. Our selections hastily made, we ordered coffee and found our seats. The *pirozkis* were quite good, but the coffee was awful.

After lunch we visited a *Beriozkya* shop. The word *Beriozkya* means birch tree. When driving on the highways, one sees mile upon mile of birch trees. The *Beriozkya* shops are for foreigners; they are all over Russia. In the Ukraine, they are called *Kashtan* shops, which means chestnut tree. These shops, as I said, are for foreigners, because you can purchase only with hard currency, such as dollars, francs, marks, yen, crowns, pounds, etc., but not with rubles. The government needs hard currency. The shops are a combination gift, arts and crafts, liquor, and domestic food shop, with a smattering of some imported foods too. The prices are as much as 50 percent less than those in the regular retail shops. Vodka and caviar are two items in this category. Some of the arts and crafts items, mostly all hand made, are exquisite, particularly the enameled boxes. We didn't buy anything, just looked and admired.

Next we started walking to the Winter Palace. We didn't quite know the way, so we stopped and pulled out our city map. In less than five minutes, a pretty young girl asked us, in quite good English, "Can I help you?" We told her what we wanted to find and she directed us. Then she asked, "Have you been to Petrodvorets?" We replied, "We haven't even heard of it." She then said, "It is the former summer palace of Peter the Great, also called the Water Palace. You absolutely must go and see it." This aroused our interest and we asked, "How do we get there?" "By boat," she answered.

At this point we began to inquire about her personal life. She said her name was Elena, but preferred to be called Lena; she was a university student and today was her last day in school, as the summer vacation was starting. She was nineteen years old, taller than average, quite attractive, self-confident and at ease with us, and struck us as being very intelligent.

With this bit of information, we asked her if she would be our guide and take us to this place. She agreed, but first she had to call her mother and inform her that she was going with us. She called and then told us it was all right with her mother.

It was a bit of a walk to catch the boat to Petrodvorets. This palace was built in the early eighteenth century by Peter the Great on the southern shore of the Gulf of Finland. Our boat was a hydrofoil and soon we clambered aboard with many other passengers. It wasn't long before we disembarked on the Palace grounds.

We had hardly started walking through the grounds when we realized what Lena meant when she said a visit to Petrodvorets was a must. Everywhere we looked we saw exquisite statues and fountains by the score, of every description. Most of the fountains and some of the statues bubbled, sprayed, and spouted water in countless fascinating patterns. We also saw many unusual and amazing waterfalls, several very colorful and uniquely designed flower gardens in full bloom, life-sized statues on the Grand Cascade, and much more. The Morskoi Canal, which divides the park, was a spectacle to behold. This magnificent park and the summer palace of Peter the Great provide a mixture of the beauties of nature and the creativity of man. These two elements are blended to perfection. Petrodvorets is absolutely breathtaking. Words cannot possibly describe it.

With deep regrets, we had to leave this majestic place. We walked back to the boat dock, sat on a bench, and waited for our boat to take us back. By this time, we had spent over three hours going through the Palace grounds. Lena was like an old friend, as we sat on the bench chatting away without regard to time. Much to our dismay, we realized we'd been so busy talking that we'd missed our boat.

Unknown to us, this was a cause for concern. Lena explained, "Each ticket is numbered to identify the boat you came to the Palace on and you must return on this same boat! One of the boat captains is a real meanie and he's liable to refuse to let us on his boat." When the boat docked, she cried, "Oh my, it's the mean captain's boat!" As I said before, Lena was a bright young lady, so she told us to hold our ticket so as to conceal the number. This we did, but to no avail. The captain wasn't fooled and indicated that we couldn't board. Lena then went into action. She half shouted, gesticulated wildly, spoke with machine-gun rapidity, and finally broke the captain down. He let us board. It was important to us to leave on this boat, as we had tickets for a performance by the famous Ukrainian Folk Dance Ensemble; if we missed this boat we would also miss the performance.

After we got settled on the boat and were underway, we asked Lena what she had told the captain. Briefly, she told the captain that we were Americans and that we had to get back to Leningrad; otherwise, we would miss our plane! What a break for us! Bless Lena.

Then Lena took us, by way of the metro (underground rail), right to the door of the Cultural Palace where the performance was being held. By the way, the metro station was beautiful, the trains quiet, fast, and efficient, and the fare was just five kopeks (eight cents).

Here we said *do sveedahnya* (good-bye) to Lena. She was an exceptional young lady, and it was a stroke of good fortune that we found her. She made it possible for us to enjoy a most memorable afternoon and add one more page to our book of memories.

The Ukrainian folk dancers were marvelous and their native costumes were dazzling. It was a terrific show. By the time we left to go back to camp, by way of the metro, train, and then bus, it was near midnight and still not dark! We really had a full day that day, about sixteen hours long.

The next morning was sunny and warm. We once again headed for Leningrad, this time to see the Winter Palace and the Hermitage Museum, one of the finest museums in the world.

As we approached the museum, we both got thirsty. We noticed rows of dispensing machines where people waited to buy drinks. These machines dispensed *Beriozkya* juice, a drink made from the extract of birch trees. The drinks cost three kopeks apiece. We had no three kopek coins. A *babushka* (elderly lady) standing close by was aware of our dilemma, and gave us a couple of three kopek coins.

The juice, however, is not dispensed in containers. Standing on the top of the dispensing machines were several ordinary drinking glasses. What one does, after previous customers have drunk from the glasses, is to take a glass and rinse it with cold water from a tiny faucet in the dispenser, insert your coin, and the juice then comes out of another faucet. You drink, and then place your glass among the others—strictly sanitary, Russian style! However, the juice was good, had a very unusual taste, and did quench our thirst. This possibly unhealthy procedure never deterred us from drinking this juice whenever the need arose. We figured that if the Russians do it, so could we.

Soon we reached the Winter Palace (built in 1762) and adjacent buildings that house the Hermitage. These buildings were built by the finest Italian and Russian architects, in the Russian baroque style.

The Hermitage is one of the world's largest museums. It houses nearly three million exhibits. It is a treasury of world art. Just to see the rich parquet wood floors, the huge crystal chandeliers, the gorgeous paintings on the walls and ceilings, is a rare treat. The quantity, quality, and variety of the artifacts were indescribable. We spent nearly three hours viewing just a minute number of these artifacts. It is no exaggeration to say we could have spent weeks in this museum without seeing it all.

We had just a couple of days left of our stay in Leningrad. We tried to see more, but as all travelers know, there is never enough time to do justice to any major city. There is always so much to see and so little time. This is especially true of Leningrad, the Hero City.

The Piskarevskoye Cemetery in Leningrad is a must see. In World War II, Leningrad was under siege by the Nazi armies for nine hundred days. During those days, almost six hundred thousand Leningraders died of hunger, freezing temperatures, bombs, and bullets. However, the city lived on, fought, and finally won! The will of the people turned what threatened to be certain defeat into victory. This is perhaps one of the greatest examples of courage and fortitude. It shows unparalleled dedication and patriotism by a people. This is why Leningrad is called the Hero City.

As you approach the cemetery, you first see a pit about two feet deep and several feet square, surrounded on all four sides by slabs of dark blue marble. Within the pit burns the eternal flame. Directly ahead of the pit is a six-foot-wide concrete walkway. Parallel to this walkway, on each side, are gardens nearly as wide. Then, parallel to the gardens, also on both sides, are narrower concrete walkways. All of this stretches for about three hundred yards. There, at the very end stands a tall, magnificent statue (I believe it represents Mother Russia). The statue is surrounded on both sides by tall trees. On either side of the walkways are large, slightly raised, grassy plots.

This cemetery is the resting place of several hundred thousand victims of the siege of Leningrad. There are no individual graves here. The grassy plots are mass graves. Each plot is the resting place of five thousand people. There are no markings, crosses, headstones, or anything on them. Only a small plaque lies in front of each. To stand there viewing the profound simplicity of Piskarevskoye cemetery is an emotional experience hard to comprehend or describe. It is a heart-wrenching example of the horrors of war. To see it, to feel it, is to significantly understand why war is hell. It is sure to make one a "Peace-nik."

Gypsies must move on, it's true, so we left beautiful, exciting, historic Leningrad with but one regret: we didn't have nearly enough time to see and savor all that was available in this most remarkable Hero City.

Our route took us to Novgorod, then on to Kalinin. Novgorod was of no particular interest, with one exception. Instead of a small cabin, we were housed in a rather large building in individual rooms, similar to a hotel. The building was under construction, and nearly completed. To our amazement, it was deteriorating almost while we looked at it! It was a very poorly constructed building. Our room was clean and adequate, but the toilet facilities were an abomination! The toilet was filthy, messy, stunk, and didn't work properly. The Russian campers, and there were many of them, appeared to be drunk and unfriendly. It was quite a contrast to the Russians we met in Leningrad.

We met a young Australian couple and invited them to join us for a beer. They had some rather negative things to say about their camping experiences in Moscow and other parts of the USSR. They had been to cities that we planned to visit. We didn't give this much thought, because in our previous experiences we learned that traveling is a very subjective activity and other peoples' tastes are not necessarily our own.

However, we did heed their warning to us to take the windshield wipers off our car or they would be stolen! The only reason for the Russians to do this, they thought, was their desire for souvenirs. The Aussies' warnings were correct. From then on we noticed that in the campgrounds, especially, we saw no windshield wipers on foreign cars. We soon discovered that many Russians were very much taken by American things, especially Levi jeans. And they would take them if they had the chance! There was little to see at the campground, so, with the Aussies, we took off for the city of Novgorod to see the sights.

Novgorod is an ancient medieval city, founded in the ninth century. It was a major commercial and cultural center and was the chief center of foreign trade. It has a long and varied history. It went through many governmental changes until it came under complete Moscovy control in 1478 and lost its freedom.

It is one of the birthplaces of Russian architecture. The magnificent architectural monuments of Novgorod earned it the name of the "Museum City." One of the finest examples is the eleventh-century St. Sophia's Cathedral. We visited a couple of other unusual churches, the Yaroslav Palace, and the monument in the center of the Kremlin marking the thousandth anniversary of Russia. In World War II it was held by the Germans and suffered great damage. Many of the buildings have been restored, but much of its architectural glory has been lost forever.

We went back to the campground for dinner. The Aussie couple were having dinner also, and again we invited them over for a beer. Our Russian waitress added our Australian friends' dinner to our check, but we didn't mind. The entire check came to just $5.75, total. Wow!

Up and away we went the next morning. Not too unhappily, we put Novgorod behind us. We noticed that while we ordered tea with our breakfast, the Russians in the camp were drinking beer and vodka! To each his or her own.

Kalinin was our next stop. It was cold in the early morning, but soon the sun warmed us. It was a nice day for driving. The highway from Leningrad to Moscow was fairly similar to California state highways. They had just two lanes, which were not overly wide.

At this point we became aware that, along the entire distance, the highways were lined with trees on both sides. It was interesting to see that whenever the buses stopped to let the passengers off, we would see them disappear into the woods via footpaths. No buildings would be visible! It was eerie. Obviously their dwellings were back in the woods.

Along the highway, groups of mostly elderly people, primarily women, were cutting what appeared to be high weeds using long, old-fashioned scythes. A horse and large wagon followed them as they loaded the cuttings onto the wagon. We later learned that these peasants not only kept the sides of the highways neat, but they also gathered feed for their animals. Late in the afternoon, without any trouble, we found our campground near Kalinin and checked into the Intourist office in the Tver Motel.

This campground was quite pretty, neat, and clean, with lots of trees. It was a big improvement over Novgorod. The cabins were attractive and inviting. Our cabin was a cute little nine-by-twelve-foot, A-frame cottage built in typical Russian style, painted in pastel hues of yellow, red, blue, and green. The architecture was similar to the small wooden cottages of the workers and peasants we had been seeing as we drove through the countryside. The cabin had rather wide eaves. Hanging from the eaves, in front of the house, we noticed wide fascias. The fascias had cut-out artistic designs, and curlicues. We found this very attractive. After getting settled, we went to the Intourist office and arranged for our free guided tour of Kalinin.

We went back to our cute little cabin to read and write postcards. The night was turning cold and our beds lacked sufficient blankets. I went to the office and asked for another blanket for each of us. The lady told us flatly that they didn't have any. What could we do but suffer in silence and brave the elements? About half an hour later, a young lady knocked at the door bearing two blankets for each of us! The Intourist personnel were very good to us, maybe because of our age.

The next morning, after breakfast, our very sweet young lady guide, Valya, met us and we drove to the city in our car. Valya was very knowledgeable and articulate. She was easy to understand.

The most impressive feature of this tour was our visit to a World War II memorial. It was a very simple concrete and stone edifice with an eternal flame burning soft and low. The flame was from the eternal flame at the war memorial in Moscow and was carried by foot to Kalinin. While the flame burned, we heard a steady beat, like a heartbeat. As the flame glowed and the heart beat, soft, somber classical music emanated from within.

This experience was so emotional, so overpowering, so heart-wrenching, that both Dorothy and I had tears in our eyes. For those few moments, it was difficult to even breathe. What a powerful indictment against war the monument was. It so graphically reflected the attitude and feelings of the Russians against war, "never again," and the overpowering desire for peace. We suspected that Valya intentionally brought us to this memorial so that we, too, would get the message of the horror of war.

While in the city, we shopped in a *Beriozkya* shop. There were many lovely handmade gift items including amber jewelry, but we weren't in the gift and souvenir buying mood quite yet. We did buy some cookies and candies and a liter of vodka. The vodka wasn't expensive at only $2.25! We also bought a box of candy and cookies for Valya.

As we walked up the steps to the entrance of the hotel, we handed Valya the cookies and candy in the plastic bag that had the *Beriozkya* logo imprinted on it. Then something strange happened: Valya took the bag, climbed a couple of stairs, turned and handed us back the bag. Then, rather surreptitiously, gestured for us to wait. In a few moments, she returned with a plain plastic bag, transferred the candy and cookies into it, thanked us, and bade us good-bye!

Dorothy and I looked askance at each other, shook our heads in bewilderment, then left for our cabin. Once there, we tried to analyze this unusual incident. We suspected that, knowing the Soviet citizens don't shop at foreign currency stores, the question would be, where did she get the foreign money? For a Russian to be carrying a *Beriozkya* shop bag might cast suspicion upon him or her. This might make them suspect that they might be involved in some devious or illegal activity with foreigners, especially Americans.

This was our first experience of this nature. From this strange incident, we deduced how fearful the Soviet government was of another horrible war like World War II. In this war they lost over twenty million lives and nearly one third of their county, the most productive areas being destroyed.

During our time there, the Cold War was very intense. The Russians, unfortunately, suspected everybody and everything. The government was paranoid in its reaction. This was not true of the people we met. However, they couldn't help but reflect this fear and suspicion, if ever so slightly, in their behavior. How truly sad.

Our tour was over early, so after eating a bit and washing our clothes, we took the bus back to the city. We checked out the markets and other interesting shops, then went back to the *Beriozkya* shop. This time, Dorothy bought a simple amber necklace which cost us seventeen dollars! Its value in the US would be many times that. By this time, we felt tired, so went back to our little hut to rest, relax, and dry out. We got soaked in the rain on our way home.

The hotel had an attractive dining room. We both felt hungry, so off we went to indulge in Russian cuisine. Music greeted us as we entered the dining room. It was coming from a four-piece band with a female vocalist. They played, of all things, loud rock music! Their playing wasn't very good, and for us it was disappointing. Here we are, thousands of miles from home, in a foreign country, being entertained by American rock. And the Russians were disco dancing and loving it! They were not only dancing exuberantly, but also drinking vodka with the same exuberance.

This was our first real experience mingling with the Russians when they were "out on the town." Unlike in the West, their drinks were served to them in bottles, not glasses. They mixed these drinks themselves with mineral water, mostly, and sometimes champagne!

During the weeks we spent in the USSR, we realized that the Russians drink wholesale! This also applies to the Finns whom we met. On rare occasions when we did see them order a drink in a glass, it was a minimum "double shot." Yes, the Russians take their drinking and dancing seriously.

Shortly after we were seated at a table, another couple, probably in their mid-fifties, were seated at our table. They came from a small city in Sweden. As usual, we went through the formalities of introductions and small talk (their names were Ivy and Walther). Walther was tall, handsome, and nicely dressed. He didn't dress like a camper. He had the bearing of a military officer and was very outgoing. Ivy was nearly the opposite. Physically, she gave the impression of one who had known hard work. She looked older than Walther, yet we could discern a subtle gentleness in her features, particularly in her eyes. She looked like the motherly type. In a matter of minutes, we became almost like old friends. Walther spoke good English. Ivy's English was not good, but she understood quite well. They were also camping here.

After dinner, we joined the other dancers and carried on delightfully until eleven o'clock. In all fairness to the dance band, they did play some Russian songs, which we thoroughly enjoyed.

During the evening, a drunken young man seated at a table near us asked a young lady nearby for a dance. She refused and, much to our horror, the man doubled up his fist and swung wildly and viciously at the woman! She was alert enough to duck, and he missed her and fell with a crash to the floor. We expected a bouncer to immediately toss him out on his rear. Instead, a waitress picked him up, whispered in his ear, and led him back to his table. A few minutes later, he tried to stand up, started to lose his balance, leaned on his table to steady himself, and the table, with all the dishes and glasses on it, came crashing down. What a mess. This time for sure we thought he was going to get it, but again a couple of waitresses picked him up and coolly and calmly led him to a bench outside.

It was quite cold outside when we all left to go to our bungalows, and there he was, still sitting on the bench, stoned! Before we parted with our Swedish friends, they invited us to have breakfast with them at the community kitchen in camp. Despite the unpleasant scene with the drunk, we enjoyed a rather full, interesting, and exciting day and night, and had found new acquaintances.

We woke up early, and as prearranged, we had breakfast with Ivy and Walther. Dorothy and I supplied a real treat: peanut butter and jelly. Ivy made typical Swedish coffee, hot and strong! During our conversation at breakfast, we learned that they also planned to drive to Moscow. Our itinerary listed the Mozhaisky campground, located about twenty minutes from downtown Moscow, as our next stop.

Again, as was the usual pattern for us, we got lost! It seemed almost a certainty that this would happen. It was never anything worse than a real annoyance for us, especially me. After asking directions a couple of times, we pulled into the Hotel Mozhaisky parking lot. And who should we meet? Ivy and Walther! However, they didn't intend to camp there. They stayed at the hotel.

Our accommodations here were much like the others, only our cabin was a bit larger and we had to use the campground toilet facilities, which were pretty bad. Dorothy described the women's toilet as terrible! There was no toilet paper available. You used either *Pravda* or *Tass* (national newspapers), unless you had your own toilet paper.

The campground offered one nice feature to the hotel guests and the campers: a free bus that ran from the hotel to downtown Moscow, near the Kremlin, every hour, on the hour, from eight in the morning until eleven at night. This enabled us to go to town right after breakfast, do our sightseeing, have lunch, and then go back to our cabin and take a nap. Later, we would eat dinner at one of the dining facilities in the hotel, mostly at the buffet. Ivy and Walther joined us in this routine. Then, because it was still light and the weather warm, the four of us would hop on the bus, and ride to the end of the line. We would do more sightseeing, and then catch the bus back. This procedure we followed for nearly all the four days we traveled together. It was always nearly midnight, and still light, when we got back.

During the days we spent with Ivy and Walther, we kept constantly busy sightseeing. One day we took advantage of the free, three-hour tour of the city. Our tourist guide, a comely young woman, like the other Intourist guides, spoke English in a voice we could clearly understand. She knew a great deal about the history, culture, and interesting features of Moscow. She kept us fully engrossed during the entire tour.

Moscow is more than captivating. There is so much to see that a three-hour tour just can't do it justice. This is mainly because the culture, religion, history, and the many varied languages of Russia are different from most of Western Europe. There are nearly 150 different ethnic groups that live in this vast land. The USSR covers nearly one sixth of the globe and lies in eleven time zones. When it is morning in Leningrad, it is night in Vladivostok.

Physically, Moscow is one of the world's largest cities in population and area. During the summer there are millions of tourists, mainly from the other socialist countries.

Mature, fully-leafed trees lined the wide *prospekts* (major streets or boulevards), even in metropolitan Moscow. The many tiny Moskva and Fiat automobiles were an amusing sight. They looked like weaving, darting, multi-colored beetles. In the center of the *prospekts* was a well-marked lane used exclusively by police, fire, and government vehicles. Unknowingly, when I first drove in the city, I was driving in this lane because there was so little traffic there. I later learned that this was illegal.

One day, just Dorothy and I were walking along the Kremlin wall when we came upon a bridal party taking photographs. It was clear that the wedding had just occurred. The bride and groom were attired in traditional wedding garb. The bride was holding a lovely bouquet of flowers. Immediately after the picture-taking, the party walked a short distance to the monument that contained the eternal flame memorializing the Great Patriotic War. Surrounding the flame lay many, many bouquets of flowers. The bride then carefully placed her bouquet among the others. This was a very touching scene.

Later, the couple got into an automobile decorated like our "just married" cars would be bedecked, with multicolored streamers and ribbons. Tied to the radiator was a large teddy bear. Fortunately, I had taken pictures of this entire event. It was so unusual, I wanted a record of it. Curious about the teddy bear, we learned that this was a common practice. If the newlyweds desired their first-born to be a boy, they would signify this with a bear. If they desired a girl, they would signify with a girl doll. This was another event to remember.

All my adult life, I had longed to visit Lenin's tomb. I would guess that many people have either seen it or seen pictures of it. In order to get inside the tomb, one must queue up in a very, very long line. We were determined to see Lenin, and waited for three hours before we could enter the tomb. At the entrance stood two military honor guards standing at attention so rigidly that they looked like statues. We could not tell if they were even breathing. Another soldier, standing at the entrance, took my camera—no picture-taking. We then slowly and somberly walked past the glass-covered casket. Lenin's face looked as though it was carved from marble. We were not permitted to stand and gaze at him. We had to keep moving. This took us less than thirty seconds. This was a real emotional experience for us. We realized that this mere mortal, while living, was responsible for one of the most dramatic and historic events in human history.

Ivy and Walther joined us and we ate our last dinner together in the main dining room. We splurged for the occasion and ordered some very expensive, but excellent, caviar as an appetizer. We watched the Russians and tourists from other socialist countries eat, dance, and drink to the loud, rank, rock music, loving every minute of it.

I mention tourists from other socialist countries because there were very many of them. One reason for this was that the currency of all the socialist countries was not convertible, and therefore not accepted in Western countries. Here, their currency was acceptable. Secondly, during the time we were in these countries, it was extremely difficult for citizens of the socialist countries to get permission to travel anywhere except to other socialist countries.

The four of us left after the band stopped playing at a half past ten. We strolled around a bit, and then went up to Walther and Ivy's room to say our final and sad farewells. The next day, they would head for home. Dorothy and I had to leave the next day for a one-night stay in the ancient city of Suzdal.

Before we parted, they presented us with a small cushion for Dorothy's back. They also gave us a handsome, pump-type coffee thermos. They certainly surprised us by such unexpected generosity. The five days we spent with Ivy and Walther were five marvelous, memorable days that we will cherish forever. The gods were certainly smiling upon us. This fairy tale experience of our meeting with Ivy and

Walther didn't end with our emotional farewells that night in the Mozhaisky Hotel.

Again, when strangers meet, especially foreigners, the common practice is to talk about your comings and goings. Nearly always you exchange personal information, including addresses and invitations to visit. With Ivy and Walther, it was more than just a formal gesture. On our part, and theirs, the invitations were sincere. We developed warm feelings in the short period of time we spent together.

Unexpectedly, these feelings bore fruit. Ivy and Walther visited us twice. We, in turn, spent eight unforgettable days with them in their home in 1984. Who could have possibly dreamed that from this chance acquaintance such wonderful happenings would occur!

From Moscow, to the Ancient City of Suzdal, and Return

Meanwhile, back to our travels. When we were planning this trip, it was arranged by our travel agent from San Francisco. In order to get permission to spend ten days in Moscow, we would have to take a one-day break to another city after five days before we could return. In our case, the other city was Suzdal.

Trying to find our way to Suzdal was a bummer. Moscow is a very large city both in population and area. It is encircled by two rings of highways, an inner circle and an outer one. I can assure you that before we found the road leading to Suzdal, we were going around in circles! Once we missed our exit, there was no turning back. We had to complete the entire circle to try once again to find the correct exit. On our second trip around I spotted a small kiosk in a grassy, park-like area in the center of the circle. I noticed a man in a uniform, either police or military, standing in the doorway. I parked the car and walked over to the kiosk. I wanted to get directions to Suzdal.

Before I got to the entrance, this man, with an authoritarian look on his face, held up his hands as if to push me back. As he did so, I did get a quick glance of the inside of the kiosk. I saw there three other uniformed young men staring at me. The kiosk was also full of electric and electronic equipment. By this rapid glance I realized that this was more than a police station. I was quite uneasy about being there. I pulled out my map and pointed out Suzdal to the officer. I then pointed to our car. He realized our predicament and relaxed considerably. So did I.

Next, he indicated through gestures that I would have to complete the circle in order to come to the exit to the Suzdal highway. This would be quite a trip. With a look of dismay on my face, I pointed to the highway on the other side of the circle. He carefully looked me over then indicated that I could drive across the grassy parkway onto the highway. I got into our car and crossed this area while he stood in the road holding up traffic so I could drive onto the highway. What a break. We were relieved.

For this one night in Suzdal, we were booked into a fairly new and quite large hotel. This hotel was only one story, but seemed to wander all over the place. We got completely lost in the hotel looking for the Intourist check-in desk. Like so many other buildings we saw, this one also showed poor construction and evidences of deterioration. It's sad, as it appeared to be a nice building. After rambling around like lost sheep, we finally found the check-in desk, only to be told that we should have checked in at the nearby town of Vladimir! No one told us! However, the nice Intourist lady got us straightened out and escorted us to our room.

Our room was nice, large, and sunny, with toilet and shower, but hot water only at a certain time of the day. We were also allotted only ten squares of toilet paper! It's hard to imagine that a country that could build this large hotel, a remarkable subway system, and even put a man in orbit couldn't provide hotel guests with toilet paper! These are just a few of the contradictions we experienced in Soviet society.

At about two in the afternoon, we ate lunch in one of the several dining areas in the hotel. It was a nice lunch, "soup (borscht) to nuts." We then decided to "do the town."

Suzdal is one of the oldest cities in Russia. It was first mentioned in the chronicles in 1024. It became an important city of the grand duchy of Vladimir-Suzdal in the twelfth century, and the religious center of northeast Russia. The city was destroyed in 1238 by the Mongols under Batu Khan.

Tourist attractions include ancient buildings and churches. Many of these unusual buildings were built of stone and wood, and the architecture is very unique. About one hundred of these historical monuments have survived. Unfortunately, we had time to visit only a very few, but enjoyed very much what we did see. Our last stop was at a *Beriozkya* shop, where we bought a few souvenirs, candy, a hard bagel, and some bread, then headed back to our hotel.

On the way back we spotted a small tank-truck where an elderly lady was dispensing *kvass*. We had heard that *kvass* was a popular drink with the Russians, so we decided to give it a try. *Kvass* is a fermented drink made from rye, barley, rye bread, and unusually flavored with an unknown substance. There was a short line of customers, nearly all with their own containers—some as large as a gallon—waiting to be served. There were glasses for those without containers, as at the *beriozkya* juice stands, only this time with a garden hose to rinse the glasses. Sanitary? Hardly!

This sight was an intriguing bit of Russian culture, so naturally I wanted to take a picture. Standing nearby was a small group of men who appeared to be workers, chatting and smoking. Russian men not only drink a lot, but are also fairly heavy smokers. I started to focus my camera, but all I could see was something black. I looked up to check my camera and there, standing directly in front of me very close to my camera, was one of the men. When I saw him and I had this puzzled look on my face, he shook his finger and said, "*Nyet*" (no). I had no idea why he didn't want me to take this picture, but I surmised that, recognizing us as foreigners, he was reluctant for us to record this bit of primitive activity. Perhaps he felt it would be demeaning. Naturally, I respected his wish, whatever the reason, and we proceeded to get in line and order some *kvass*. The lady rinsed out a couple of glasses with the garden hose and filled our glasses from a wooden spigot. The charge was a mere pittance, but even this was too much because it was gruesome! How and why they drink it we couldn't figure out. Obviously one had to have an acquired taste for it. Later, in another town, I was able to get a picture of a *kvass*-dispensing rig. I got it quite surreptitiously.

It was too late for dinner at the hotel by the time we got back, so we munched on the bagel, some cheese, and the candy. It was hardly a wholesome repast!

That night, after we went to bed, I found I had trouble sleeping. The reason will seem unbelievable. I have a very sensitive sense of smell, and the soap in the bathroom had such a heavy strawberry odor (not fragrance) that it disturbed my sleep. I had to get out of bed and close the bathroom door before I could fall asleep again!

The next morning I wanted to shower, but there was no hot water. C'est la vie! Breakfast was included in our cost for the room, so we headed for the dining room where we lunched the day before. When we got there they refused us, indicating that we would have to go to another, smaller dining room. We found the place, which was like a coffee shop, and they refused us there also! This was a bit too much! We then went back to the first dining room and started to protest rather vociferously. A very nicely dressed, quite handsome and professional-looking middle-aged lady came over and took charge. She was clearly the manager. She seated us immediately, before the others waiting to be seated, and in a very short while returned with our meal and served us, ahead of everyone else. Our breakfast consisted of fried eggs, and it was rather unusual how they were served. There were two eggs fried with small chunks of pork, served to us sizzling hot in dainty little individual fry pans with two handles. We also had tea and bread. It was certainly a novel way to fry and serve. It was a bit too greasy for our tastes, however.

After breakfast, we packed up and left for Moscow. When we arrived, we were assigned our same cabin. We were tired, so we had a beer and took a short nap. Beer in the Soviet Union left a little to be desired. We were always served different brands, none of it really good—just fair, but drinkable.

With our new friends, Ivy and Walther, on their way back to Sweden, we were now on our own. The next six days in Moscow we spent taking in as many of the sights and scenes as we possibly could.

Perhaps one of the most outstanding events was our night at the Moscow Circus. The performers, men, women, and animals, were truly amazing. Soviet circuses are acclaimed worldwide. To our knowledge, every major city has a circus that performs locally. Some do travel, but they're not constantly on the move like American circuses.

During this period, we mostly used the free bus. Occasionally, when necessary, we used taxis. Rarely did we drive our car. I indicated previously that driving in Moscow is an experience in itself. It is not for the weak at heart. Riding in taxis is bad enough, but at least the taxi driver knows the traffic laws. For strangers, there is a great danger of violating some law. There are traffic policemen everywhere and they are very strict about enforcing the law.

So now, footloose and fancy free, we set out for new adventures. They weren't long in coming.

The following morning, after eating our usual meager breakfast of bread and butter, Russian cheese (like Russian beer it is not the best), and powdered coffee in our cabin, we got ready to take the free bus and go sightseeing. I went to get my camera, but it was gone! We searched everywhere to no avail. We thought that I might have left it in Suzdal. We went to the Intourist office in the hotel and told them what had happened, and that the camera might possibly have been left in Suzdal. One of the clerks called Suzdal and was told there was no camera found. I sadly remembered that on our first day in this campground, when we were shown our cabin, the camp director pointed out to us the long, narrow windows and emphatically told us that when we left the cabin we must lock the windows and door. The reason was that there were campers here from all parts of the world and one should be careful.

Then we recalled that on our first day after we got back from Suzdal, we were gone the entire day and failed to lock the windows. We then assumed the camera had been stolen. Without a camera I felt naked. We went to a camera shop in town and I bought (not too cheap) a Russian camera with instructions in Russian! The clerk gave me a five-minute oral course of instructions and sent us on our way.

With low spirits, even after purchasing the new camera, we went to the famous Gum Department Store and indulged in ice cream cones. There may be many negative things about the USSR, but one must admit their ice cream ranks among the best. And purchasing it in the Gum Department Store is an experience in itself.

When you see a line of at least twenty-five people in Gum, it is surely a line waiting to purchase ice cream cones. Why the long lines and the long wait? It's easily explained as the result of Soviet efficiency. Typically, a middle-aged Russian woman somberly dressed with a white *babushka* around her head, carries a metal tray with about twenty holes to hold twenty cones. It is strapped around her shoulders with the tray resting against her tummy. It takes her less than five minutes to sell out of cones, with people jostling, shoving, and pushing to get ahead in line and those in the front of the line cursing (we suspected) and reprimanding the pushers and shovers! The cone, by the way, costs about fifteen cents.

In less time than it takes you to read this, she is usually sold out and disappears. In the meantime, the line waits and grows. In approximately ten minutes, she returns with twenty more cones and the scene repeats itself!

While on the subject of ice cream and Soviet inefficiency, we purchased tickets for a live performance of an operetta based on a Russian folk tale. It was held in the Palace of Congresses in the Kremlin.

The performance was a bit slow, but the singing and especially the dancing were superb. Before long, there was an intermission and it appeared as though nearly the entire audience rushed out. Dorothy and I remained seated. About fifteen minutes later, the performance resumed. Again, before long, there was another intermission. This time our curiosity got the better of us, so we too joined the exodus and saw the people falling into at least three lines. There was a line for food, a line for drinks, and a line for ice cream. We got into the ice cream line. There was a "Gum-like" lady serving, only she was dishing out ice cream into lovely, silver-plated sundae dishes. She had no ice cream scoop. She was using a tablespoon and after every filling she would put the dish on a scale; if it appeared to be too heavy, she would scrape a little off with her spoon. I rarely saw her add any. This operation was so inefficient and time consuming that several of the customers didn't get served before the show started again. It was really amusing to see this "performance." We were fortunate to be served!

One night, while we were preparing some food in the camp's community kitchen, we met a young couple from West Germany. Of course, what happened before happened again. They struck up a conversation with us. It seems that folks from other lands recognize Americans and like to converse with them, regardless of how well they speak English. In this case, Andrea and Rolf spoke English quite well. They were truly "gypsies." They were traveling in a regular car, carrying all their food and other necessary items in the trunk of the car. While we were chatting, they were opening cans of food and eating from them. We chatted for just a short while and invited them to our cabin after they were finished eating. Sure enough, at about eight o'clock, they dropped in and we spent until midnight "shooting the bull."

In the course of the conversation, they told us that they had a summer cabin near Freiburg, which is near the Black Forest in West Germany, and that we were invited to spend the weekend with them there if we were going that way.

Before this came up, we had no intention of going to Freiburg. However, our son, who was director of the University of Colorado Medical Library in Denver, had done some favors for a man-and-wife team of doctors who had done some important research in blood pathology. They were visiting professors at the medical school and were from Freiburg. Our son told us that they were now back in

Freiburg and that we should go visit them. Since we had been invited by Andrea and Rolf, we decided to go there. We told them we would call them and let them know when we would be in Freiburg. We would then also visit the doctors.

The next day was a full one for us. This time we drove to town and visited the Russian State Historical Museum and a cathedral (now a museum). They were both in Red Square, and were filled with fabulous displays of Russian art and culture from ancient to contemporary times. The art we'd seen so far on the trip was absolutely awesome. It definitely proves there is no limit to the creativity of humankind.

After our museum trips, we went back to the Intourist hotel, where we had purchased tickets for a guided tour of some of Moscow's subway stations. At the hotel we met our guide, a very nice young lady, who took us on the tour. I believe we visited about four stations, each one completely different, and each one another example of Russian artistic creativity. They were spotlessly clean. For us, this was quite a revelation after riding the New York and London subways. In those places, and especially in New York, it was hard to find a clean spot!

To cap off our day's adventures, at the Intourist office we had made reservations for dinner at the Ukrainia Hotel. This hotel was allegedly designed by Joseph Stalin. Many people think it is a bit grotesque. Tickets for the dinner had to be purchased in advance at the Intourist office for twenty-five dollars each! It seemed a bit steep and a bit rich for our blood, but once in a while you have to live it up. We were anxious to have an authentic Russian meal. We especially wanted to taste Russian cabbage borscht. Since our parents came from Russia, both of our mothers cooked mainly Russian food. My mother wasn't a terribly good cook. Dorothy's mother was, and Dorothy is also a fabulous cook. Her hot cabbage borscht is excellent.

So we went back to our cabin to shower in the crummy camp bathroom, put on our best bib and tuckers (Dorothy wore a skirt instead of slacks for the first time in weeks), and then drove back to the Ukrainia Hotel.

The street was very wide and, like nearly all the streets and highways in Russia, was tree-lined. There was very little automobile traffic on this *prospekt*, and no place to park until you turn off the *prospekt*. In order to get to the hotel, we had to drive nearly into town to find an exit, then turn around and come back. However, we found a place to park across from the hotel and walked to it across this wide street.

As had happened before, we had difficulty finding the dining room. Ultimately, we found someone who took us by the hand and led us to our table, where we were almost entirely by ourselves. We didn't know whether to feel honored or slighted. It turned out to be the former. We were treated like royalty.

Our waitress was very pleasant. She soon brought us our first course, a small plate of caviar, smoked salmon lox, and a liter of wine. Next came a platter of thin-sliced, cold roast beef and a platter of cold, sliced turkey covered with a delightful white sauce. And, of course, lots of tasty, hearty Russian bread and butter. At this point, our nice server said, in German, "*ah, gutten appetite.*" To me, this meant that was all we were going to get for our fifty dollars, and I said so to Dorothy. She, with her practical mind, said, "No way! We haven't even been served the borscht yet, and I'm sure we are to get some." I, on the other hand, stuck to my opinion and ate generously of what we had been served, including a liter of wine.

Sure enough, Dorothy was right. Out came a tiny casserole with something unfamiliar, but hot and delicious. And then came a big bowl of borscht! By the time we polished off the borscht, we were beginning to feel full and ready to quit. But now we were served the main course. It was a kind of stew with potatoes, sausage, beans, and gravy, very hot in temperature, served to each of us in an earthen jar. Then we were given another liter of wine. Dorothy and I were nearly *platzing* (yiddish, meaning bursting), so the best we could do was to eat a few spoonfuls. Our waitress saw our look of despair and started to smile as if to say, "It happens to everyone." What was maddening was that it was so delicious that, if we hadn't pigged out prior to this, we could have slopped down the whole jar full!

Finally, after all this food, we were served a bottle of apple juice, I guess to wash down all the food, a dish of ice cream, and coffee. All the food and the wine was extremely luscious. We certainly felt that we'd gotten our money's worth, and then some.

It seemed that we had been eating and drinking for about an hour. There was still a bottle of wine left that was not touched and we asked the waitress if we could take it. She indicated, "Of course." We thanked her profusely for her excellent treatment (there was no tipping in the Soviet Union at that time), and then waddled our way out of the hotel to our car.

Our car was parked across the street, and, as I said previously, it was quite a drive to the exit where we could turn around to head back to camp. This was a "No U-turn" street. Dorothy said, "Look, there's practically no traffic on the street. Why don't you just make a U-turn?" I did, and as I completed the turn, there stood a policeman, by his motorcycle, waiting for us with outstretched arms. He was tall and very handsome—he looked like a Hollywood movie star. He saluted us and said, *"Papiers* (passports)?" We didn't have them with us, as they were being held at the Intourist office at the campground, which is customary. You get them back when you leave. Meanwhile, Dorothy had the bottle of wine in her hand and tried to hide it from the policeman. Anyway, we tried to explain to him why we didn't have our passports and why we made the U-turn and of course he didn't understand one word of what we were saying. In the end he waggled his finger at us in admonition, saluted, and waved us on. This was quite a night.

There was still so much to see of Moscow, and one way to see it was by boat down the Moscow River. Our free bus took us near the Kremlin, where we could arrange for a trip. With very little trouble, we found a short line at the kiosk where we could purchase tickets for the boat. Dorothy and I were discussing what a trip would involve, regarding distance, time, and cost. Immediately in front of us stood two men, a woman, and a young girl. One gentleman turned to us and, in quite good English, asked if he could help us. We discussed our minor problem with him and he did help us. We purchased our tickets, boarded the boat, and seated ourselves near them.

The man who spoke to us and the woman were man and wife. The young girl was their daughter. They were from Warsaw, Poland, and were visiting the other man, a Muscovite. The adults appeared to be in their mid-forties. The girl, we learned later, was ten years old. The wife's name was Maritza, the husband, Miroslaw, and the daughter, Kate. The Russian was named Valery.

No sooner had the boat taken off when Valery disappeared, but soon returned with his arms laden with soda pop and beer. Of course he offered us some, so we had a beer. As almost invariably happens, the usual conversation of who, how, when, and where took place between us and Miro (short for Miroslaw). We told him where we'd been and also that we were headed for Poland after we left Russia. We asked about the availability of modest accommodations in Warsaw. I showed him our planned itinerary for traveling to Poland. He recommended that we alter it and come directly to Warsaw and visit them and he would arrange to have a flat available for us!

We chatted a lot with him, enjoying the boat ride, the lovely views of Moscow, and contentedly drinking beer. The Russian couldn't speak English, but seemed to understand a bit, as did Maritza. Kate also could understand and did speak a little English. I wanted to give Kate a gift of some sort, but having none, I gave her a quarter as a souvenir. Immediately, the Russian gave me a silver ruble. (It's on my key ring now.)

We had a great time together, despite the language barrier, and made arrangements to meet the Poles in Warsaw. They got off the boat, we gave them our thanks, said our good-byes, and returned by boat. In every way it was a most gratifying experience.

The next day was our last day in Moscow. Right after breakfast, we drove to a petrol station nearby to get some diesel, but it was Sunday and the station was closed. Back to camp we went to inquire where else we could find a petrol station. An Intourist lady called several places and found one quite a distance away. We knew we could never find it on our own. A young college boy who was volunteering to work at the camp said he would take us if we would bring him back. This was fine with us, so off we went, found the station, and filled up.

By the time we got back it was too late to leave for our next camp and get there before dark. The government discourages night driving, so we prevailed upon the Camp Director to let us stay another night. Surprisingly, he said yes, so we settled in for one more night in Moscow.

After resting a bit, we went to the main dining room in the hotel for dinner. Getting served in these tourist hotel dining rooms is a story in itself. There are so many tour groups visiting Moscow that is seemed as though half the world was there. We saw dozens upon dozens of tour buses everywhere. As a result, when the tour groups entered the dining room, they got served with such efficiency that it seemed that before their posteriors hit the seat they were served the first course. Their meals were all prearranged.

We poor loners got seated quite soon, but then waited and waited to get served at the convenience of the help. Not only that, but in many instances the menu was in Russian, leaving us at a loss as to what to order. We eventually got served and all went mostly well, even though quite often we didn't know what we would be served.

That night we were seated at a table with a salesman from England. We chatted a bit with him, then a few moments later another gentleman was seated at our table. He was of dark complexion, nattily dressed, and from the Middle East. It turned out that he was an ophthalmologist, named Dr. Arar, from Lebanon. A bit later, the Englishman left and we chatted with Dr. Arar. He told us that he came to Moscow every one or two years to study under the famous eye surgeon, Dr. Paderovsky. This Russian doctor had developed a new technique for eye implants after cataract surgery. I mentioned to Dr. Arar that I had a cataract and would probably need surgery in the near future. The good doctor got quite excited and said, "Let me arrange an appointment for you with Dr. Paderovsky immediately. Perhaps you can be operated on tomorrow and it won't cost you a cent!" I had to explain to him that we were to leave Moscow the next day and it would be nearly impossible to do what he proposed. He was adamant that I do as he recommended and kept repeating, "It won't cost you a cent." Dorothy and I both knew we couldn't pursue this matter, but in order to placate him, we said we would seriously consider his offer. He then said, "Call me tomorrow and let me know your decision." He was staying in this hotel.

The next morning, we tried to contact him but he was out. We did leave a note for him, thanking him, but telling him it was nearly impossible for me to have the operation. This was our final unexpected, unusual experience in this dramatic, remarkable, fascinating, historic city of Moscow.

In the course of our eleven days in Moscow, we saw very much of vast interest: breathtaking sights, exquisite art, fantastic displays of both modern and ancient churches, buildings, monuments, and more. It is impossible, in just eleven days, to see more than just an infinitesimal number of the things there are to see. It would be extremely difficult to state what impressed us the most in this marvelous city. There is just too much of everything that is so unique and artistic. Perhaps our choices would be the Kremlin (Lenin's tomb and the buildings in the Kremlin) and the underground subway system. However, I could write a list an arms-length long.

The USSR is a country of hundreds, even thousands of years of history. It has a culture that represents nearly 150 different ethnic groups and is so vast it covers eleven time zones. Much of all this is reflected in Moscow's history, art, and culture. I could fill page after page describing what there is to see in Moscow alone. However this is not my intention. This effort of mine is more a chronicle of events and experiences. It is not intended to be a tourist guide book.

One thing I must add, though. We were amazed at how clean the streets were everywhere in the Moscow metropolitan area. Wherever we walked, we saw little old ladies, always dressed in long plain black dresses, with white *babushkas* tied over their heads and with coarse straw brooms, sweeping, sweeping, sweeping the sidewalks, streets, insides of buildings, wherever!

Another fact of Russian life is the way they drive their cars. As an illustration, we were with a lady Intourist guide, in our car, on a city tour. On a fairly busy street, a woman pedestrian was crossing the street when a car came bustling towards her. She took off to keep from being hit, as the driver gave no indication that he was going to slow down. This was a bit shocking to us Californians, since we're used to the pedestrian being king and always having the right of way. I turned to our guide and innocently remarked, "I see why the Soviet athletes win so many Olympic track medals." She looked at me rather quizzically as if to say, "What do you mean?" I replied, "With the way Russians drive their cars, you have to be the fastest runner in world to stay alive while crossing the street." Needless to say, she really cracked up.

There are many, many more incidents, characteristics, and customs that reflect on the lives of the Soviet people we came into contact with in the time we spent in the USSR. You'll read more of this later.

The time came too soon when we had to say *do sveedahnya* (goodbye) to this part of European Russia. The events, occurrences, experiences, the sights, sounds, and smells, the tastes, the feel of this portion of our trip are inscribed indelibly in our minds. Our book of memories grew thicker day by day.

The gypsy life would next take us south towards the Ukraine. We weren't anticipating more unexpected adventures, but we could not deny the fact that after all we had thus far encountered, anything could happen.

Central European Russia and the Ukraine

The carefree life was urging us on, so after a good (and the last) Moscow breakfast, we hit the road. Before we left, we wisely had an Intourist clerk write, in Russian, the name of the city that would be our next destination, and the name of the campground. This, we felt, would expedite finding the campground, as well as avoid delay and aggravation. The next stop for us was the city of Orel in Central European Russia. As we neared the city, we put our plan to work. Boy did it work!

As we neared Orel, we noticed several people at a bus stop. We pulled up to the curb and motioned for someone. A gentleman came over and I showed him the card with the name of the campground we were looking for. He read the card, looked us over (just out of curiosity, I guess), gave our car a quick going over, then tried to give us directions. By this time, about five or six people had gathered, and all of them were trying to explain which direction to take at the same time. It was a sight. Each of them pointed in a different direction and were arguing with each other about who was right. It was an exercise in futility. Finally one man pointed to himself, then pointed to the back seat of our car. We nodded, he climbed in, and off we went, directly to the Orel Hotel and campground. We thanked him and, after he left, Dorothy and I exploded, from repressed laughter, over this hilarious misadventure.

The drive to Orel, about 235 miles from Moscow, presented scenery different from anything we had previously enjoyed. We left Moscow via the Outer Ring road. There were few pleasure cars on the road, but zillions of trucks. Once we got out of Moscow's suburbs, past dozens and dozens of apartment complexes, some huge, we drove along enormous farms. They apparently are State, Collective, or Co-operative Farms. They were much too large to be individual farms, if there are any in the USSR. These farms went on for miles, before we finally reached the campground. The campground itself wasn't too bad, but the buildings looked raunchy and rundown. It was not at all appealing.

While checking in at the camp office, the clerk told us that the date of our scheduled arrival time was incorrect. However, he still checked us in. A short time later, he told us someone wanted to speak to us on the phone. Dorothy answered the call and spoke to a lady on the other end who demanded to know why we were off schedule. Dorothy explained the problem we had acquiring diesel fuel in Moscow, which, in turn, made it nearly impossible to get to Orel before dark. She also explained that, first, the government discouraged night driving, and secondly, because we were older people we didn't like driving at night. Consequently we were one day late to Orel.

The lady replied, "But you are two days late." Dorothy disagreed with her. The lady then directed us to skip our next destination, which was Kursk, where we had planned to spend two nights, and go directly to Kharkov from Orel.

That night, in our cabin, Dorothy checked our schedule. Sure enough, we were, as the lady said, two days behind schedule. Dorothy was counting the days we stayed in Moscow rather than the nights. She was a bit embarrassed by her insistence that we were only one day behind. The next morning, she asked the clerk if he would please call the lady back and apologize for us.

Our room was one of two, a duplex with a shared bathroom. The room was moderately clean, but the bathroom left something to be desired. There was no seat on the toilet and no toilet paper. Only gypsies like us could cope with such conditions. Anyway, we settled into our room and then decided to go to the cafe for dinner.

As we walked out the door, we saw on the porch of a unit across the walkway a man and woman cooking hot cakes on a tiny grill. We greeted each other and the gentleman spoke to us in English. He appeared to be a man in his fifties, rather tall, blonde, and handsome. With him was a much younger woman, also tall, good looking, and well proportioned. In the course of our conversation, he said he was from Sweden, married, and had children. The lady with him was a Russian nurse from Leningrad.

His story was that he comes to Orel about once a year to buy wine for his personal use, a couple cases at a time. He claimed that it was the best there is and it's so much cheaper than in Sweden. When he comes to Orel, he picks up his female companion in Leningrad and they travel together. He claimed that his wife knows all about her!

When he was describing this fine wine, he reached into the trunk of his car, pulled out a bottle, and handed it to me. I looked it over, then handed it to Dorothy. She looked it over also, though it meant nothing to either one of us, so Dorothy handed it back to him. He said, "No, no. It's for you. Enjoy it." Once again our "fairy godmother" had presented us with another magic gift. We, of course, thanked him sincerely, and then parted company.

All of this took place in a matter of less than five minutes. We then strolled to the cafe and had a rather nice dinner consisting of a bowl of borscht, a veal patty, and mashed potatoes with gravy. The cost for both of us was about $2.50. It was a pleasant peasant meal: no frills, no special service, nothing but good, plain food.

In this camp, as in the camp in Moscow, we noticed a lot of youngsters, both boys and girls. They behaved like a very happy bunch of kids, full of fun, very animated, but not rowdy. It was pleasant to see them have a good time, like kids everywhere. (If only we adults would never grow up and start spoiling things.)

After breakfast, we packed and were on our way; our destination: Kharkov. This city is famous for a massive and critical tank battle (fought between the Russians and the Nazis during World War II), which the Russians won. This victory was important because it was a turning point in the war against the Nazis; the point at which the Russians went on the offensive. This would finally result in the destruction of the Nazi army.

Not far out of Orel, we entered an area dedicated to raising geese. We observed geese by the thousands on both sides of the highway. It seemed that wherever there was water, whether a small mud-puddle or a rather large lake, we would see them, small flocks and large. It was an incredible picture.

Along this highway, as on all the highways we'd driven, we saw many statues and monuments memorializing the Great Patriotic War. We observed that there were always fresh flowers placed on them. Even now, so many years after the war, the people had not forgotten.

We arrived in Kharkov by mid-afternoon. Due to the second grade highways and the many smoky trucks, we averaged about thirty-five miles per hour. This campground, like some of the others, looked seedy and run down. It was large, rather ugly, and exceedingly uninspiring. We were becoming well-used to this.

We checked in, then went to our assigned cabin. Once again, it was very plain and rather nondescript. It had only the basics: two single beds and a small table with a chair. There was no decoration, no pictures on the walls, nothing "extra." It was clean, though, and for that we were grateful.

As the toilet facilities were public, we decided to check them out and were aghast at what we found! The toilets were primitive. Primitive with a capital pee! It was a stand-up model. There were no stools; just a hole in the floor in which you took aim! It was a messy, smelly abomination. We could only suspect that the Russian people, in many respects, were still living in the nineteenth century. Perhaps, we surmised, only some Western countries place emphasis on living clinically clean in their habits and their lifestyle.

After this experience, we needed a drink. We opened the bottle of wine the Swedish gentleman gave us and, like he said, it was fantastic! It was bubbly, deep red in color, and had a tingle like champagne. Now, after a glass of this nectar of the gods, we felt restored and hungry.

This camp had an outside cafe, where we ordered a dish of *shoshlik*, a sort of Russian stew, served with radishes and tomatoes. This was the first time we had had these delicacies since coming to the USSR. What a treat. The *shoshlik* was quite good. We even bought some tomatoes and some excellent chocolate candy.

So far in our travels in the USSR, we'd had very little in the way of fresh salad vegetables and fresh fruit. We are both big fruit and vegetable eaters and sorely missed them. I recall one day in Moscow when we saw several shoppers, mostly elderly ladies, carrying bags of oranges. We got all excited and, with gestures, found out where we could buy some.

The store was about two blocks away. We were amazed to discover that the "store" consisted of one man, one woman, and perhaps fifteen crates of oranges standing on the sidewalk. There was a line of customers easily a block long! As much as we desired some oranges, there was no way we could wait in line for the hours it would take for us to be served. In addition, as we compared the amount of oranges to the number of customers, we felt quite sure they would all be sold before it was our turn to buy. It was rather disappointing, but it made us appreciate something we take for granted in the West!

Back to the Kharkov camp. After a breakfast of delicious ham and lousy coffee, the guide, Gennady, who was to give us our free tour of the city, showed up. We were very fortunate on these tours because, in most cases, we were the only English-speaking campers. This meant we would have the guide all to ourselves, making it possible to be more informal and friendly with him or her. The only exceptions, so far, occurred in the larger cities of Leningrad and Moscow, where we were in groups.

The highlight of this tour, the most impressive and yet the saddest, was a monument to which Gennady took us. Like the monument in Kalinin, it had the eternal flame, the sound of the beating heart, and the somber music. More than this, there was a path about one hundred yards long paved with deep red bricks. At the end of the path was a very large statue of Mother Russia. In her eyes was a look of deep sorrow. Gennady explained to us that the path was called the "Avenue of Blood" for at this spot the Nazis exterminated thirty thousand Russians! Thinking about this devastated us. We Americans just can't comprehend or visualize the horror, the slaughter, and destruction that the people and the country suffered at the hands of the Nazis. The impact of this is beyond belief, and the extent of the barbarity of the Nazis is indescribable! No wonder the Russian people desire peace with all their hearts and souls. They vow they will never let it happen again.

I've hinted at the relationship that developed with Gennady, which, in turn, enabled us to be more intimate and personal with him. As a result, we began to ask more personal questions of each other.

He asked about our occupations, and we explained that we were both retired, but had been employed at a state college in Southern California in non-teaching positions. He told us he was a college student, and the director of the camp was a principal of a high school. They both worked at the camp in the summer.

Because we were connected with an educational institution, Gennady asked us if we would be willing to meet with the director and himself to talk about the educational system in the United States. He said they'd like to put it on tape. We explained that we weren't really qualified to tell them much, but we would be glad to inform them of what we knew about the California system of education.

With some time on our hands, we parted company with Gennady and went shopping in the *Kashtan* store. The store was similar to the *Beriozkya* shops, previously described. They are just called differently in this part of the USSR (the Ukraine). We purchased some vodka, an electric razor for me (cheap, and would just about shave the hair on a billiard ball), some *halvah,* a milk shake, Russian style (mostly shake), some chocolate candy, and some cheese. From a street vendor we bought some *pirozkis*, which were not bad.

Back to camp we drove. In the pavilion in the camp, a lady director was leading the campers in all sorts of games, dances, and songs. The people appeared to enjoy every minute of it and were shouting, laughing, joking, and having a ball. We enjoyed watching them immensely. This was contrary to what our mainstream press had been telling us all along: that the Russians don't laugh and don't have fun.

Dinner included some good hot borscht, for a change. The rest of our meal was good, also, and quite inexpensive.

Later in the day, we met Sasha, the director, and Gennady. Dorothy and I went to Sasha's office for our chat on education. Gennady wanted to tape record our conversation, but couldn't find the recorder, so he took notes.

After about an hour discussing education, we began to talk of politics and the Jewish question. At this point Gennady rose, went to the door, and closed it! This was a very graphic example of the fear the Soviet people have of their government, and the lack of democracy in their system. We had experienced instances of this nature before this occurrence, and several after it. The Cold War was taking its toll on the Russian people and, to a considerable degree, on Americans as well. Nevertheless, we continued our conversation in this vein for about another hour. Our Russian friends defended their political system and said, "Yes, there was anti-Semitism in the country, but it was manifested mainly among the intellectual class."

How little we all knew, or anticipated, what the future had in store for this great country. We had a very interesting and memorable stay in Kharkov. It is the third largest city in the USSR and, while it is not pretty, it has a lot going for it. Our itinerary called for us to be on our way to Kiev, so on we went with considerable excitement, for in a little village just outside of Kiev, Dorothy's parents had been born.

The road to Kiev was better than we expected and we traveled the 310 miles to it without any trouble. Kiev is the capital of the Ukrainian SSR, and is one of the oldest and most beautiful cities in Europe. It stretches along the picturesque banks of the Dnieper River. It is the hub of large industrial enterprises, higher educational establishments, and major historical and architectural monuments with worldwide significance. Kiev is also the center of the Ukrainian people's culture.

One of the major accomplishments of the Soviet government, in its early years, was the construction of the huge Dniepropetrovsk Dam on the Dnieper River, near Kiev. This was also the site of one of the Soviets' most tragic events. During the Second World War, when the Nazi armies marched unimpeded into the Ukraine, the Soviet government blew up the dam to prevent it from falling into the Nazi's hands.

As in the past, we registered at the Intourist office and were shown our room. It was in a unit of three separate rooms, with just one bathroom to be shared by all. When we entered our room, it was dirty, unkempt, and cluttered with used dishes. Our hostess was so disgusted that she took us to another room. It was much better but still not very appealing. It was late that evening before we got hot water in the shower.

While we were registering, we had asked the Intourist ladies if they could possibly locate any of Dorothy's relatives. Dorothy's uncle, in the US, had told her he was sure there were none left in the village of her parents' birth. As it turned out, we were informed the next day that the office could locate none.

The next day, Dorothy and I were both ill with the "Stalin's Revenge." We had purchased tickets to an all-male Ukrainian choir and *bandura* (similar to a guitar) group for the next night, but felt like canceling out. Luckily, we had brought some medication from home just for this illness and by late afternoon we were both feeling better.

Urged to go to the concert by the Intourist staff, we decided to try it. It was a fortunate decision. The singing was fabulous and the *bandura* playing was superb. I might add that the quality of Soviet entertainment in general is hard to beat.

The next day, our guide, twenty-one-year-old Svetlana (who was as pretty as her name), took us for a tour of Kiev. Again there was just too much to see in too short a time.

One of the highlights we witnessed was the changing of the guard at a World War II memorial. The guards were boys and girls, fourteen to sixteen years old, Young Pioneers who were selected for this honor because they were exemplary students. Their dress, for both boys and girls, is similar to our Boy Scouts uniforms, the exception being the regulation red kerchief around their necks, which is the symbol of the Young Pioneers. They performed the changing of the guard with the precision and solemnity equal to that of the soldiers at Lenin's Tomb. It seems that all socialist countries have Young Pioneers, or similar organizations. The major difference between these groups and our Scouts is that, in socialist countries, these organizations are much more involved in community service and social activities. A very touching part of the memorial included tributes performed by recent brides, who place their bridal bouquets on the monument.

Another unusual sight was the oldest pharmacy in the USSR. Svetlana took us inside and it was indeed something to see. This pharmacy was several hundred years old and still dispensing drugs! The entire store was an antique shop.

While with Svetlana, we discussed several controversial subjects, such as the Jewish question, the educational system, employment for college graduates, and politics. The answers we got, typically, expressed the party line, as we expected.

We both felt better the next day. We met Svetlana and drove to the Babi Yar Monument, a tremendous, gruesome edifice. It was here that the Nazis slaughtered 100,000 Russians. In one day, the Nazis killed twenty-five thousand people. They then shoved the bodies in a ravine and covered them with dirt, using a bulldozer. Some of the victims were still alive!

Svetlana took us to the catacombs of the Greek Orthodox Monks. The catacombs were in caves that had been excavated in the pre-Christian era. The monks first occupied them in the eleventh century.

Some of the monks were buried there and the remains became mummified.

Later we went to the museum, in the area called the Lavra, to view ancient and contemporary artifacts and handicrafts. We saw many beautiful and charming items. The ancient Russians were superb artisans.

We left Kiev with mixed feelings; our impressions of the city ranged from very good to bad. There are a lot of good things that can be said about Kiev, too much to be presented here. As for the bad things, we discussed them openly with Svetlana: the high cost for the use of the inadequate camp cabins, the poor and inefficient facilities, and the unsanitary conditions of the bathrooms, among others. Her excuses and rationalizations were, to us, insufficient.

Rovno was our next stop. The drive through the countryside from Kiev was prettier and more interesting than the drive to Kiev. There were lots of ducks and geese and a greater variety of trees. The peasants appeared to be more prosperous and better clad.

There was no campground in Rovno, so Intourist booked us into the Hotel Mir (Peace). Our room was very pleasant, with its own working (!) toilet, short on toilet paper, but clean; and our own shower. We felt exhilarated by this qualitative change in our accommodations.

Rovno is a pretty city. Here we saw the nicest apartment buildings thus far on our trip through the USSR. These apartment houses did not resemble the dull, drab, uniform structures we had been seeing up to now. These looked more like Philadelphia row houses. The apartments here had more color, were better designed, and were often built at different heights. All of this enhanced the attractiveness of these complexes. More practical thinking went into the design of them than we had previously seen. For example, in the taller buildings, which rented to families with small children, the architects had built playgrounds on the roof. There were safety precautions, and adequate equipment was provided. It surprised us when we walked into a mini-supermarket located right in the complex. We also visited a very large store that sold only clothing.

Once again we visited a World War II memorial to the eighty-two thousand people killed in a concentration camp by the Nazis. We also visited a flax factory that employed seven thousand people. (Flax and wheat are very important crops in the Ukraine.) Last, but not least, we saw a beautiful small park and lake built entirely by the Young Komsomols, a communist organization of young people in their teens to early twenties. This was very impressive, and another example of how Russian young people were involved in community service.

Rovno left a very good impression on us. Everything we saw, did, and ate had a positive and pleasant effect on us. We wished we could stay longer, but leave we must.

Our final stay in the USSR was in the city of Lvov. It was quite a change from Rovno—for the worse. Once again, Intourist booked us into a hotel because there were no available campgrounds. The area was jammed with people: workers, tourists, etc. It was somewhat disappointing after Rovno. I wasn't feeling too good, so that may have affected my feelings about this city. Dorothy seemed to be cured, though.

I asked the Intourist clerk if she could get me a doctor. I told her my troubles. She replied, "If I call a doctor, you will be put in a hospital." I was a bit disturbed by this and told her, "Oh no, I just want some medicine." She smiled, then got on the phone and in about ten minutes a lovely, rather tall, well-dressed, and professional-looking woman was introduced to me as the doctor. The Intourist clerk explained my problem. The doctor could not conceal a smile as she left, and in about five minutes she returned with a small packet of pills. The Intourist clerk read the directions to me, and that was that. There was no charge for the doctor or the medication!

After this little episode (and after I took some pills), Dorothy and I went window shopping. We went into some jewelry shops and were absolutely astonished at what we saw. The store was jammed, primarily with young people buying gold watches, rings, necklaces, earrings; all quite expensive! They were standing in lines three people deep trying to make their purchases. You would have thought that they were giving the jewelry away! The Russians here must be very wealthy; we thought.

Later we went to a beauty parlor in the hotel. I got a haircut for ninety cents. Dorothy got the full treatment for one dollar and forty cents. We both were quite pleased with the results. We then went back to the hotel for dinner. We indulged ourselves and had a small helping of black caviar, at three dollars and sixty cents each, for an appetizer.

I was feeling much better the next morning, though still a bit weak. The pills must have been working. Our guide took us on a city tour. We saw some churches with fantastic decorations, paintings, and wood carvings in the interiors. Some were more resplendent and ornate than others. The walls, ceilings, and statuary had been painted primarily in tones of gold and deep, somber reds. It reminded us of many of the Catholic churches we'd seen in Mexico.

The following morning, we would leave the USSR for Poland, and in all honesty, we weren't too unhappy about leaving Mother Russia. We looked back on all we saw and did; the good, the bad, and the mediocre. We remembered the many people we met, all that had happened to us during our month in the Soviet Union, and the nearly three thousand miles that we covered in that vast country. It left our emotions tied in knots: we had experienced so many contradictions! There was unbelievable beauty in the Russian art and culture, and yet so much unpleasantness in their slavish love of alcohol. The Russians built space ships requiring technical and scientific expertise, and yet when a toilet bowl leaks at its base, they pour gobs of cement around it to stop the leak instead of fixing it properly. Their underground subway stations are spotlessly clean, artistically decorated, and the peak of efficiency, yet their toilets everywhere, except in the better hotels and restaurants, are an abomination. Neither the toilets, nor the other bathroom facilities in most cases, work. The Soviets provided their own country, and many others, with the most complex and sophisticated military hardware. However, they could not provide toilet paper, or wrapping paper to put around a loaf of bread! They built and exported the finest of farming equipment, yet throughout the countryside their own people used ancient scythes to cut grain. The list goes on and on.

The greatest contradiction, however, was in their political system. This system was built on an alleged philosophy of equality, egalitarianism, and democracy. Yet much remained to be desired by the Russian people. There was subtle evidence of fear, and the submissiveness and resigned acceptance of the people toward their government's policies was universal.

Through all the contradictions (the lack of the good life promised the people, the Cold War and the hot one, the evils and mistakes of their various leaders), Dorothy and I hoped that ultimately the Russian people would work through their trials and tribulations and eventually have the life they dreamed of. Dorothy and I believe in the axiom, "There can be no socialism without democracy, nor democracy without socialism." History is yet to be written.

As a footnote to the above observations and thoughts: nearly all the Intourist people we met urged us to return in five years. The new Five Year Plan was supposed to concentrate on producing consumer goods of improved quality, and to provide the Soviet people with products they had yearned for (and waited patiently to receive), for many years.

Subsequently, we did return in five years. However, the hopes of the people, and the assurances of Intourist, did not materialize. Instead, the conditions continued to worsen. The Cold War became "icy" and the people's level of fear became alarming. It was a tragedy for all people, Russian and American.

Poland, A Lesser Socialist Country

We arose early in the morning anxious to get going, but had to wait for breakfast. Shortly after our meal, we headed for the border, just fifty miles away.

At the border, we had to go through the Russian guard station before entering Poland. Boy, did they give us the works! They searched our luggage, purses, and papers, including my daily trip log. They investigated our car, top and bottom, inside and out. They even had me play the tape recorder to see if it was fake! They treated us as if we were counter-revolutionary, smuggling, drug dealing terrorists, all rolled into one! I suppose there must be a reason for this sort of treatment. We certainly did not experience this when we entered the country.

When the guards finally let us out, we both breathed huge sighs of relief. It was a sense of paranoia that we experienced throughout our stay in the USSR. Our only explanation for this was that the fear of another war was so pervasive; their government reacted in an irrational spirit of overkill.

After this ordeal with the Soviet border guards, dealing with the Polish border guards was a breeze. They checked our papers, asked a few questions, then sent us to an office where we had to exchange our money. It was mandatory that we exchange our currency for their zlotys at the rate of fifteen dollars per person per day. The zloty was worth about three and one half cents. Since we were committed to spend fifteen days in Poland, we wound up with approximately thirteen thousand five hundred zlotys. We felt like millionaires!

Because it was raining when we reached the border, we decided to get accommodations as early as possible. Our travel books told us of a P.T.T.K. hotel in the next town about nine miles away. The P.T.T.K. hotels and hostels are government owned and operated and are lower priced than regular hotels.

The town we were headed for was called Przemysl. We asked the guard for directions to this town and to the P.T.T.K. hotel. He replied that the nearest P.T.T.K. was in a town called Shemesh. I looked on my Polish map and could not find Shemesh, and told him so. I tried to pronounce the name of the town listed in the book and on the map, but to no avail. Finally I pointed out the town on the map. He replied, in broken English, "Ya, that is Shemesh!" We then realized our problem. Polish words are made up with mostly consonants and few vowels! And we thought the Russian language was difficult.

Now, as in our pre-USSR experience, we were completely on our own, with the help of our travel books, of course. We had to once again rely on our wits and gypsy instincts.

Przemysl (Shemesh) is one of the oldest towns in Poland—over one thousand years old. With some help from a local, we found the P.T.T.K. Poland, here we come! Like many of the buildings in the USSR, this hotel also appeared to be one thousand years old. It was an ugly, concrete building. It looked dank and dirty and very uninviting, but we had no choice but to stay for the night.

We went inside and it was worse than the outside. It not only was dark, but it also had a very strong odor of urine. Naturally, any place that had been peed in for all the years this place appeared to be standing would smell to high heaven. To add insult to injury, it wasn't a cheap place. We paid $22.40 for the night. We had the impression that Poland would be rather inexpensive. We asked the desk clerk to write a menu for us and then went to Centrum, the center of town, to a restaurant. Our dinner was a seven on a scale of one to ten, plus it was inexpensive at $5.25 for the both of us.

Later, in strolling around, we spotted a very nice campground nearby where we could have gotten a nice bungalow with four beds for only $17.50.

The town itself looked its one thousand years. The buildings were drab, sordid, broken up, and decrepit. Russia, in comparison, was much cleaner. The one exception we noticed was the campground. It looked fairly new. The camping area was on a lush green lawn and some of the shrubbery was pruned in the shape of animals.

After our first day in Poland, we had a rather negative attitude about the country and were a bit apprehensive of what lay ahead. But we had committed ourselves to spend our fifteen days here, come what may. After all, gypsies can't be too choosy.

Being anxious to get out of this drab and dreary hotel, we got up early and drove on to Lublin, where we stopped at a local restaurant for breakfast. We were having a little difficulty ordering, but with sign language and a smattering of Yiddish-German, we made the waitress understand that we wanted scrambled eggs and coffee. To indicate we wanted two orders, I held up my forefinger and middle finger. Guess what? We received three orders of half-raw eggs and three glasses (not cups) of coffee! Why? Apparently if you indicate the number of whatever you wish by holding up your forefinger and any number of fingers after it, your thumb is included! Try it and see how it works. This so amused us that we just couldn't be put out about it.

Recall now that when we met the Polish people on the Moscow river, the husband, Miroslaw, checked our itinerary and rerouted us to Warsaw, where they lived. So from Lublin we headed for Warsaw as our first major stop, rather than the way we had planned to go. Miroslaw said that they had no phone, so in order to find their place we should take a taxi.

The drive from Przemysl to Warsaw was a real revelation. On both sides of the highway were beautiful small farms. I would guess they measured anywhere from two to fifteen acres each, all planted in garden vegetables and flowers. It appeared that every farm had a portion planted in poppies, all colorfully in bloom. Adding to this, the farms were arranged in attractive geometric shapes. They were a very pleasing sight. Our opinion of Poland went up a couple of notches.

We later found out that nearly 80 percent of the farms in Poland were privately owned and some were subsidized by the government. As a result, farmers in Poland were a fairly well-to-do class.

Again, while traveling towards Warsaw, we were keenly aware that everything we saw was much nicer than in Russia. There were flowers everywhere, in the yards, the gardens, along the streets, and particularly in the small parks. The newer houses and apartment buildings were much more attractive and better kept than in Russia. The stores were more modern and, finally, the buses and trucks were not so abused and decrepit.

Seeing all this certainly gave us a more positive impression of Poland and definitely lifted our spirits. I must confess that after our month in the USSR and our first day in Poland, we felt somewhat depressed. However, this passed.

Warsaw wasn't far distant, and as we approached the outskirts of this large city we spotted a campground and pulled in. What a pleasant surprise! This campground was much nicer than nearly all those we saw in Russia. At $3.75, the price for a nice room in half of an old, but clean, bungalow was about a quarter of what we paid in Russia. We didn't have private toilet facilities, but there was a community bath house, which also was cleaner and less odoriferous than those in Russia.

We settled in our half of the bungalow and later had a snack at the camp snack bar. We inquired about getting a taxi and were told there was a taxi stand just a short walking distance away. By this time it was nearly five o'clock. We strolled to the taxi stand and saw a luscious blonde young lady climb in the front seat of a taxi and give the driver a big kiss. I saw this and thought, "A taxi driver, a beautiful young lady . . . you know?" It turned out that she was his wife (so much for an evil mind), that she was off work and he was off duty, and they were on their way home.

Before he could drive off, I hurriedly showed him the paper with our friend's address written on it. He was inclined to refuse, but his wife prevailed upon him to take us. Evidently, the address puzzled him, so he took out his map and he and his wife both tried to figure out where we had to go. They came to some conclusion and off we went—in circles! He drove and drove, checked his map, and drove some more. I would guess we were riding around for at least twenty minutes. Finally, he stopped at a rather large apartment complex and pointed to one of the buildings. Dorothy told him to wait while she verified the address. Sure enough, the taxi driver was correct. We thanked him profusely and wanted to pay him. He shrugged his shoulders as if to say never mind! Nevertheless, I gave him two American dollars and he was thrilled. With these two dollars he could get a lot of zlotys on the black market if he was so inclined.

On the subject of black market money exchange, we discovered that we would be hustled for money exchanging wherever we went, and quite openly. This was vastly different from the USSR. To exchange money illegally in the Soviet Union was a serious offense. If caught, both the buyer and seller would be severely punished.

There we were, about to visit our new friends, not knowing what to expect. We climbed the three flights of stairs, came to the correct apartment, and there on the door was a note. It was written in English and addressed to us. The note said, "We are gone now, but will be back in a very short while." This was quite a surprise, as our arrival date was not that specific when we arranged our visit on the boat on the Moscow River.

In about fifteen minutes, Miro and his brother-in-law arrived. We entered their apartment and exchanged greetings, and shortly afterward Miro's wife Maritza (a lovely name) arrived. We all gathered around the dining table, which was in the very small, cluttered dining room. Maritza brought some bread, lunch meat, cheese, and, of course, vodka, and we ate buffet style. The next few hours we spent getting to know one another on a more personal level. We told them much about ourselves. They did the same.

Miroslaw is a chief test engineer in a factory that produces heavy road equipment and small cranes. Maritza is a doctor, a second level general practitioner, which means she is next to the top. When we were told that Maritza was a doctor, we related to her the event that I experienced in Lvov, USSR, when I had diarrhea. She was curious to know the medication the Russian doctor gave me, but we didn't know and I had no pills left. She left the room and returned with several pills. Through Miro, we were told that one type of pill was for diarrhea. The other was a sulfa pill that was to be taken if the first pill didn't work. Since neither of us needed them at this time, we packed them away. Kate, the young daughter we'd met in Moscow, was with her grandparents in another town. The older daughter, a fifteen-year-old, was away at a government camp. In our conversation, we talked only to Miro. Maritza could understand a bit of English but could not speak it. We found this true with many couples we met in Europe.

Near ten o'clock, we decided we'd better arrange to get a taxi and get back to the camp. Miro said, "It's not necessary, we'll join you and walk there." Dorothy and I were truly puzzled! Walk there after it took the taxi driver nearly twenty minutes to find their place! We told them the story. They both laughed and said, "Let's go." In about fifteen minutes we arrived at the camp! The taxi driver had been going around in circles trying to find their apartment, and here it was, just a few blocks away. Before we said good night, they insisted we come stay with them. Since both girls were away, we could have their bedroom. This was fine with us.

Yes, the "good fairy" had certainly been singling us out. As far as we were concerned, she was working overtime! The next morning, after breakfast, we packed and drove to our friends', where we would spend the next eight days.

Their apartment was very small, with hardly enough room for two, much less the four who lived there. The girls' bed was barely adequate for Dorothy and me. Maria (her anglicized name) and Miro also had a small bedroom. In the living/dining room there was a sofa bed.

The bathroom was the "prize," though. It consisted of a small tub with a hand-held shower that was manageable and proved barely adequate. In front of the stool was a tiny washing machine, with so little space between the toilet and the washing machine that one had to sit sideways on the stool to use it! There was also a terrible lack of closet space throughout the apartment. But, as the tour books say, "If things are not quite as they are at home, then don't leave it!" Dorothy and I had long ago accepted this bit of travel philosophy and managed quite well.

In the eight days we spent with these very gracious, hospitable folks, we saw and did many things; too many to be listed here. I will briefly tell about some of the highlights of the city of Warsaw and the experiences we encountered there with our friends.

First I must confess that we did take advantage of the very lax black-market money exchange law. It happened as a consequence of Miro needing a part for his very small Fiat automobile. Paying for the part with zlotys, he said, would take forever. But with US dollars, he could get it immediately! Another black market operation, I suspect. So in a sense of obligation I said I would help him out, and we exchanged fifty dollars for five thousand zlotys! Considering that we now had these five thousand zlotys plus the nearly one thousand zlotys per day we had to purchase by Polish law, and keeping in mind that we were paying nothing for our room, you can imagine why we felt like millionaires! We had a similar experience in getting oil for our car. With US dollars we got it immediately.

Now, with my wallet stuffed with money, we paid for nearly all the expenses that occurred while we stayed with them. Dorothy and I really felt stinking rich, and behaved accordingly.

Warsaw had been nearly destroyed by the Nazi military machine during the war. As a result, we now saw practically an entirely new city, and a beautiful one at that. The outstanding exception was "Old Town" Warsaw. Even there many of the small shops had been nearly demolished; those that remained standing were pock-marked with bullet holes.

The government did a magnificent job of restoring Old Warsaw. It is a tourist's delight, primarily because it doesn't cater to tourists by offering a clutter of souvenir shops, gift shops, rinky-dink fast food establishments, and the like. As a matter of fact, there was one quite old and rather nice restaurant that served only duck in various ways.

One night, when Maritza was on the night shift at the hospital, Miro took us to this restaurant. We had an excellent dinner, including a liter of outstanding Hungarian red wine. At first, Miro was a bit reluctant to drink any wine. Drinking and driving in Poland, as in the Scandinavian countries, is a real no-no. He didn't drink too much. We finished up this delightful repast with ice cream and delicious coffee— for a change. I picked up the tab. With the tip (unlike in Russia, tips are accepted in Poland), the dinner came to $22.50. With our black market money it came to $7.50. That's living high off the hog (or duck!) all right.

Another time, the four of us went sightseeing. We visited the Wilanow Palace, the palace of a former Polish king. As usual, it was a marvelous structure both inside and out. This is generally true of royal palaces and castles throughout the world. Near this palace was a restaurant called the Horseshoe. It specialized in wild game dishes. Dorothy had wild duck and I had wild boar; it was quite a treat and quite good. For dessert, we had a dish of wild strawberries covered with *smetana* (similar to sour cream). We went "wild" over this meal! Our waiter spoke excellent English; we found out that he had lived several years in Chicago.

One day, they took us and their sister-in-law to the small village of Zeluzowa Wola. This village was famous because Frederic Chopin was born here, and it was where he composed some of his music. We visited his house, but only saw it from the outside. We were fortunate because this was a Sunday, and every Sunday afternoon, a free concert is given in this village. A very talented pianist played the piano inside the house, while the audience sat on folding chairs in the yard, enjoying Chopin's beautiful music, amplified. This was a real delight.

Later in the day, we visited a tiny village which had been converted into an outdoor museum. It was an exact replica of the seventeenth-century village. An enchanting place, each small wooden cottage had gaily-decorated wooden fences surrounding the house. At the top of the fences, the peasants had carved wooden, colorfully painted farm animals.

But most fascinating of all were what appeared to be tree stumps. They were just vertical standing logs, about two to five feet high, carved as busts of humans. They appeared to be caricatures of monks, priests, and noblemen. They were also painted, but in somber colors. There were eight or more of them in the yard near the cottages, and there may have been more elsewhere. The most astonishing thing about them was that they not only displayed artistic innovation, but served in a functional capacity. They were bee hives! The bees flew in and out through the mouths, eyes, and ears. When it came time to harvest the honey, the peasants would remove the hats or heads from the figures and extract the honeycombs from the bodies, which were hollow. It was extremely clever, and we thought that it was a very amusing sight.

Dusk was approaching, and so we traveled from this unusual outdoor museum to another small village nearby. We spotted a very small, wooden, and rather nondescript restaurant, where we decided to dine. It appeared as if this restaurant could have been from the seventeenth century also. Like the village itself, the outside was of rough hewn, drab, and dusty boards. It was not much different on the inside, but it was moderately clean. Being a small place, it didn't have a large staff. The cooks and waitresses were not young, appeared to be middle-aged. They were rather portly, a bit coarse, peasant-like but extremely friendly. They wore plain, long, white cotton dresses and white hats that were somewhat like bonnets. The atmosphere was very rustic and the service was more family-style than professional. A rather robust woman seated us at a rough wooden table that was covered with a white tablecloth made of a coarse material. We sat on heavy wooden chairs. We had the feeling that we were eating in the home of a Polish peasant.

There was no menu. The main meal consisted of a bowl of soup, a helping of meat, mashed potatoes and gravy, and some dill pickles. It was typical peasant fare, simply served, and simply good. I paid for all five of us and the bill came to $4.20! Unbelievable. We were told that, in Poland, often it was cheaper to eat in restaurants than to eat at home. I believe it. It was getting late, so we headed back to the apartment and relaxed over tea and some sweets.

At eight o'clock it was still light, so we decided to take the tram to Old Warsaw, one of our favorite places. We strolled around the square. Many of the small shops were closed, but an ice cream shop was open, so we indulged. It was good, but not as good as Russian ice cream. By this time, we all were tired, so we took the tram back home. Incidentally, the fare on the tram was three cents. The bus cost five cents. Did I mention that we really liked Poland?

In the few days left to us in Warsaw we took in as many sights as we could. We traveled the city by tram, by bus, and by foot. We were usually accompanied by Miro, although once in a while Maritza would go with us when her work schedule permitted. A few times we went alone. One thing was sure about this family: they did like to walk. While with them we walked so much that Dorothy and I would be ready to collapse before we got back to their home.

The many places we visited included several very ornate Catholic churches (Poland is about 90 percent Catholic). We also saw some outstanding palaces, fine museums, and other interesting historical buildings. One such place was the very elegant Opera House. It had been destroyed by the Nazis. After the war it was restored beyond its original splendor.

However, the most dramatic structure we saw was the monument to the Jews in the Warsaw Ghetto. Here, the Jews (surrounded by huge, heavily armed Nazi guards) refused to surrender. For weeks they held out against the might of the Nazi war machine. Thousands were killed, and just a bare handful survived. It was a breathtaking monument, painful to look upon and heart-rending in its significance. It presented a depth of sorrow that actually could be felt by those observing the memorial.

Inevitably the time came for us to say farewell to Warsaw and to this very gracious, friendly, and warm-hearted family. During our stay with them, Maritza, though unable to speak English, had understood much of what we were saying. What she was unable to communicate verbally she expressed in her pleasant manner and her kindness towards us. Miro was a plain "good guy;" very smart and street-wise.

This family, and all the relatives we met, had one thing in common: they all disliked their system of government! They yearned for capitalism; even longed passionately for it. It was obvious to them that, under capitalism, they could be quite well off. In a sense, they were right. What they had overlooked was the great amount of social amenities their system provided to the great mass of Polish people, despite the negative factors of the system.

As with Oskar in Stockholm, Miro and I would stay up late, sipping vodka and discussing politics. I played the role of the devil's advocate. We both enjoyed these political tête-à-têtes. The last night together, before retiring, Miro made out an itinerary for us to follow for the rest of our tour through Poland.

"The time had come the walrus said" to pack our bags and move ahead. So, after a light breakfast, we hugged, kissed, and shed a few tears, and said our good-byes. Maritza packed us a box of goodies, which included a box of liquor-filled candies. And off we went. Tziganers don't stay put. They are always on the move.

Krakow was our destination, not too far distant. Merrily we rolled along, enjoying the Polish countryside, discussing, as we went, the events of the past few days. It was hard to imagine that another amazing experience might befall us. It almost gave us goose pimples to think about the extraordinary events we had experienced thus far on our trip.

At about noon, we found a shady spot off the highway and stopped for lunch. After our snack, much to our dismay, I discovered that the lock on the trunk lid of our car went kaput. Not being very mechanical, I lashed the lid down and we drove on, hoping to find a mechanic.

I don't think we had driven more than two kilometers when we spotted a small highway sign bearing the symbol of a wrench on it. Naturally, we drove to it. It was a building all by itself in a forest area several meters off the highway. A rather well-dressed young man came over to us and I showed him our problem. I just knew he couldn't understand me, but he nodded and called over a mechanic. This man was really a sight: big, burly, and wearing a pair of overalls that were covered with grease from head to toe! The "boss" showed him the problem. The mechanic analyzed the problem correctly, but did not have the needed part. So he created one! He had the trunk fixed in less than twenty minutes.

I tried to determine how much I owed for this service, but merely got a shoulder shrug. Unsure, I gave them each a dollar bill; the reaction was amazing: they both had big smiles on their faces and certainly appeared well-satisfied. We shook hands, and both men kissed Dorothy's hand. Apparently that was a Polish custom, and a very nice one for her.

It was late afternoon when we arrived in Krakow and began looking for campgrounds. The first one we came to was for tents only. The second, and last had no vacancies. A lady standing nearby was aware of our dilemma and motioned for us to follow her. She led us to a very large house, located just a block away from the campground. We were given a quite large, fairly clean room with swayback beds. The cost was twelve dollars.

We indulged in our customary repast: a cold deli dinner consisting of bread, cheese, cold cuts, and raw vegetables. In this case, we enjoyed cucumbers and tomatoes, a delicious Polish salami, and pretty fair Polish beer, which we had purchased at the campground.

Later, I went to shower, but the tub was full of clothes. Oh well! The next morning, I tried again. This time, the tub was empty of clothes, but there was no hot water. I couldn't win. Dorothy and I just scraped off the mold, used a lot of deodorant, and went on our merry way.

Our destination for the day was the town of Oswiecim, where the infamous Nazi concentration camp and crematoria is located: Auschwitz. We had a bit of trouble finding it, and when we did, we were amazed at the large number of buses and cars parked there. Auschwitz is now a museum and people from all over the world come to see it. The Poles come by the thousands.

Over the front gate was a large, lace-like filigreed sign, made of black ornamental iron with the words (in German), "Work Makes You Free."

Completely encircling the camp was a rather high chain link fence, electrified with enough voltage to electrocute anyone who attempted to climb it, but now without power.

Inside the camp were all the original buildings that were used to store the worldly possessions of the hapless, doomed inmates. Each building still contained the items that had been confiscated and deposited there. For example, one building had all the empty luggage of the inmates. Another held nothing but shoes. All that another building housed was eyeglasses. In yet another, nothing but children's toys. The most macabre building of all, and the most heart-wrenching, was the one which had mounds and bales of human hair. There were several more such buildings containing other personal possessions of the victims.

Then there were the shower rooms, where the victims were forced to shower before they were taken to the gas chambers! After being gassed, the bodies were placed on a motorized dolly, which took the bodies into the crematoria. The ashes were later removed, also by a motorized container, to be disposed of.

After witnessing the horrible physical aspects of this death camp, people then proceeded to the museum where the visual aspects of the Nazi barbarism are presented. Auschwitz is called history's single most monstrous battlefield! It is estimated that as many as four million innocent souls perished there! It is impossible to record the emotions one feels in this ghastly place, or to stretch the imagination to calculate the magnitude of man's inhumanity to man! We wished that every human being would, somehow, be able to visit the Auschwitz death camp. We felt that this would have a very definite effect in preventing the needless, senseless method of waging war to solve problems between nations.

With heavy hearts, we headed back to our abode, stopping en route at a restaurant in a small village, where we again had a full, simple dinner of meat, potatoes, and ice cream; it cost $2.75 for us both. By the time we got home, we were both physically and emotionally drained. I headed for the shower immediately, only to discover that not only did we not have hot water, we had no water at all! It seemed we'd have to settle for sandpaper.

Later, our landlady served us hot tea and homemade cheese cake. This unexpected treat somewhat assuaged our hurt feelings over not being able to bathe. This had been a very trying day for us, so we went to bed early.

The next day dawned with a slight drizzle, but this did not deter us. We'd had so much rainy weather already on this trip that a slight drizzle could be categorized as liquid sunshine! Our next venture was a day trip to the city of Wieliczka, where Poland's famous salt mines are located. We had heard that the mines were quite interesting. Other than that, we had no idea what to expect.

I'll start by saying that, after our trip through a small portion of the mine, we were ready to proclaim it the eighth wonder of the world! The mine is a working mine. The portion open to tourists goes back as far as the seventeenth century. We entered the mine by descending 394 stairs to the floor of the mine. This section of the mine was solid rock salt.

During the time the miners worked, and were exploited, those with artistic talent sculpted various scenes in their leisure time. This artwork depicted the miners' lives, religious figures, and culture. One could call them the "salt mine artists." The tour took us past several chambers, or galleries, where generations of these men sculpted the most exotic, mystifying, and miraculous works of art imaginable.

The Blessed Kings Chapel is an example. It is a huge room, lit by five very large chandeliers, hand carved and decorated with salt crystals. In this chapel are a main altar, two side altars, two large bas-reliefs, and still more; all carved by hand from rock salt! It's absolutely indescribable. As if this wasn't enough, there is also the timbering throughout the mines. It is an example of master carpentry skill. We never dreamed we would be so taken by the pure artistry of a bunch of logs, so skillfully arranged, that do nothing but hold up walls, ceilings, and stairways. That this work was purely functional, and intended for safety and transportation, did not prevent it from being artistically grand.

Finally, we saw the museum that depicts the history of these mines. Here we could visualize the story of the miners' struggles against some of the terrible abuse and exploitation they suffered. There were pictures depicting the revolutionary episodes of the workers, documents connected with the history of the miners' methods of transporting the salt, and on, and on, and on. I can truthfully say that in my opinion, if a tourist visits Poland and sees only the Wieliczka salt mines, it would be well worth the trip!

After the salt mine, we drove into Krakow to the main market square. En route we bought some cherries and apples—a real treat. In Old Town Krakow, we visited the famous Cloth Hall. The Cloth Hall was active during the fourteenth and fifteenth centuries as a gathering place for merchants who went there from all around the area to sell their wares. Originally, what they mostly had to sell was cloth, hence its name. Now it is a very active marketplace of many shops in the charming Old Town Krakow Square.

Also in the square are several magnificent old churches and government buildings. There is much history connected with Krakow, and especially with the marketplace. We went into the two cathedrals, Peter and Paul's and St. Mary's, and saw exquisite paintings, religious carvings of statues, figurines, and gorgeous stained glass. There is just no limit to the creativity of human beings. We headed home after this remarkable day and soon headed for the shower. Guess what? Still no water. "Quick Henry, the Flit!"

The next morning, we fortunately were able to get just enough water to make coffee and eat a light breakfast, pack up our "camp," and head for Zakapane.

Zakapane is probably Poland's most popular mountain resort for both winter and summer recreation. It lies due south of Krakow in the Tatra Range of the Carpathian Mountains, almost on the Czechoslovakian border. The weather was atrocious—cloudy, rainy, and very cold. It was hard for us Californians to take.

It wasn't a long drive, so we arrived fairly early. The first campground we stopped at was full. A few miles further we located another one and, fortunately for us, there was one small cabin available. This we immediately rented.

Our first impression of this campground wasn't encouraging. Due to the rain and lack of grass, mud was everywhere. In addition, the place was packed with tents. They were practically on top of each other. It seemed as though there were hundred of campers.

Our cabin also left something to be desired. It was a bit crude and very plain; more like a wooden tent. It contained just two beds and nothing else.

The bathing and toilet facilities, however, were something else. As bad as our experience was in Russia, this was much worse. It served the entire campground. The floor was covered with muddy water, the filth was staggering, and the smell was absolutely unbearable. I made one attempt to use it and that was it.

Dorothy, however, was fearless. She would roll up her pant legs, grit her teeth, hold her nose, and charge! I never thought I would live to see the day when Dorothy would have more courage in such matters than I!

The weather continued to be nasty, and we didn't want to stay in camp, as it was too depressing. Instead, we drove into the Centrum, which was the main shopping area of Zakapane. It was absolutely jammed with tourists from Poland and other socialist countries. While we were there we bought a few gifts. Since it was still daylight, we took a cable car up to a very lovely mountain ridge. It was drizzling lightly, but after the camp environment we were exhilarated by the clean, fresh, damp air and the beauty of the surrounding mountains. To add to our pleasure, we indulged in a barbecued Polish sausage sandwich (Polish sausage is the best!). It was so good we just had to have one more, and then we left for camp.

For dinner, we ate at the camp "bar." The meal was very plain, a bit meager, not hot enough, but fairly cheap. While we were eating, one of the camp employees who spoke fair English introduced himself at our table. His name was Andrew. He said he would like to talk with us, so we made arrangements for him to come to our cabin.

At about nine o'clock he arrived and began to pour his heart out. He was part of the family that leased this campground from the government and ran it as a private enterprise. Now we could understand why it was so poorly run. They wanted to make as much money as they possibly could with the minimum of service and accommodations.

In the course of our conversation, we learned that Andrew was exactly like Miro. He hated the system and desired capitalism with all his heart and soul. He, like Miro, wanted to be rich. Who doesn't? After about an hour of chatting, he got up to leave. Before he left, I asked him to write out in Polish a note saying, "Please show these people where they can find a private home or modest hotel where they can spend the night."

After Andrew left, we went to bed, but it was so cold and damp that we slept with the sleeping bags we purchased in Warsaw over the blankets on the bed and it still wasn't too warm.

For certain, the gypsy life isn't all peaches and cream. However, during the day, we did have periods of sunshine in between the clouds and rain. Despite the disagreeable portions of our stay in that unlovely camp, the surrounding mountains were marvelous.

We rode the lift to the highest peak, hiking all over and around that peak and the one we went to the day before. We had enough nice weather to enjoy our stay there. Even though we both love mountains, it was soon time to move on.

The next stop on the itinerary Miro had laid out for us was the town of Zywiec. Its claim to fame was that the Zywiec brewery was located there and the beer it produced was considered Poland's best. Miro also told us that at the brewery we would find a good restaurant.

It didn't take us long to get to Zywiec, nor did we have much trouble finding the brewery. However, finding the restaurant was another matter. We walked all around the brewery and could find no place that served food. A young man was passing by; we stopped him, and with our usual performance of sign language and broken Yiddish, we got him to understand that we were searching for the restaurant. He led us into the brewery and down several stairways. The further down we went, the gloomier our surroundings became. We felt like we were in the catacombs of ancient Rome and we both felt anxious when, lo and behold, there appeared a dimly lit, tiny food store! Not a snack bar or such, just a place where you could buy cookies, candy, and other miscellaneous prepackaged snacks. This was not what we had in mind. We indicated so to our guide, and back we climbed to the street level. Since we gave up on the restaurant, we thought at least we'd try a bottle of the renowned beer. No way: there was none available at the brewery, but we were directed to a liquor store nearby. Wouldn't you know, they were out of Zywiec Beer! By this time our mood was one of pure frustration.

There was nothing we could do about all this, so we turned our attention to finding a place for the night. We stopped the first person we met on the street, a middle-aged man. I pulled out the note that Andrew had written for us regarding sleeping accommodations, and handed it to him. He read it, looked us over, and then motioned to

someone across the street who was waiting at the bus stop. An elderly lady came over, and the man spoke with her and showed her our
note. She also scrutinized us carefully and seemed to be a bit hesitant.
I then said, "*Ein nacht*" (one night). Her response was to indicate that
she approved of us. I motioned for her to get into the back seat of our
car. We thanked the gentleman, then drove away. We drove only a
short distance before we arrived at her house, a modest wooden bungalow, the front yard of which was completely planted in flowers and
vegetables. This made a good impression on me because I love gar-
dening and have a rather extensive garden at home.

Her husband, a large man on the stout side, greeted us with a
reserved but friendly smile. You could see he was a bit puzzled at seeing us, total strangers and foreigners, but his wife apparently explained
our situation and all was obviously settled and acceptable to him. What
little luggage we needed was brought in, and our hostess directed us
to what appeared to be the living room. The house was furnished with
old-fashioned, dark, rather bulky pieces of furniture, none of which
matched. Our bed was a large sofa bed in this living room. This was
quite a treat, as it was the first time in weeks that we were to have a
large bed all to ourselves. The others we'd been sleeping in were either
single beds or small double beds.

The lady left, and Dorothy and I tried to converse with the old gentleman. He spoke very poor German, so our discourse was rather limited. I did, however, manage to make him understand that we had
been to the brewery, could not find the restaurant, and couldn't even
buy a bottle of Zywiec Beer. He immediately arose, went to the small
refrigerator, and proudly presented me with a bottle of it. He opened
the beer, and I toasted him with a gesture and drank. To my taste, Miro
had overrated it. Nevertheless, I enjoyed it, and Dorothy and I polished
it off.

The weather was pleasant, so Dorothy and I took a nice walk
through this comfortable working-class neighborhood. It was an area
of well-kept, small, wooded homes. Nearly all of them had lots of flowers that were planted randomly and were in bloom.

When we returned, we wanted to bathe, but again there was no hot
water. It became evident that, throughout Europe, electricity is quite
expensive. Unless you stay at better hotels, you are apt to find hot

water a treat, and restricted in availability. However, after we dried off, the cold bath made us feel good.

While we were bathing, the folks were eating dinner. As for us, we didn't know what to do. We didn't know whether we would be fed or not. If not, there really was no place nearby where we could eat. We just sat, tried to relax, and waited to see what would happen.

At eight o'clock, our hostess motioned us to the table, where we were served a customary evening meal in Poland: a platter of cold cuts and a dry cheese somewhat like cottage cheese. With this she served us homemade dill pickles, which were the best we'd ever eaten; the smell of them was divine. (We are "mavins" on dill pickles, as Dorothy puts them up from the pickles I grow.) We couldn't help raving about how delicious the pickles tasted, and Dorothy tried to find out what she did that made them so good. She tried to tell us but, with the language barrier, it was next to impossible. We did gather that she put leaves in each jar, but what kind? Finally, she rubbed her eyes with her fists, made facial grimaces as though she was crying, and, like in charades, we caught on. She used horseradish leaves! We regaled in laughter.

All through the meal they sat with us at the table, and, despite the language barrier, we chatted, laughed, and just had a real fun time. We got the feeling that taking in paying guests was rather new to them.

It was a very pleasant day, despite the brewery disappointment. The novel way in which we contacted our hosts and the lovely time we spent with them was a new experience for us, and a most enjoyable one. We all retired; Dorothy and I looked forward to spending the night together in a single, comfortable, large bed!

At seven o'clock, we got out of bed to a warm and somewhat muggy day. At least it wasn't raining. Our breakfast was on the table and was not only good, but plentiful. We each had two soft boiled eggs, rolls, hot tea, jam, honey, and homemade cottage cheese—delicious! A bit later, we parted with fond farewells, again with the feeling that we were leaving friends, not strangers of a twenty-hour acquaintance.

The next three days were spent traveling through many small, quaint, sleepy little villages and some larger towns. The going was a bit slow, as we traveled off the main highway.

This part of Poland, the western region, is mainly agricultural. We encountered mostly what we'd driven through before: rolling hills; very curvy, narrow roads; and small farms made attractive by their plots of gorgeous flowering poppies and their fascinating geometrical designs.

Farming in Poland is about 80 percent private. The rich farmers have very handsome homes, some that are three stories high. These homes are made entirely of wood. The exception is the downstairs front wall. This was made of large round stones that were embedded in concrete, and arranged in unusual designs.

In one of the small towns, we found a barber shop owned by a man and wife. Since we both needed tonsorial attention, we went in; I got a haircut and Dorothy had a wash and set. It cost us ninety cents each! Ah! Poland!

During these few days, we stayed in small hotels and ate in small restaurants, when we didn't eat in the hotel dining rooms. As it had been throughout our tour of Poland, hotels were rather expensive in relation to other costs. These class II hotels were not the best. Restaurant prices, with a few exceptions, were very cheap; the food was plain, not in large portions, but, on the average, quite good.

On Monday, 23 July, we neared the border of East Germany. As we said good-bye to Poland, we felt mixed emotions. We'd had many memorable experiences; some pleasant beyond description, and others best left forgotten. We felt much less tension here than in the USSR, and had much more freedom to travel anywhere we wished. Shopping was more efficient, but there appeared to be less to buy. One striking feature that we greatly appreciated was that the toilets, with very few exceptions, were cleaner and worked more efficiently.

One very glaring disparity between Poland and the USSR became obvious as we drove through Poland. It concerned the statues and memorials we saw very often along the highways. In Russia there were many statues, monuments, and shrines in memory of the Great Patriotic War. There were also many billboards and banners, some permanent, others not, dedicated to the civil and political life of the people and the country. In Poland, where the people are nearly all Catholic, we saw religious statues, icons, figurines, and monuments of every description on the roadsides. The Poles apparently take their religion seriously. We saw war memorials also, but these were mainly in the cities or at places where some significant or momentous event took place.

Another fact of life in Poland that we became pleasantly aware of was the extent of art in the country. For some reason, our preconceived picture of the Polish people was of a nation of peasants and hard-working laborers, whose life and culture were rather circumscribed and provincial. But after going through the salt mine, the magnificent cathedrals, and the ancient village museum where we saw the bee hives, and after listening to the Chopin concert, we learned how little we really knew about Poland. This is a very good example of the value and benefit of travel, especially to foreign lands.

Finally, there were the people. In all truthfulness, we felt that the Russian people, by and large, were a bit friendlier than the Poles. We certainly had much more contact with the Russians, and on a closer, more personal level. Since we had spent less time in Poland than in Russia and much of this time was spent in Warsaw with our new acquaintances, we had less contact with Polish people on a one-to-one basis. Be that as it may, thus far on the trip we found the people everywhere to be wonderful! I believe that our incredible experiences confirm this.

So much for Poland, a country full of surprises for us. Not only was our book of memories filled with pages of this interesting country, so too was our book of knowledge. We left feeling that our three weeks spent there were very enlightening and gratifying.

Germany, East and West

It was about noon, 23 July, when we crossed the border, leaving Poland and entering East Germany, the German Democratic Republic. Our destination was East Berlin; we had booked a week's tour when we first arrived in London.

In just a couple of hours, we passed through customs of both countries with no inspection whatsoever except for the necessary official documents. These being in order, we drove on to East Berlin, just sixty miles west.

With little trouble, we arrived at our hotel, the Berlinstadt, a five-star hotel. It was a rather new hotel, quite attractive, several stories high. Our room was very nice, spacious, and on the third floor. The windows looked out onto a small square with lovely, beautifully designed gardens. All the flowers were bursting in full bloom. It was a very pleasant sight to look down upon.

After settling in our room, we next met our group leader, who gave us our itinerary, plus the information we needed, and told us that we were now to go on an hour-and-a-half-tour of East Berlin via bus.

It soon became obvious, as we toured the city, that Berlin had been heavily bombed by the Allies during World War II. Many of the buildings appeared to be either entirely new or fully restored.

The tour was interesting and informative. We saw many nice buildings and apartment houses. Rent, in all the socialist countries, was subsidized by the government. It never exceeded 10 percent of the income of the highest paid member of the family. We saw many shops of various descriptions, and restaurants and hordes of people everywhere.

This tour was not exciting, with one exception. There happened to be a sports festival, representing the youth from all over East Germany; they congregated near our hotel. Hundreds of youngsters, both boys and girls, had gathered together. They were dressed in colorful sports outfits. It appeared that they had been divided into groups, and each group wore its own color combination. There were many such groups; it was quite fascinating to see so many color combinations.

Sports in the socialist countries are a national pastime. Many of the people, young and old, participate, as opposed to Western countries where the people are mainly spectators. We saw this as wholesome cultural activity, and it was widespread throughout the Eastern Block nations.

Briefly, what we saw in Berlin was a clean, neat city of many people hustling and bustling along the street. Only one thing made a vague impression on us. We got the feeling that there was a certain aura of conformity, not only in the buildings, especially the large apartment houses, but in the people themselves. There seemed to be a similarity in their dress, behavior, and mannerisms. This was merely our subjective observation, but during our week here, it seemed to hold true.

As of our first day in East Berlin, and for the week to come, we were no longer traveling like gypsies. We went on a structured, organized tour and we were bound to a time schedule. Our entire tour was carefully planned. Time pretty much determined where we went and what we saw and did for most of the day. The nights, generally, we had to ourselves. However, there was very little for us to do on these free nights. We didn't wander far from our hotel. We mostly saw saloons and disco-bars. At our age and habits, neither appealed to us. Occasionally we had an afternoon to be on our own.

During these seven days we spent touring East Germany, we visited Dresden, Leipzig, Erfurt, Weimar, Eisennach, and Potsdam. We saw many churches, statues, homes of famous Germans, etc. Words cannot begin to describe what we saw. (As I have noted before, this book is not intended to be a tourist guide book, but I will briefly describe some of the more unusual, amazing, and elegant things we did see.)

In Dresden, almost 80 percent of which was destroyed by American bombers, we visited the Green Vault, a museum of priceless art objects, mostly collected by Augustus the Strong, who reigned from the late 1600s until 1733. We admired fabulous pieces of gold and silver jewelry done by a goldsmith hired by Augustus, as well as art work made of porcelain, shells, precious stones, and other materials. There was a thirty-two karat green diamond that reputedly cost Augustus the price of three castles. We saw, hanging by a fine string, a cherry pit that was intended to be looked at through a powerful magnifying glass. Only then could one see that one hundred faces had been carved into the pit! It was the most amazing thing we'd ever seen!

Next, we drove to Leipzig to visit the world-famous Meissen porcelain factory. It is impossible to describe the superb beauty and craftsmanship of the hundreds of pieces of porcelain on display there.

The Meissen factory policy, we were told, was to make two pieces of everything they were commissioned to make: one for the buyer, mainly museums and private collections, and one for the factory itself. We also enjoyed the excellent dry white Meissen wine produced here, for $1.25 a glass.

In Leipzig, we visited the Karl Marx University, called the Wisdom Tooth (!), and the St. Thomas Church, where J. S. Bach is buried. Here in this church, Martin Luther gave his first speech on the Reformation. It was also the scene of the infamous Reichstag Fire Trial, where Georgy Dimitrov, a Bulgarian Communist leader, was tried for the fire and found not guilty. The fire had been set by the Nazis as a plot to frame Dimitrov. This was the beginning of the Nazi party's influence and Hitler's rise to power.

Our next stop was Weimar. There we visited the Goethe National Museum. Goethe, the German philosopher, poet, and dramatist, lived and died in Weimar. So did Johann Schiller, also a poet and dramatist. There are statues of both of these great men of letters in front of the new Opera House. This was once the site of the old Opera House where the Weimar Republic was founded in 1919. J. S. Bach and Franz Liszt at one time also lived in Weimar. This city was, and is, truly a city of history and culture.

From Weimar, the bus took us to see another infamous Nazi death camp, Buchenwald. We did not know that in the vicinity there were over one hundred smaller concentration camps connected to

Buchenwald. Despite the horrible history of Buchenwald, it was mild in comparison to Auschwitz. Nearby stood a very elaborate monument and tower, dedicated to the many thousands who perished here.

Next we went to Erfurt, a very quaint town of striking half-timber houses and small buildings. Half-timber houses are quite common in Germany as well as in England. Briefly, the exterior construction of these houses consists of heavy timbers holding up the roofs. The timbers are painted in dark colors, mostly brown. Nearly all of the roofs are quite steep, so the timbers are set up in interesting angles. The area in between the timbers is filled with stucco, generally white. The dark, angled timbers exposed within the white stucco, and, in almost every case, the window boxes with red and pink geraniums combine to make these houses very quaint and picturesque.

In Erfurt, we visited several churches, which, like churches most everywhere, are decorated with fantastic works of art. We saw stained glass windows, religious paintings, wood-carved statues, figurines, and elaborate pulpits.

Next our bus took us to Eisennach, a beautiful and very old hamlet nestled in a lush valley. We visited the Wartburg Castle, high on a hill, where in the old days donkeys were used to haul water to the castle. The donkeys were still there, but they hauled children to the castle instead. Then we went back to Erfurt and our hotel.

The next morning, we left Erfurt and headed for our starting point, East Berlin. En route we drove through the lush Hartz Mountains. The going was slow but very pleasant, and we ended up in Potsdam, picked up our local guide, and visited two palaces built by Frederick II. One palace was old, the other somewhat newer.

Here again we saw displays of baroque and rococo architecture, furniture, and the like. The interior of the palaces contained a mishmash of paintings, artifacts, and antiques, which represented untold wealth, but were not necessarily in good taste, due, perhaps, to the way in which they were displayed. Frederick II lived in the palace for forty years, and named it Sans Souci (Without Care). It was built, I believe, for his girlfriend.

The highlight of our trip to Potsdam was to stand in the same room in the Cicelien Palace where Winston Churchill (prime minister of Great Britain), Joseph Stalin (premier of the USSR), and US President Harry Truman met during the period of 17 July to 2 August. There, they clarified and implemented the agreements reached at the Yalta Conference held in the USSR. At that time, Churchill had been defeated for re-election and Clement Attlee took his place. A picture of that historical scene hangs on the wall behind the table at which they sat when they signed the agreement. It was quite an emotional charge to stand before that table and try to visualize the historical event that took place nearly thirty-five years ago.

Our group consisted of thirty people. Of this number, only four couples spoke English: one couple from London, a younger couple from Kennington near London, a couple from New York City, and Dorothy and I. The older couple, from London, were very reactionary. They found nothing good about anything and bad-mouthed everything. The couple from New York, several years younger than us, let us know quite distinctly that they wanted to be alone. They acted a bit snobbish. The couple from Kennington, also much younger than us, was our saving grace. They were very friendly, seemed to be quite liberal in their thinking, and very pleasant. We got along nicely, but unfortunately we really didn't get together until the night before we returned to East Berlin. However, we did exchange addresses and go through the usual formality of, "If you ever come back to Europe (or come to America), please come and visit us." We were sincere and felt that they were also.

That last night, we had dinner together and the next morning we ate breakfast together. Then we said our fond farewells and parted. This ended our tour of East Germany. We headed for "Checkpoint Charley."

In thinking back about our week's tour in East Germany, we realized how different and, in a way, disappointing this trip was compared to our travels up to then. During this week, we made no contact with East Germans other than with hotel and restaurant employees. The others we met, exclusive of those on our tour, were also tourists. Since we spent our nights in hotels and ate in either hotel dining rooms or restaurants catering to tourists, our personal contacts had been almost exclusively with other tourists.

As I stated earlier, on this tour we traveled on a rather rigid time schedule. Although we saw a lot more places (in considerably less time) than we could have on our own, we saw nothing in depth. We were constantly on the go. As a result, neither Dorothy nor I recall much of what we saw and did during this week. The tour had no fairy tale type of memorable experiences. No, the gypsy life was more to our liking, even with all its trials and tribulations.

Be that as it may, we have no regrets about our tour. In traveling in foreign lands, there is always something of interest, something new and different that adds to your store of knowledge, helps to break down barriers between different races and cultures, and makes the concept of one world, living in peace and harmony, more possible. *Auf Wiedersehen*, East Germany!

It was a warm, bright, and sunny morning in July when we left East Berlin, footloose and fancy free. We headed for "Checkpoint Charlie," or the dividing line in Berlin between Soviet-controlled Berlin and the US-controlled part of the city. Berlin, itself, was divided into four parts that were controlled by the US, the USSR, Great Britain, and France.

The euphoric state we were in didn't last long. When we pulled into the US side of "Checkpoint Charlie," an American soldier greeted us quite cordially and asked to see our papers. Everything was OK, except we didn't have our car insurance paper to drive into West Germany. We knew we'd purchased it and searched high and low to no avail. It was gone. The only explanation was that it had not been returned to us, either by the border guards in Poland or East Germany, when we crossed one of those borders.

The soldier was adamant about not allowing us to cross the border without it. The price for insurance was fifty-five dollars, which we willingly would have paid, but the guard would accept only West German marks; he had no means to exchange money.

It was Sunday, and there were no banks or money exchange offices open on the East German side. Our only option was to exchange money on the West German side. The banks would not be open on the West German side, either, but the guard said there was one money exchange office open in West Berlin. It was in the heart of the city. I suggested that I drive to this place, exchange the money, and return for the insurance. "No way," he replied! I then said, "I'll leave my wife for the deposit." He laughed, but wouldn't yield. I was really concerned. I would have to travel by bus and tram, in a huge city, with no directions, to try to find the exchange office. Just at this moment, when we both were in the depths of despair, a US sergeant drove up in a jeep to inquire what the problem was. The guard explained our situation to him. The sergeant then turned to me and said, "Hop in." He drove me to the exchange office while Dorothy stayed behind. I got the proper West German marks, returned, paid for the insurance, and we were finally on our way. What a blessing! What a relief! Another fairy tale for our collection.

By this time, it was late in the afternoon and had started to rain. We had spotted a small, rather old hotel nearby and got a room. The cost was a bit high. The room, however, was very clean and smelled nice, for a change. It did not have private toilet facilities, but we were quite content. The weather cleared a bit, so we took a bus to the Berlin Zoo, one of Europe's finest. Our spirits had climbed several notches and we were feeling fine. While at the zoo, we bought foot-long hot dog sandwiches. They were good, but not quite up to Polish sausage.

The zoo was very nice. There were lots of baby animals, but we couldn't stay long, as it started to rain quite hard. We took the bus back to our hotel.

What we saw of West Berlin while strolling, as well as riding on the bus, was certainly a revelation when compared to East Berlin. West Berlin was like any large American city. There were billboards, glaring neon signs, long-haired boys, sexy girls, restaurants, movie houses, porno shops, sex shows, peep shows, and crowds of people everywhere. The people appeared well dressed, many in blue jeans.

They were obviously fairly well-off and not loath to spend their money. They appeared to enjoy a hedonistic lifestyle, almost 180 degrees from what we saw in East Berlin. Like so many large cities in Western Europe we'd been to, American culture and influence was quite pervasive.

Close to our hotel, we found an Italian restaurant. We ordered a large pizza, with salad, wine, ice cream (we eat a lot of ice cream), and coffee. What a glorious treat after weeks of Russian and Polish food. It was, however, quite expensive. With a tip, it came to $18.50. What the heck! We were living it up.

In reviewing our first day in West Berlin, it was easy to see why East German youth were so attracted to the living standards and lifestyle of West Germany, and why they wanted to go over the "Wall." The next day, we took the bus into the downtown section and purchased another camera. I just wasn't satisfied with the Russian one. We also wanted to buy Dorothy a pair of shoelaces, but we had no luck finding any.

We'd been trying to buy these ever since we left home, whenever we could remember it. They weren't anything real special. It was just frustrating. Back to the hotel we went, and dined again at the small Italian restaurant; later we went to bed. The next day, we would head into West Germany proper.

Almost the entire next day was spent crossing borders and always being checked. First we crossed West Berlin into East Germany. After driving about 150 miles, we crossed the border into West Germany (the Federal Republic of Germany). By the time we got through both borders, it started to rain fairly hard and we were both exhausted.

We came to the city of Brunswick and spotted an attractive *gasthaus*. At this point, we weren't concerned about our budget. We needed shelter, warmth, and rest. Instead of a room in the main building, we were given a tiny, single-room cottage with all the toilet facilities. It was clean, cozy, and comfortable. We unpacked our bags and immediately took a nap. An hour later, after freshening up, we went to the dining room. Much to our surprise, it was much larger than we expected, and nicely appointed. The waiter seated us at a table, which, again, was quite a surprise; our table overlooked an attractively landscaped indoor swimming pool. It was very unusual to find a swimming pool in a *gasthaus*. But, from what we saw of this establishment, it appeared to be more like a small hotel than a guest-house.

This ambiance put us in the mood to indulge ourselves, regardless of the budget! We had an excellent dinner, after having a large tankard of good, cool, frothy German beer. The dinner was complete—everything from soup to nuts. Both the beer and the dinner were budget-busting, but we were not quite adjusted to Western European prices. We had spent too much time in the USSR and Poland, and were a bit spoiled. After this, we went back to bread, cheese, cold cuts, and the like, for dinners; the operant word was "economize."

After a nap, the fine beer, and the excellent dinner, we felt more relaxed and less tense than we'd felt for weeks; we were almost exuberant. After a good night's sleep and an early morning shower, we went to the dining room for breakfast, which was included in the price of the room. This place was just full of surprises! In the middle of the dining room was a huge table laden with food, the likes of which we hadn't seen since the trip began! There were several kinds of juices, cold cuts, cheeses, bread, and rolls. There were eggs in the shell, butter, jelly, and sweet rolls. A carafe of hot coffee was placed at our table! Our jaws dropped, not only at this overwhelming assortment of food, but also at the thought of stuffing it all between those open jaws. It was a do-it-yourself table and we did it to ourselves, over and over again, even to the point of making ourselves husky sandwiches for lunch, which Dorothy stuffed in her Tasha (tote bag)! What a repast. We then waddled to our room, packed, paid our bill, and left. The bill, for everything, staggered us. It totaled $64.80. It easily exceeded our daily budget. Nevertheless, we felt like "contented cows" (perhaps "pigs" is the more appropriate word here). We didn't object to the cost for three reasons: first, everything about this place pleased us, and we felt that we deserved the occasional splurge; second, after the many weeks we spent in Russia and Poland, we thought we should indulge ourselves; third, we have a standing joke between us: whenever we overspend, we say, "Charge it to our daughter, Beverly!"

We would next be traveling through a section of West Germany called Franconia, and we would be driving on the "Romantic Road." I drove over two hundred miles through what we called picture-postcard beauty. This wasn't a heavily traveled road, which pleased us, and the countryside was absolutely enchanting. We passed through many tiny, sparkling villages where most of the old, very well-kept houses (some half-timbered) had colorful red-tile roofs. Here also, the houses, barns, and even some small commercial buildings were adorned with many window boxes of bright and colorful flowers. As we had seen before, they were mostly geraniums. It was so very charming.

This area was wine country, producing mostly white wine. The little villages were nestled in small, picturesque valleys surrounded by low-lying hills; vineyards were everywhere. Nearly every village had its own small winery producing its own special wine.

We eventually stopped at one tiny village named Sommerhauser and located a *gasthaus*, a *fremmden zimmer* (friendly rooms available) called "Weinhaus Unkel" (Wine House Uncle). What a cute name.

Sommerhauser was as charming a little village as you'll find in that area. Not only did it have lots of charm, but also it had considerable history. It was founded in the seventeenth century and previously occupied by the Romans during the medieval period. Located near the Main River, it was surrounded by low, lush hills and idyllic valleys that supported small farms and vineyards. As you enter the village from the highway, you pass through a narrow archway built into a thick rock and mortar wall. This was apparently part of the wall the Romans built to surround the city. You travel perhaps three or four blocks on narrow cobblestone streets, then turn left, go another few blocks, and there stands another portion of the wall; also with the same arch. While walking, one could see where much of the wall was deteriorating and, in many places, was completely gone.

Above both of the arched entrances, as part of the wall, there are small structures with windows. These, we surmised, were the guard quarters used at the time the wall was built, as lookouts against enemy forces. The ancient Germans also poured boiling oil on enemy troops attempting entry through the archways. Now, however, these guardhouses have been pleasantly transformed. The one over the arch, where we entered, is now rented to a British writer. The other guard-house is rather unique. It is being used as a theater for live drama and is alleged to be the smallest theater in Europe. It contains only forty seats.

Walking these few blocks was sheer ecstasy. On both sides of the streets were tiny shops, gaily decorated with attractive flower boxes. Over the doorways of the shops were small, black, wrought-iron fili-greed signs, many of which had symbols describing the type of shop it was. For instance, a flower shop sign would have a bouquet; a shoe shop might have a shoe; a saloon, a beer stein; and so on. These signs were not only charming, but artistically well done.

Last, but not least, to add to our pleasure was the fact that it was easy to let our imaginations stray. We could mentally picture what this lovable small village must have been like in the ancient days when the Romans occupied it.

Our delight increased when we noticed that in front of our *gasthaus* was a concrete statue of a small boy with his mouth wide open as though he was laughing. He appeared to be standing in a shallow well. Earlier, I mentioned that this entire area was wine producing country. Sommerhauser had a reputation for producing several varieties of fine white wine.

We also learned that in a couple of days the people in the area were to celebrate their annual Wine Festival. Traditionally, at our *gasthaus*, someone poured several gallons of wine into the little boy statue through pipes inside the building. The wine flows from his mouth and the citizens help themselves to free drinks!! This is a feature of the festival that certainly adds to the festivities.

This fascinating stroll through the village had made our day. It was so different from anything else we'd experienced. Before returning to our room, we purchased some fresh fruit to snack on, then later went to the dining room for dinner, which was only mediocre. However, we each had a glass of Sommerhauser wine—two different varieties. The wine lived up to its reputation and compensated for our dinner. Later, we ate a peach, the first one for us that year. It was delicious in the extreme.

The next day, we drove to the ancient city of Rothenburg, on the Tauber River, for a day trip. This city of fifteen thousand people is one of the best preserved medieval cities in Germany. It, too, is a walled city. The walls were built in the fourteenth and fifteenth centuries, as in Sommerhauser, and the entrances to the city were through similar archways in the wall. However, over the main archway that we entered, instead of a small structure over the arch, there was a rather large stone head that is best described as a gargoyle with a hideous face and a wide-open mouth. Through the mouth, the defenders of the city would pour boiling oil on enemy invaders—gruesome, but perhaps effective.

There is much of great interest to see in Rothenburg, but I'll just name a few highlights. Over the main beer hall, where in the olden days the town councilmen would gather to "council" and drink beer, stood a most unusual mechanical clock, which had an extraordinary history connected with it.

Legend has it that, in ancient times, the city was about to be attacked by a very large enemy army. The councilmen realized their forces would not be nearly strong enough to prevent the invasion of the city. However, the mayor had a plan that he thought just might work.

As the approaching army neared the city, the mayor went out to greet the enemy commander and made him a proposition: that he and the commander sit down and drink beer, and if the commander drank more steins than the mayor, the city would be his. But if the mayor out-drank the commander, the army would not invade and they would make peace! The commander accepted the proposal, and, as legend would have it, the mayor out-drank the commander and the city was saved! Another story is that the mayor drank a three-liter tankard of wine in one draught! To celebrate this extraordinary event, this large clock was erected. Now, every hour, on the hour, the intricate works inside the clock depict the drinking scene by animating the characters on the face of the clock. It shows them lifting their steins to their mouths and drinking. It is not only clever but also comical, and keeps accurate time.

At this point, we joined a rather large tour group led by a middle-aged German woman. Like all tour guides, she was very knowledgeable. It was fortunate that we had little trouble understanding her. With the group, we visited the St. Jacob's Church to see the famous central altar, a fantastic work of art. One man devoted much of his life to carving this magnificent altar from a single large tree. Over the altar hung a dazzling crystal receptacle, which allegedly contained three drops of Christ's blood! The altar was called the "Blut Altar." After our guide clearly explained the history of the altar, I wise-cracked by saying, "No wonder people could produce such remarkable art work. This was before television!" The crowd cracked up.

The old city of Rothenburg itself was, like Sommerhauser, quite pleasing to stroll through. It, too, had streets lined with charming small shops that displayed the interesting wrought-iron signs, window boxes with colorful flowers on nearly every building, etc. Many of the houses were of the half-timber construction that Dorothy and I love.

Later, it started to rain and it was time to head home. We bought some cheese, wurst, bakery goods, fruit, beer, and a bottle of Sommerhauser wine. This was to be our dinner. We left Rothenburg well-pleased with all we saw and did in this fabulous town. We added another page to our memory book.

When we got back to Sommerhauser, the locals were busy erecting booths and stalls in preparation for the following day's Wine Festival.

"And the rains came." It was pouring when we woke up. It would be no fun to stay for the Wine Festival under these conditions, much as we wanted to. We showered, but ran out of hot water. Then, we left to continue south along the Romantic Road; our destination was Bavaria and the Bavarian Alps.

The traffic was much heavier, but the countryside, after the rain, was glorious. The hills were steeper and the valleys deeper and more lush. On both sides of the highway, the farms appeared to be in the peak of production. Our mouths watered at the thought of eating the fresh fruit and vegetables that we knew grew there. In more ways than one, this was a romantic road.

En route, we passed quite a number of *zimmers* and *gasthauses*. By about three o'clock, I was a bit tired of driving as we entered the little village of Peiting, which appealed to us because of the many half-timber houses with their red tiled roofs and flower boxes.

After a few moments of driving through Peiting, near the outskirts of town we noticed a rather old, two-storied house. Connected to the house, and behind it, was a rather long, one-story building. Like so many buildings we'd seen thus far in West Germany, we noticed the traditional flower boxes all around the front and side windows of the building. The entire building was white stucco with the usual red tile roof. Surrounding the house was a low, wrought-iron fence and a flower garden in the front yard. On the fence was the sign *"Zimmer Frei."* This was exactly what we were looking for. The village, the house, and its surroundings attracted us very much.

A rather elderly lady answered our knock. She was a very comely, pleasant, sturdy lady with a friendly face, ruddy cheeks, and twinkling eyes. Like "All State," we knew we were in "good hands." She spoke no English, but with our Yiddish we made known to her our request for a room. The room she gave us was large and airy, with several windows that we greatly appreciated. Like the rest of the house, it was typically Germanic—sparkling clean—as was our hostess, Mrs. S.

It didn't take us long to get well-acquainted. In the course of our stumbling conversation, we learned that the house was seventy-five years old, and we judged our hostess to be about the same age.

It was mid-afternoon when we got settled, so we decided to drive to Garmisch in the German Alps. Garmisch-Parlenkirchen (its full name) is in southern Bavaria. It is an international winter resort in the Bavarian Alps at the foot of Germany's renowned mountain peak, the Zugspitze.

The weather so far in Germany had been a mixed bag—rain, clouds, cool, warm—a bit of everything but snow.

Driving to Garmisch was super. The sight of the small, lush farms along the road, nestled on the low hillsides, with the proud, pretentious German Alps and their snow-covered peaks for a background, was glorious.

Added to this were the incredible carvings, made of wood and carved by hand, that are common in Bavaria and sold all along the road to Garmisch. We stopped at one woodcarver's place and became fascinated by his artistic ingenuity. He was an elderly man and obviously had a terrific sense of humor, for nearly all of his carvings, large and small, were in a humorous and satirical vein. They were carved from logs, trees, stumps, and branches. We had the greatest admiration for his talent. Naturally, we just had to buy something from him, we were so impressed with his work.

At Garmisch, a tourist town loaded with Americans, we inquired about the trip up the Alps to the famous peak, the Zugspitze. The trip was a bit expensive, but we decided not to deny ourselves this pleasure.

Back to Peiting we went, driving in heavy rain, to our comfortable room at Mrs. S's. As we entered the hall, we noticed on the wall the mounted head of a buck deer. We explained to Mrs. S. that where we live we see deer all the time. We also told her that we have a tiny farm, on which we have a small orchard, a fairly large garden, grapes, berries, and about a dozen chickens. She smiled and motioned for us to follow her.

She led us through the kitchen, through the back kitchen door, and into a short hall. From there we went through another door into the long, single-story building, that we had noticed attached to the main house. To our utter amazement she had beckoned us to see her "farm."

Her "farm" was primarily a dairy farm; there, in separate stalls, were about twenty-five dairy cows. Before we got to the cows, there was a separate room which contained the most modern electrical milking and milk processing equipment. This farm was operated by Mrs. S., her son, and her daughter-in-law.

She then took us to see her chicken pen and hen house. The pen held at least double the number of hens that we had. Lastly, we came to the hay barn section of the building, and witnessed how skillfully her ten-year-old grandson operated a mechanical skiploader moving bales of hay. At this point, grandma saw the need to feed hay to the cows and, grabbing a pitch fork, began tossing them hay as we watched in admiration of her strength.

This entire tour through her "farm" was really something. Everything was spic-and-span, very well organized, and, surprisingly, not very odoriferous. Little did we realize that the structure we first saw not only contained a home for humans but also a "castle" for cows and chickens! And grandma grinned from ear to ear when she saw the look of amazement on our faces. This was indeed an experience.

The weather the next morning was atrocious. It was raining cats and dogs, but we were getting sort of used to this non-California weather.

After a light *fruhstuck* (breakfast), we headed for the town of Fussen, about thirty-six kilometers away, at the foot of the Alps. The closer we got to Fussen, the better the weather got. Eventually we basked in bright, warm sunshine.

On the outskirts of Fussen stood two grand castles built by King Ludwig I. We first went to visit the Hohenschwangau Castle where Ludwig had resided. It was built high on a hilltop, as were so many castles, and it was quite a hike up this steep hill.

Ludwig I, because of his eccentricities and his intimate relationship with the dancer and courtesan, Lola Montez (who once lived in the town where we lived) fell into disfavor with his subjects. This forced him to abdicate to his son Ludwig II. The castle was really nothing exciting to see, both inside and out.

From Hohenschwangau Castle, it was just a short, but again steep, climb to the Neuschwanstein Castle built by Ludwig II. To get to this castle, we first hiked along the shores of the Forgennsee, a lake. This was a nice, easy hike and interesting because of the large number of swans that populated the lake. Ludwig II named the castle after the swans. However, Ludwig II was called the "Mad King." It was said that he went insane and ultimately drowned himself in the Lake Staruberg in Bavaria. This castle was also of no great consequence, but the panoramic view from both castles was spectacular.

From here we drove to the village of Weis, to see a Catholic church! Once, again, we became overwhelmed by the elaborate embellishments and rococo decorations, such as the ornate marble altar and splendid marble pillars holding up the ceiling. It was sheer beauty! To us, every church is like a museum.

It was later than usual when we crawled out of bed the next morning. After our *fruhstuck* of rolls, butter, jelly, and lots of good, hot coffee, we pointed ourselves towards Garmish.

It was Sunday, 5 August, and it was an extraordinarily beautiful morning. As I noted in the log I kept, it was the best morning we'd had on the trip so far! This was due, perhaps, to being in the foothills of the mountains. Everything was so invigorating. The drive to the mountains was also very pleasing to the eye. The hills rose higher and the valleys dropped deeper than anything we had seen thus far. The entire landscape and the small farms that nestled on the hillsides appeared more luxuriant. The hills, cloaked in many shades of green, resembled gentle rolling waves in a sea of pines.

Soon we arrived in Garmish and purchased tickets for the trip up to Zugspitze, the highest peak in Germany. What a trip! First we went by train, then by cog-wheel train, then by a breath-taking heart-stopping funicular high, high above the ground. The lift was only a four-minute ride, but to us (scaredy cats) it seemed more like hours.

We landed atop the Zugspitze, and by walking around the peak we had a 360 degree view of the surrounding countryside below us. What fantastic views! We stood nearly on the Austrian border. Everywhere we looked we saw incredible sights. Around us was an awesome chain of barren, solid granite mountains. Below us, in every direction, we could see gorgeous, green-carpeted valleys. There were also low hillsides studded with houses, barns, and other buildings, nestled amongst the tiny luxuriant farms. It was like a fairy land.

Not surprisingly, the peak was crowded with lots of tourists, like us. For people who love mountains, this was the place to be. We took the long lift down to the base of the peak, got our car, and headed home. En route, we passed over the Ammer River. We viewed it from the bridge and it was truly a stunning sight. The river ran swiftly through a very narrow canyon of verdant trees and shrubs, several hundred feet below us. It was a photographer's delight!

When we got back to our *zimmer*, Mrs. S. greeted us with a pitcher of delicious "homemade" milk and cookies. We then went to our room and ate our "poor traveler's" dinner. We often ate dinners in our room, wherever we stayed. This was especially true in Western European countries, where all costs are fairly high, and would be budget busting if we didn't do so.

Before retiring, we took a leisurely stroll into town, walking and gawking till bedtime. This had been a fabulous day for us, one of our nicest! We had no hassles, no traumatic experiences like getting lost, and best of all, our entire day was spent in viewing the beauties of nature. We went to bed fully satiated. We were completely relaxed from the day's events.

The next day our destination was Freiburg. This meant driving through an area of the *Schwartzwald* (Black Forest). The morning was warm and muggy, and soon we were ready to take off. It was time to bid our sorrowful *auf wiedersehen* to our friendly Mrs. S. and her family. She had knocked off a couple of marks from our bill, and then handed us a present of a box of homemade cookies! What hotel manager has ever done this for you?

En route to the *Schwartzwald*, as it had been since entering West Germany, we passed through many small towns and villages; some more charming than others. We went via very curvy roads that became quite narrow when going through the towns, and were heavily traveled.

We noticed that in nearly every instance, when passing through a town, we would see a local brewery. It appeared that each town brewed its own beer. For my part, drinking the beer reminds me of what the drunkard said about liquor, "It's all good, only some is better than others!" We're convinced that we drank more beer and wine and ate more ice cream on this trip, thus far, than we'd consumed in years.

As we approached Fussen, we noticed the traffic backed-up for nearly seven miles; coming in to Fussen from the opposite direction. It pleased us to know that we didn't have to go that way. As we neared Freiburg, we looked for a *zimmer* close to Lake Constance. This was a very attractive area. For this reason there was nothing available; so we drove on.

Before reaching Freiburg, we stopped at a *zimmer* in the small village of Eigeltingen. It was a bit warm that evening, so we joined our landlady sitting on a bench outside and spent some time in small talk with her. The weather continued along the similar pattern that we'd experienced for days, nearly always warm, muggy, and overcast with some rain.

Fruhstuck, the next morning, was more elaborate than we'd been having. It included an egg, wurst, sliced cheese, and good strong coffee.

Eigeltingen was just a short distance from Freiburg. En route to Freiburg, we drove along the shore of beautiful Lake Constance. It's a rather large lake and is partly in Germany and partly in Switzerland. Freiburg is the home of the famous Freiburg University. It is a very old university, founded in 1457. The city itself is very old and has a reputation for being a famous cultural center. Many of the medieval buildings, including the university, are outstanding examples of fine Gothic architecture. The city is quite large, with a population of nearly 150,000.

Because it is so large, we had trouble finding a *zimmer*. At the sign of the little "i" (an information center), they sent us to a small hotel *gasthaus* right next to the *banhoff* (railway station) and in front of the Lowenbrau Brewery. It was pretty noisy, for the brewery worked day and night. We did have a nice, large, clean room, and as an added bonus we got to smell the beer being brewed at no extra charge!

Shortly after we got settled, we called the Von K.'s. These were the people our son had suggested that we get in touch with. Dr. Von K. and his wife (also a doctor) had spent some time at the University of Colorado Medical school, in Denver, doing some highly specialized hematological research. They are both specialists in this field. Our son was director of the Medical Library there, and knew them both quite well. We were invited to their home.

It was mid-afternoon before we arrived, and after the formalities of introductions, Mrs. Von K. invited us for a light snack, their four o'clock tea. Their home was very nice, rich with fine paintings and other furnishings that even we recognized to be of superior quality. The part of the house we saw revealed that this was the home of people of culture and good taste, and, evidently, a substantial income.

Soon, our hostess seated us at the table. The tablecloth and napkins were of fine white linen, the glassware was sparkling crystal, the silverware was silver, and our cups and saucers were delicate porcelain, beautifully designed. It was a sumptuous setting. Our snack consisted of delicious homemade cakes and very tasty and aromatic coffee. The entire ambiance was so formal that we felt out of our element. However, we had a pleasant chat (they both spoke excellent English) for about an hour. During our conversation, they both spoke of a serious concern: that there was a noticeable drift to the right by their government. They showed considerable alarm that there could possibly be a resurgence of Nazism!

When the hour was up, we parted in a very cordial manner. Although the atmosphere had been rather stifling, we enjoyed the visit. They were not haughty or aloof, just a bit stilted. We weren't accustomed to this level of cultural environment. After all, we're gypsies.

While in Freiburg, we did considerable walking in the center of town and especially in the Munster Market Plaza. We walked so much because the day before, without knowing it, I pulled a real boo-boo. I drove right through a pedestrian-only area that was like a shopping mall. I soon found out my mistake when we got lots of yells, horn tooting, and hand waving by the few cars that were allowed there.

We always enjoy going to the open, as well as closed markets. There was always something new, novel, and different to see. After nearly five months and thirteen countries spent searching, we finally found a pair of shoelaces for Dorothy's shoes. And would you believe it? They were a bit short! Does this really matter to gypsies? No.

Our car was being serviced, so we walked until late afternoon, window shopping, people watching, and admiring the unusual architecture, mostly Gothic, of the buildings and especially the churches. While in the market, we purchased lots of goodies for our lunch and dinner. Then we picked up our car and drove back to our *Gasthaus*. Before going up to our room, we stopped in the bar and had a beer. The patrons, as was obvious by their dress and mannerisms, were workers. They appeared friendly, and seemed to enjoy their leisure and their beer. I would have liked to spend more time with them, "drinking beer with the boys."

The following day, we opted for a guided bus tour of the city. We learned that Freiburg was heavily bombed during the war. They certainly did a great job of restoration. We saw many interesting things on the tour and learned much about the people who lived there during the medieval period. We were told about their beliefs, superstitions, religion, and culture. We especially liked the sign over the main building of the university which said, in German, "The Truth Shall Make You Free." It was a very interesting city, and we were pleased with the tour. Taking the tour of the city saved wear and tear on our nerves. We could also see more in one fourth of the time we would need if we were going on our own. The additional benefit was having a guide to explain at what we looked.

One rather unusual and droll sight pointed out to us was on a very old Gothic building. On the outside of this building, about two stories up, we saw painted carvings of unearthly and grotesque gargoyles. It seemed that each one had some specific significance. One in particular was really fascinating. It was the figure of a man carved so that his bare behind was facing the street. His purpose was to ward off evil spirits!

On the way back to our room, we shopped for dinner and the next day's lunch. Our dinner was an eight-course spread. We dined on roll-mops (pickled herring), chicken sandwiches (we'd purchased a barbe-cued one), stinky cheese (bier Kase—and, boy, did it smell), tomatoes, grapes, beer, and, for dessert, cookies and candy! It was some feast.

After this luscious repast, we remembered to call Rolf and Andrea, the couple we'd met in the Moscow campground. We got the impression that they were married. And, for some reason, based on nothing at all, we assumed that Rolf was a mechanic or skilled laborer of some sort.

We asked an attendant at the petrol station to make the call for us. After a moment's conversation with someone on the other end, he turned to us and said, "Dr. Rolf?" Dorothy and I stared at each other blankly for a fleeting moment and said, "Yes." We didn't know. We'd made false assumptions. I got on the phone and Rolf gave me instructions on how to find their weekend place. It was only about fifteen kilometers from Freiburg in a tiny hamlet called Falkensteig, not far distant from the French border. He also said that they wouldn't arrive until about seven at night.

Rain was coming down in sheets the next morning. After breakfast, we drank lots of good hot coffee. Then we drove to a Laundromat to do our laundry. It was rather expensive, compared to what we had previously experienced. Then we went back to our room to pack.

Since we had lots of time, we drove to the resort town of Titisee on Lake Titisee. Fortunately, the sky had cleared, the sun came out, and all the world looked rosy! The lake is in the *Schwartzwald*, and the town is a typical tourist town with lots of gift and souvenir shops. The *Schwartzwald* is famous not only as a unique forest, but also as the area where the famous Black Forest hams, bacon, and sausage are produced. There are numerous shops vending these products, as well as many wood carvings, and the usual gamut of souvenirs of every description. We bought a small handmade pair of bellows, for our barbecue, which had interesting designs depicting nature carved on both sides.

Both the town and the lake of Titisee were very appealing. The surroundings were beautifully kept, with flowers everywhere and fascinating wood carvings, wooden buildings, and wooden fences. For the first time in our lives, we saw people windsurfing on the lake. By the time we'd seen a good portion of what there was to see, the time was approaching to drive to Falkensteig to meet Andrea and Rolf.

We arrived at about a quarter past six. It had started to rain, and turned cold. We located their house by inquiring of a neighbor, but we couldn't drive to it because there was a tiny stream that ran in front of it with only a wooden foot path to get to it. So we had to park our car off the road across the highway.

There was really nothing nearby but a *gasthaus*, which had a restaurant. We could only sit in our car and wait. That we did until nearly eight o'clock. By this time, we started getting a bit panicky because no one had showed up. We decided that we had better get accommodations for the night. We went to the *gasthaus* and fortunately got a room. We then went to the dining room, as we both felt hungry and depressed. Just as bowls of hot soup were served, Andrea popped in, all alone. Rolf was unable to come; he had forgotten, when we talked with him on the phone, that this weekend he had to be on duty at the hospital.

Andrea was in her last year of medical school. I guessed her to be in her late twenties, a few years younger than Rolf. She was slightly taller than average, well-proportioned, and shapely. Her hair was medium blonde and shoulder length; her face was plain yet pretty; and her eyes spoke of intelligence and self-assurance. We knew we would have no trouble getting along with her.

Andrea joined us for dinner. We made a deal with the landlady to pay her half-price for the room (but not to stay), which she accepted. After dinner, we removed our things from the room and moved into the weekend house. This house was an old, somewhat dilapidated, wooden two-story home. Andrea and Rolf rented half of it. At this point, we found out that Andrea and Rolf were not married, but were "cohabiting."

When we entered the house, we were shocked. It felt damp and smelled musty, which was to be expected, as it was used only on weekends. But aside from this, here was one instance that was an exception to a rule. In our experience, German people were very neat, clean, and orderly. This house was exactly the opposite. It was dusty, with cobwebs everywhere. Wine bottles, both full and empty, were strewn all over, and pots, pans, and assorted dishes were scattered hither, thither, and yon. It was the nearest thing to chaos you could imagine. Well, no one said the gypsy life was all strawberries and cream. There was nothing to do about it but grit our teeth and bear it. After we had drunk a bottle of wine and gabbed until eleven o'clock, it was time to retire.

Because this old house was divided in half, for two tenants, Dorothy and I had to sleep in a loft. In order to get to the loft, we had to climb up a ladder. Dorothy inquired about the bathroom, which we both required occasionally during the night. This posed no problem for Andrea. She simply fetched us a couple of chamber pots and all was well.

It was still raining when we came down for *fruhstuck*. In the kitchen was a small wood stove, and it gave off considerable heat. It was warm and cozy, and Andrea had prepared an elaborate breakfast for us. We were both hungry and did justice to the meal.

Later, in Andrea's car, we drove through part of the *Schwartzwald* and through several small medieval villages. We went over hills and through valleys, never getting bored. In a couple of the villages we stopped to visit, there were fascinating baroque churches. We shopped in a small village for some smoked Black Forest ham, bacon, and sausage, and then went back to the house.

Andrea prepared a delicious lunch and we ate like pigs. She was quite adept in the kitchen. She treated us like a "Jewish mother." To most Europeans, what we consider lunch is the main meal of the day; it is a rather large meal.

The rain had stopped, so the three of us went for a hike. We stopped at a phone booth and Andrea called Rolf. We also spoke with him, and he was profuse in his apologies to us. We then went strolling along on a regular hiking trail. We'd never seen anything like it. The trail was wide, smooth, and cleared, like a path in a botanical garden might be. It was at least as well marked as our California freeways. Signs and arrows were painted everywhere; you couldn't get lost if you wanted to! In addition, every so often there were benches for resting, picnic areas, and even a fire pit to cook in. In all our years of hiking, we'd never seen anything like this. Most surprisingly, nothing was vandalized, covered with graffiti, or shot at for target practice. To us it was almost unreal. We enjoyed it all.

The clouds appeared again, so we turned back towards home. Andrea then served cold cuts, bread, cheese, and smoked tea (something we'd never tasted before). She then opened up a bottle of wine and we sat around and chatted until ten o'clock, when there was a knock on the door.

Andrea opened the door to welcome a young couple about her age, friends of hers who were returning from a weekend in Basel, Switzerland. After introductions, they joined us, and we proceeded to indulge in more wine, conversation, and laughter. This lasted until midnight, when we retired. Because sleeping accommodations were limited, the friends had to use the floor as a bed. In addition, there was a shortage of blankets. Fortunately, in our car we had the two sleeping bags we'd purchased in Poland. I went out to get them and everybody was happy—and sleepy.

Morning dawned bright, sunny, and warm. It was a blessing, for the night before had been cold. We all felt chipper, and Andrea decided we would have *fruhstuck* outside near the garden. She then proceeded to prepare and serve a huge breakfast of Black Forest sausage, bacon, and scrambled eggs—the works. Dorothy had to fry the bacon and sausage, as Andrea said she didn't know how. Breakfast is my favorite meal (Dorothy's is dinner), so I was in heaven. The weather was perfect.

This was the grand finale of a very memorable weekend. We prepared to say *auf wiedersehen* to Andrea and her friends and head for Switzerland.

I noted above, in a somewhat negative manner, the condition of the weekend house, how unkempt and littered it was. But I must state, unequivocally, that what the house lacked in cleanliness and comfort, Andrea more than made up for in her treatment toward us. She was as kind, gracious, and considerate as anyone could expect. And again,

Dorothy and I marveled at the rapport we seemed to have with much younger people. We rarely experienced a "generation gap" syndrome.

So now we will leave the two Germanys. Again, it's a bit overwhelming to begin to describe all that we experienced in both countries. What you have just read is a brief and sketchy record of some of the highlights of what occurred while we were there. The Romantic Road was all that the name implied. For us, it was a several-hundred-mile road of romance, with people, places, and things that are unforgettable.

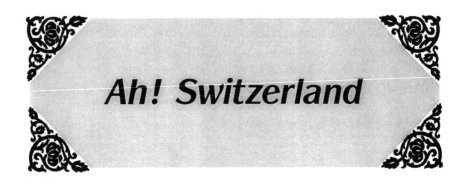

Ah! Switzerland

Shortly after leaving Andrea's place, we drove through a very unusual natural rock formation. It was a narrow canyon, perhaps not more than a half mile long and two hundred feet high. The sheer walls came right down to the road's edge. This place was called *Hollental* (Hell's Valley). On the very top of each hill stood a statue of a buck deer, silhouetted against the clear blue sky. In a leaping position, they posed facing each other. It was an unusual sight. It was called the *Hirschsprung*. We stopped to take pictures and then noticed a pretty little stream which flowed serenely alongside the highway through the valley. The effect of this setting was absolutely inspirational. A short while after leaving this remarkable scene, we reached the Swiss border and, without any trouble, went through customs. We now entered Switzerland.

Several days earlier, we had casually met a young man from Switzerland and he had recommended we stay some place near the center of the country, for convenience. He suggested Interlaken. We checked out Interlaken in our guide books and noted it was a popular and rather expensive resort city. This is not for penurious gypsies. We would settle elsewhere.

Soon we came to the pretty little town of Spiez, not too far from Interlaken. We liked what we saw. We spotted a *gasthoff* and rented a room. This place was nothing special, and a bit more than we figured to pay, but we got settled and decided to check out the territory, so we drove to Interlaken.

Spiez is on the shore of the Thunersee (Lake Thun) with a backdrop of the Swiss Alps. It is quite impressive. Further on, on a narrow strip of land that lay between the Thunersee and the Brienzsee, is the city of Interlaken. We parked our car and started walking through town. Interlaken is an interesting town, but it didn't take us long to discover that it looked and smelled of money. It was obvious to us that this city was too rich for our blood. Also, it was too touristy, in a refined way, and too crowded.

Back we drove to Spiez and stopped at the train depot for a meager dinner. We were told that Switzerland was rather expensive; since our budget was getting tattered, though not yet torn, we had to be a bit frugal. A Tourist Information Office was in the train depot. It was closed, so we decided to check it out the following day.

Just prior to reaching Spiez, Dorothy and I discussed our future travel plans. We were four and a half months on this trip so far. Our original plan was to spend a year in Europe. Dorothy turned to me and said, "You know, I'm getting a bit tired of traveling." And I, somewhat to her amazement, said, "You know, I am too!" It seemed we both felt homesick for our little "farm," family, and friends. We decided we would continue until we completed six months of the trip. Then, in a very stern voice, Dorothy said to me, "Now I don't want you to go telling everybody that it was on account of me that we terminated our trip!" I assured her that this wouldn't happen because I, too, felt somewhat stressed and strained. After this discussion and the decision we made, we both felt relieved.

What little we saw of Switzerland on this first day wasn't very impressive. It was less appealing than the area of Germany we'd just driven through. The next morning, we walked to the Tourist Office and told the young lady what we desired in the way of accommodations. After two phone calls, she gave us the address of a *zimmer* close by. We went back to get our things, and with just a little trouble found the place we had been directed to. We rang the door bell and were greeted by a plain but friendly-looking woman. I guessed her to be in her early fifties. We introduced ourselves and she identified herself as Mrs. Luci "S." She then took us to our room upstairs. This was a large, light, and airy room with a fantastic view. It had two large windows and a glass door that opened onto a small balcony. Luci spoke no English, but we did OK with our Yiddish and her Swiss German. She spoke rapidly and frequently gestured with her hands. She had a very expressive face, smiled a lot, and would often break out in boisterous laughter.

The house sat on a sloping hill, sloping from front to back. It was an older wooden house with a steep pitched roof, three stories high, but only the two top floors were for living. The ground floor was a basement. The front of the house faced a narrow alleyway. The back had a big yard, in which was a very nice vegetable garden, flower gardens, a rabbit pen, a few fruit trees, and some ornamental trees and shrubs.

Outside our room, on the third level, was a narrow balcony, about four feet wide, with a wooden railing. We could look down from the balcony and get a bucolic view of all the backyard. We had such a fantastic view toward the horizon that only a poet could do it justice. Both from this balcony and from our bedroom window, the view was indescribable. If ever there was a picture postcard that described Switzerland, this was it.

We looked over a huge verdant meadow dotted with trees and shrubs, with houses and small shops scattered along the edges of the meadow. A small colony of buildings nestled in the foreground. Our eyes then traveled beyond into the soft blue, unruffled waters of Lake Thun. There, off to the left on the edge of the lake, stood a small, lovely, "fairy land" castle. It was all white, with its stately spires and steeples reaching to the sky. Surrounding it were several large trees, one of which was especially large, in full foliage. This picture-perfect scene of the white castle majestically standing on the edge of the lake with the green meadow in front, the blue waters of the lake behind, and the azure blue sky above was absolutely dazzling! But this was only half of this marvelous scene. Our eyes traveled beyond this, beyond the horizon, high into the sky at what can best be described as a miraculous sight. We were gazing transfixed at the Bernese Alps, and directly before our eyes were three of the most spectacular snow-capped mountain peaks we'd ever seen: the Eiger, the Monch, and the Jungfrau. Just picture us gazing at such an incredible sight upon awakening in the morning and viewing it for as long as our hearts desired!

It should be obvious that our first, rather low opinion of Switzerland was destroyed after this scene. This "picture perfect" sight, to this day, is as alive and as impressive as that day when we first laid eyes upon it. With us it was love at second sight.

As soon as we got settled in our spacious room, we realized that we still had a lot of time on our hands, so we drove to the village of Zweilutschiner in the Bernese Mountains. We bought tickets at the train station for the trip up to the peak of the Jungfrau. This fantastic two-and-a-half-hour trip cost us one hundred dollars. We started on a cog-wheel tram. We later changed to a regular tram that took us part way through a long tunnel to our destination. The first part of the journey, on the cog-wheel tram, was absolutely fabulous. Wherever we looked, we could see tiny little villages, some not more than a few buildings. They were painted white with either red tile roofs, slate roofs, or roofs covered with large rocks, which were a protection against collapse by heavy snow. These tiny dwellings and barns were nestled in lush green valleys located high upon the mountainside.

We got out of the tunnel and off the tram near the top of the peak. The view was spellbinding! For 360 degrees we were enchanted by the sight of blinding snow fields (the sun was so brilliant), glaciers everywhere, the awesome peaks I mentioned earlier, and the other snow-capped peaks of this range that we could see in the distance. It was pure, unadulterated beauty.

For the "frosting on the cake," very near the top we walked through a tunnel 150 meters long carved right through a glacier! Somewhat like the salt mines in Poland, several figurines, elf-like, stood carved into the walls of the glacier. There was also a nearly life-sized auto—it looked like a Model T Ford—sculpted in the wall. Surprisingly, there were electric lights embedded in the ice walls.

We were so mesmerized by all this splendor that we spent hours walking around over the snow, gazing at the enchanting tiny villages far below us and drinking in all the magnificence of our surroundings. This was almost like a dream come true. We left for home, and the trip down the mountain was breathtaking and scary.

The drive home was a pleasure. What we could see of the scenery was rich. The road was narrow and winding with lots of traffic, both cars and bicycles. We dropped out of the mountains and skirted the shores of Lake Brienz and Lake Thun.

We shopped for food. When we got home, around seven o'clock, we cleaned up, relaxed, and Dot prepared dinner, which we ate in our room while casting adoring eyes at the gorgeous triad of mountain peaks framed by our bedroom window—the Eiger, the Monch, and the Jungfrau. What a way to end a day of all days!

The fourteenth of August was another lovely day, which put us in the mood for sightseeing. We knew that our hiking and camping club had a cabin near Grindelwald, and we wanted to see it. The drive to Grindelwald was the same we took the day before. Fortunately, there was less traffic, so I was better able to enjoy the scenery.

Grindelwald is a popular town for both summer and winter sports. There are many excellent hiking trails in the summer and very good skiing in the winter. Because of this, the town attracts more tourists.

After having to ask for directions a few times, we found the cabin owned by Nature Friends (our club), and what a gorgeous location it was. It was a bit more than a cabin. It was more like a small alpine chalet. The structure, architecture, and painting were just like what would expect to see in the Swiss Alps. The location of the cabin was heavenly (both literally and figuratively). It was high up in the mountains, situated so that it looked out upon a luscious, brilliant green Alpine valley, and was directly below the back side of the Eiger, so when we looked up toward heaven we could see the snow-covered top of this stately peak and more of the Bernese Mountain Range.

After spending a couple hours fully enjoying all this beauty and talking with the young Chicana caretaker, who surprised us by saying she lived in Los Angeles, we took leave, much as we hated to, and headed back to Spiez.

It was mid-afternoon when we arrived at the Thunersee and, as it was such a lovely day, and since Dorothy had packed a nice lunch, we found a bench near the shore of the lake. Like the gypsies that we were, we reveled in the food and the ambiance. We were at peace with the world. Before going home to our *zimmer*, we stopped at the town of Faulensee to inquire about a trip to the Matterhorn the next day, weather permitting. The young lady at the Tourist Office suggested we drive. She said it was a beautiful drive.

The sun was out when we awoke, and after breakfast we headed for Kondersteg, not far away. Here we drove our car onto a car-train, and sat in our car while the train went through many tunnels. It arrived in Goppenstein, where we disembarked and got back on the highway.

The next several miles en route to Tasch made for a hair-raising drive. The road was very steep, downhill, narrow, and circuitous. In several places I was required to drive one-lane, hairpin curves, after first checking a parabolic mirror (located on my side of the road) to see if the way was clear. However, my vision is a bit weak, so I would be into the curve before I could get a clear view in the mirror! Every time I had to do this, I felt as if I had lost a few days of my life and gained gray hairs on my head! It was extremely frightening for me and my wife.

Finally, after what seemed like hours, we arrived at Tasch! I was so tense I couldn't enjoy one minute of this spectacular drive. We boarded another tram at Tasch, sans auto this time, and rode to Zermat. Here we took the cogwheel train and, after what seemed like an almost vertical trip, landed at Garnergrat. We were 10,335 feet up, at the foot of the massive Matterhorn in the Pennine Alps.

Throughout our lives, we'd seen many pictures of this most famous mountain. It was really awesome. We craned our necks to see this stupendous hunk of rock that appeared to be standing all by itself. It poked its snowy white head deep into a clear blue, heavenly, sky. It stood there solemnly, looking to me like a guidepost directing not "lost souls," but souls that appeared to be lost, headed for Heaven. I could close my eyes and visualize an ethereal scene of souls winging their way from the mountain top. What a sight! It was equally dramatic to see, again, the tiny villages and isolated buildings nestled in the small lush valleys, hanging on for dear life to the steep mountain sides.

Dorothy was feeling a bit woozy from the altitude, so after a quick snack of a glass of warm milk and a sweet confection each for $5.50, we decided to go back home.

Back to Zermat we went; it was jam-packed with tourists. Once there, we went into a few gift shops and bought some postcards, but no gifts or souvenirs, and headed home. When I got to thinking about that horrendous drive from Tasch to Goppenstein, I chickened out. We learned that we could drive to Brig and put the car on the car-train to avoid that stretch of highway. It cost a bit more money, but it was well worth it. My nerves just couldn't take more of that driving.

We arrived at Luci's at about seven o'clock, just as it started to rain. Dorothy was fixing a cold but good deli dinner in our room, when suddenly the sky darkened, the wind howled, and the rain poured. In a matter of seconds, the rain turned into hail and thundered down upon the roof. Luci came dashing into our room and quickly closed the window shutters. In doing so, her hand was pelted by a hail stone and instantly raised a large welt. The hail stones easily measured half an inch in diameter!

This was an unusual hail storm as it cut a swath probably a quarter mile in width and lasted just about three or four minutes. Its path was from our *zimmer* to the edge of the lake at the castle grounds.

Luci left to check out the garden. We met her on the balcony; with tears in her eyes, she pointed to the gardens and said, *"In finif minuts altes kaput!"* (In five minutes all was lost). Their entire garden was beaten into the ground. The vegetables, flowers, and considerable fruit from the trees were lost. This was a rather unhappy ending to an otherwise extraordinary day. C'est la vie!

Earlier, when I was describing the small castle by the lake, I mentioned one very large tree on the castle grounds. When we went out after the hail storm, we noticed that this gorgeous tree had been felled by the storm. What a shame. We also noticed a number of people at the tree picking off small branches. Our curiosity got the better of us, so we walked down to see why. We learned that the castle was 150 years old and the tree about the same age. It was not a native tree and it was the only one of its kind. The people, apparently, took the branches for souvenirs.

There was a little more rain, but mostly it was fair weather the following day. Off we went to visit the city of Lucerne on the Vierwald Stratter See. The city is right on the edge of this large, park-like lake. The lake abounds with many ducks, swans, and other waterfowl.

Because of the many tourists, we couldn't find legal parking, so we parked our car in an illegal zone and went walking. Lucerne has a population of nearly seventy thousand souls and equally that many tourists. Like all fairly large cities, it was busy, crowded, and not too interesting to us. There is, probably, much of interest to see in Lucerne, but we didn't feel in the mood to do much sightseeing. We did buy a small gift for Luci.

A bit later, we walked back to the lake, sat on a park bench, ate our lunch, and fed the waterfowl. We relaxed a bit more and then went off into the mountains towards Spiez.

We returned by a different route and this was somewhat hectic. As we climbed up the mountain road over a high pass, we ran into heavy mists that soon became dense fog. Driving on Swiss mountain roads under these conditions is anything but fun. I drove in second gear for several miles. It was scary. I was wound-up as taut as a watch spring, my knuckles aching from my death-grip on the steering wheel. I didn't relax until we got down off the mountain and out of the fog.

The next morning, because of heavy rain, we just took it easy, stayed in our room, read, and relaxed. After lunch we went out for a walk. The rain had eased a bit, and we wanted some air. At a shop nearby we bought a small gift for our host, Ernst "S." and his seven-year-old son, Roland. Ernst worked for the railroad, and we didn't see much of him; he was a very quiet man. We spoke very little with him because he was difficult to understand. When he came home from his job, he would go to work in the garden, tend to the rabbits, and then cut the grass with a small hand sickle. He always did these chores, both before and after dinner. Later, we returned to our room to read and write postcards.

It was getting a bit too cool in our room, as the temperature had dropped the past couple of days. We decided to indulge ourselves and go out for dinner. There were two small hotels with dining rooms close by. We selected the better one, the Desalpes. However, it was just six o'clock, and the dining room was not yet open. In much of Western Europe, people eat their evening meal much later than we at home. In order to kill time, we had a glass of wine at the bar. Shortly afterward, the dining room opened and we seated ourselves. For a while, we were the only patrons. Although this wasn't a fancy hotel, the dining room was elegant. The tablecloth, napkins, silver service, wine goblets, glasses, and dishes were spotless and sparkling. We felt like members of the petite bourgeoisie.

On the menu, for an entree, was listed fresh fish caught in "our" lake Thun. This struck our fancy, so we ordered it. Dorothy ordered hers plain, while I had mine with a delightful, spicy, French sauce. The fish was served piping hot and smelled heavenly. A couple of bites confirmed that it tasted heavenly too. We had more wine and finished this excellent meal with a delicious dessert and good hot coffee. We hadn't yet had a bad cup of coffee in Switzerland. It was, for us, a rather expensive meal at thirty-four dollars for us both, but we enjoyed it immensely. We felt entitled to a bit of luxury after eating so many delicatessen dinners in our room.

Well-satisfied, we went back to our cold room. Apparently the cool weather was unusual for this time of year, and the heating system had been turned off. We stayed up and played cards, read and then went to bed. The thick, soft, lightweight feather *pereneh* on our bed was most appreciated.

Time was running out on our stay in Switzerland. For the few remaining days, we drove to a number of cities to see the sights. We drove to the old and beautiful city of Bern. While there, we strolled through the *zentrum* (pedestrian market place), as we loved doing, and went to the Bern Historical Museum. There we viewed the large statues of *berns* (bears), after which the city is named, and generally had a nice, unexciting, and uneventful few hours.

Next we visited the cities of Montreux and Lausanne. The weather was really crazy. It was only halfway through August, but so cold that we had to dress in winter clothing. En route, we stopped on a high bank above the Simm River to watch a kayak slalom race. This is a very exciting sport and can be dangerous. The river was very swift, but the young racers were extremely capable. We saw no serious accidents. This drive, like all the drives we'd taken in Switzerland, was just one scenic wonder after another. If nothing else, Switzerland offers fabulous scenery. We never got bored—scared sometimes, but never bored. Both Montreux and Lausanne are on the eastern end of Lac Leman. Actually this was more a driving pleasure trip, as we spent little time in either city.

Upon our return, we again indulged ourselves and went out to dinner at the smaller and less expensive hotel. The dining room was not as elegant, but the food was equally as good, as was the service, and it was more plentiful. We had six vegetables with our steak dinner. It was a complete dinner, as opposed to the a la carte dinner at the other hotel, and everything was super and inexpensive.

Because of the cold in our room, Luci invited us to come downstairs where there was heat. We did, and we socialized till bedtime. This was to be our last night in Switzerland with Luci, Ernst, and their son. While visiting with them, Luci brought out a round of cheese called Alpine cheese, which I would guess to be about ten inches in diameter and four inches thick. The cheese was so dry and hard, you couldn't slice it. You would scrape slices as thin as tissue paper with a special cutter. It was strong, but very tasty.

The story behind this unusual cheese is that when the farmers drove their dairy stock up to those high Alpine meadows in the summer, they would graze there for the entire season. But there was no way to dispose of their milk. The herders had round receptacles into which they would pour the milk, and by some process they would dry it until it became as hard as a brick! At the end of the summer, when it was time to bring the herds back to the farms, the farmers would pool all their rounds of cheese, sell them in the cities, and divide the profits equitably. It was a very ingenious way to produce and market the cheese.

Those tiny little white buildings that we saw everywhere in the mountains, sitting snugly in the small Alpine valleys, were mostly the barns and quarters for herders. On this subject, another fascinating sight was seeing the hayricks standing in fields, wrapped with new cut hay. They looked like soldiers standing in perfect alignment, row after row. They were jokingly called the "Swiss Army Men!" This scene, often repeated, was very typical of the Swiss culture. Everything was neat, clean, and orderly. We would laughingly joke about how everything was so clean we thought they washed their houses, barns, and even their cattle. As an example, we once drove into a petrol station to gas up. The lady attendant not only filled the tank, but checked the oil and washed every single window, including the head lamps! Ah! Switzerland!

During the eight days we spent with Luci, Ernst, and Roland, they treated us as though we were the best of friends. At no time, ever, did we feel like we were buying such gracious treatment. The cost for our room was twenty dollars a night. For this, we had the very nice room that I described earlier, and simple, but ample breakfasts. Next to our bedroom was a very convenient half bathroom (a toilet and sink). For bathing, we used their personal bathroom, which had a hand-held shower. This type of shower is very common throughout Europe. However, before either one of us became adept at using it, we would be washing the ceiling, walls, floors, everything but our bodies! When the weather was nice, we would sit out on the balcony in the evening and savor the magnificent view that lay before us and the majestic sight of our three favorite mountain peaks high above us.

At about nine-thirty the last morning, we packed and got ready to roll. We affectionately hugged and kissed Luci good-bye. She had tears in her eyes and it was all we could do to hold back ours.

Ah! Switzerland! This had been a fantastic eight days for us. Being partial to mountains, this country had it all. We're certain, without a doubt, that we will forever recall the wondrous, incredible sights we saw during our stay in this enchanting country, as well as Luci's charm and friendliness.

We know that there will be many who will find Switzerland a bit too orderly, too neat, too dull, perhaps even too stifling. But for Dorothy and me, who spent so many years in frenetic, smoggy, overpopulated Los Angeles and who love the mountains, Switzerland was our heaven on earth!

Once again footloose and fancy free, we pointed ourselves in the direction of Austria on a morning that was nice and warm, for a change. So long, Switzerland. *Auf wiedersehen!* We'll never forget you, but gypsies must wander.

Other Parts of Europe East and West

Our travel plans would next take us to Austria, Czechoslovakia, France, England, and finally home. We had no definite itinerary. We went where our gypsy blood directed us.

The drive from Spiez to the Austrian border, by way of the tiny Principality of Liechtenstein, was anything but dull. We went via Brienze over the Grimsel Pass, and viewed the incredible Grimsel Glacier, then through the Furka Pass, and finally on flat ground onto the autobahn. Driving these mountain roads, twisting and turning through the high passes, up steep roads and down others, is nerve racking. It also detracts from the pleasure of seeing all the marvelous sights which abound in the area.

By the time we got on the autobahn, we both felt relieved from the tension of the drive. The autobahn in Switzerland is nothing compared to the autobahns in West Germany, where the crazies tailgate at one hundred miles per hour!

Soon we entered Liechtenstein, the world's only German-speaking monarchy. It is a little fairy tale land with no military forces of any kind. There are no cities, nightclubs, department stores, and practically no crime. Some beautiful old castles, wonderful scenery, lush small farms, and orchards—a land of peace and quiet is what Liechtenstein is all about.

We spent little time in this tiny jewel of the Alps. We had no trouble crossing the border into and out of it into Feldkirch, Austria.

It was getting toward late afternoon as we crossed into Austria, so we started looking for a place to light for the night. We located a small pensione and flopped, both of us a bit stressed out from the drive.

We took a short walk in the area before dining, but there was not much to see. We went back to our room to clean up for dinner. We ate in the pensione dining room and had a full course dinner. Dorothy's entree was lamb chops, and I had pork chops. Both were quite good. The total cost was $13.60. The pensione cost us $23.20 for the night. I frequently mention the costs we incurred to show how they related to our budget. Lately, the relationship was not doing so well.

You will recall that, when we planned this trip, we naively thought we could get by spending one thousand dollars a month. It didn't take us long after first landing in London to see that this figure was a bit underestimated. We then increased our monthly budget to twelve hundred dollars. After our time spent in West Germany, Switzerland, and now Austria, we again realized that this sum was unrealistic and we needed to boost our monthly budget to fifteen hundred dollars. With this amount, we felt we could get by fairly comfortably.

Breakfast in this pensione was pretty standard and adequate. There was sufficient food to "steal a roll" (not really steal it; Dorothy just tucked it in her tasha), with some wurst for our lunch. We packed up and drove off to Innsbruck.

To get to Innsbruck, we had to drive through the Arlesberg Tunnel. It was several miles long and cost us nine dollars! Unexpected expenses like this forced us to increase our budget. When we finally came out of the tunnel, we again had to drive through the mountains and over the Fern Pass. This was not nearly as bad as driving in Switzerland.

It was just noon when we arrived in Innsbruck. Through a Tourist Agency, we got a room in a private home. Mrs. A. was our hostess. This very nice and very friendly elderly lady took us to our room, which was very similar to our room in Spiez. We were delighted with everything about this place, especially our hostess.

After bringing up our clothes and our utensils (for our meals in our room), we walked to "Old Town." We saw the somewhat usual sights: old buildings, old churches, and very intriguing narrow streets, crowded with tourists buying souvenirs and gifts. The tourists were also patronizing the sidewalk cafes. Innsbruck is a popular tourist town for both summer and winter activities, and dining at the sidewalk cafes is very popular.

By the time we got through seeing much of what there was to see in "Old Town," we felt tired and hungry. On one of the narrow, crooked streets we noticed a butcher shop that served light meals. Feeling curious and adventurous, we decided to give it a try. We had bratwurst and sauerkraut, real ethnic fare, which wasn't bad at all. With beer it cost us only six dollars, and it was an interesting dining adventure. We strolled leisurely back to our room. I napped while Dorothy read, and when I awoke, we played gin until bedtime.

The next morning, we walked to "Old Town" again, milling with the crowds and actually buying small gifts for our two granddaughters. Our stroll took us to the Inn River, where we found a bench and ate our lunch.

After lunch, we walked to the nice fountain nearby, and then to the tour bus stop. We decided to take this bus tour up into the Tyrolean Alps. The bus picked us up at 1:45 P.M. We had a young lady guide, whom we could hardly understand. The main stop-over was at a famous ski area called Kuh Tai (Cow Valley). We reached this place by driving through the picturesque Sellrain Valley. We spent an hour and a half at Kuh Tai just wandering around looking at the scenery. There was little else to see.

This tour was disappointing after our stay in Switzerland. It was fascinating to see, as in the Swiss Alps, the tiny villages high, high up on the mountain sides. It appeared as if these Tyrolean villages would fall off at any moment! Dorothy and I wondered why anyone would choose to live, let alone farm, in such isolated places.

It was windy and cold at Kuh Tai, and there was no shelter. Not only were we disappointed about this tour, but several other tourists were grumbling also. We got back to town at half past six, and went to our room to dine on another delicatessen dinner.

Our opinion of Innsbruck isn't very high. It's a pretty city and unusual in that the mountains come down almost into the city limits. The Inn River adds another dimension of beauty to it. But it is so crowded with tourists (including us, of course) that it loses some of its flavor and charm. Oh well! You can't win them all!

Off we went the next morning, destination: Salzburg. It was a nice drive through the mountains, deep canyons, and peaceful valleys—definitely more relaxing than driving in the Swiss Alps.

A few miles southwest of Salzburg, we passed through the town of Hallein and noticed a nice looking, two-story, old but well-kept wooden house that had a small *Zimmer Frei* sign on the fence. It looked inviting, so we parked and checked it out. Surrounding the house, behind the fence, was a large, nicely trimmed lawn, lots of flowers and a couple of fruit trees. It was a good omen.

An elderly couple answered our knock, welcomed us in a very friendly manner, in German, and indicated that a room was available. This room was two flights up and it, too, was very large, light, and airy, furnished nicely with three beds. It also had a sink in the room, which was very convenient for us.

The room suited us, despite the fact that we had to climb up and down the two flights of stairs to get to and from the bathroom. This was a slight inconvenience, and, we felt, a small price to pay for this nice room.

Since it was early afternoon, we decided to drive to Salzburg (Salt City) about nine miles away. Salzburg is a very old city of about 125,000 souls, and, like all renowned cities anywhere, teeming with tourists. The Salzasch River runs right through it, making it like two cities. It is considered one of the most beautiful cities in Europe, primarily because of the scenic countryside and splendid Italian Renaissance, Gothic, and Baroque architecture. It is considered one of the world's leading cultural centers. It is also noted as the birthplace of Wolfgang Mozart.

In and around Salzburg are many things of interest. We spent considerable time in Old Salzburg. Like Innsbruck, the streets are very narrow and winding, with gift shops, souvenir shops, and jewelry shops by the dozens all along the streets. There were also several very unusual water fountains, depicting horses in a variety of action poses. We never learned why there was so much emphasis on horse statues.

We had seen enough for the day, so we headed back to our *zimmer*. I got lost trying to find it. Near the *zimmer* was a *gasthaus*, where we went for dinner. We had determined that meals in *gasthauses* were generally quite good and not as expensive as in restaurants. We found this to be true here. After dinner, back to our abode, and to bed we went.

Rain still plagued us. It rained all night and was raining when we arose. We were almost getting accustomed to it—almost. The plan for the day was to visit Austria's famous salt mine, which was located near Hallein. The city and province of Salzburg were named after the salt deposits in this area. In order to get into the mine, you first must take a lift, then walk a considerable distance. Next you rented a white cotton suit with a white hood. There were quite a number of us, and we all looked like Ku Kluxers. Finally we boarded a tram that took us into the mine. We had to wear the suits because of the moisture and dust within the mine. We did a lot of walking, and twice, in order to get from an upper level to a lower level, we had to slide on our posteriors, down wooden rails. It was fun, and beat walking.

Sad to say, this mine was a big disappointment after going through the salt mines in Poland. There was really nothing much exciting to see. Perhaps if we had been to this mine prior to the Polish mines, we might have been more impressed. The total cost for this tour, including parking, was eighteen dollars. This was far more than the cost of the tour through the Polish mines.

The tour took up much of our day, and since it was still raining we started back home, stopping en route to shop for another deli dinner that we could eat in the warmth and comfort of our room. Despite the limited variety of the food we ate a-la-delicatessen, we always enjoyed it. And it saved us a heck of a lot of money.

The next morning, after our usual simple breakfast, we left. We were somewhat disappointed that we didn't see very much of Salzburg. It is the cultural center of Austria and one of the world's leading cities for classical music. It is surrounded by the Austrian Alps, with their magnificent Alpine scenery. The inner city abounds with perfectly preserved buildings of baroque architecture. These are just some of the things we didn't get to see enough of.

The gypsy trail led us once again to a socialist country, Czechoslovakia. It didn't take very long to get to the border, but once there we had to wait some time before we got to the guard station, where we underwent a very cursory inspection for only a couple of minutes. We also had to exchange twenty dollars per day into Czech crowns. One crown equaled eleven cents.

It didn't take long for us to become aware of the glaring disparity between this country and the Western countries we had just visited. The houses and most all other buildings were drab, sordid, and decrepit. The surrounding countryside also was drab and littered with trash. For us, it was quite a letdown. As we got closer to a larger town, we did see better looking large apartment buildings that had been built not many years before, and cranes all over putting up new apartment complexes. We had noticed this feature all through Russia and, to a lesser degree, in Poland.

In the late afternoon, we arrived in the city of Pilsen, world famous for its production of the beer "Pilsner," named after the city. Pilsen is an old city, dating back to the eleventh century. And it looked old.

We drove around the central square looking for a class II hotel that was listed in one of our guide books. After we found it we learned they had no vacancies. We drove around the square, headed for a hotel nearby, when a couple of policemen stopped me. They wanted to see our passports, etc. Then, for no reason Dorothy or I could fathom, they fined us one hundred crowns (eleven dollars)! I couldn't get them to explain what infraction I had committed. Of course they couldn't speak English, and they behaved so badly, to the point of being rude. They collected the fine right on the spot by giving me ten tickets, like theater tickets, each worth ten crowns. Before I was given the tickets, the cop that handed them to me tore them nearly in half. Well, this was depressing. After seeing what the country looked like, this little episode reinforced our depression.

There was nothing we could do about it, so we cursed a few times and drove to the other hotel. We could get a room for only one night. There was a Buyer's Convention being held there, which perhaps explained why the other hotel was full.

This hotel, for a class I hotel, was slightly overrated. Both inside and out, it was drab and rather joyless. We brought our stuff into our room. It had stopped raining, so we took a walk around the square and then went back to the hotel for dinner.

Seated at our table was a middle-aged Englishman. Naturally, we immediately got into a conversation. In the course of our conversation, we told him about the incident with the policemen. He smiled and then told us, "I customarily come here every year and drive my car. But nearly every time I came here I got a traffic ticket. As a result, I've since quit driving here."

After this story, I recalled our daughter and son-in-law telling us that many years back, shortly after they married, they also visited Czechoslovakia and they, too, got a traffic ticket. They also didn't know why.

In our continuing chat with our acquaintance, we told him that we intended to go to Prague next. He recommended a nice hotel there, the Yalta Hotel.

Our dinner was good, and much cheaper than we had been paying. My entree was goulash and Dorothy had Czech-style roast pork. After bidding our friend good-bye, we sat in the lobby of the hotel and got into a short, faltering conversation with a younger Czech couple. They spoke poor English. We parted company and left for our room. This day was a real downer for us.

Neither of us got much sleep that night. There was carousing, singing, and shouting outside our hotel all night until 3:15 A.M. It must have been the conventioneers. I don't think the hotel management would have tolerated it if they had been drunken natives.

After a hearty, elaborate, and expensive breakfast, we left Pilsen with no regrets. Near the outskirts of town we saw a huge, stately building that from a distance looked like a very old palace. Above the wide, arching entrance gates was a filigreed black iron sign. It was a very artistic sign. It seemed strange to see such a thing at a palace. As we got nearer, much to our delight, we could read the sign that told us this "palace" was the Pilsner Brewery. I claimed that this was the finest "palace" we'd seen in Europe, thus far.

We traveled the one hundred kilometers from Pilsen to Prague. We had no idea where we could locate the Yalta Hotel in this large city. As we drove slowly along, looking for someone from whom we could ask directions, we noticed a gentleman sitting in a parked car. I pulled up along side him and was able to make him understand what information I sought. He understood, and tried to direct me. He quickly recognized that this was an exercise in futility, so he indicated for us to wait. He pointed to a market, where we parked. Soon, his wife came out of the market and got into the parked car. The gentleman then indicated for us to follow him. We soon came to a very wide street divided by a parkway. The gentleman stopped and pointed across this street and there was the Yalta Hotel.

We waved good-bye, and then proceeded until we saw a street dissecting the road. I saw no sign indicating "no left" or "no U-turn." I had to make a U-turn to get to the hotel, which I did, then drove about a half block to the hotel. There, to greet us, stood two policemen, awaiting us with "open arms." We were absolutely stunned. We assumed that the U-turn was illegal, yet there was no sign forbidding it. And the man who directed us indicated that this was the way to go. Eventually, after much haranguing, with none of us understanding each other, they let us off. After this second unpleasant incident with Czech police, we were both so "spooked" we almost felt ready to get the heck out of Czechoslovakia.

We parked and went into the hotel, only to find out that they had no rooms available. But we did find out why the policemen stopped us. The wide street we were driving on was Wenceslaus Square and there is no parking without a permit. When we inquired as to how one gets a permit, the clerk told us, "First you park off of the square, then get your room at the hotel, and then the hotel gives you a pass which you place on the windshield of your car. Then you can park on the square." What a deal—a "Catch 22."

Be that as it may, we had to find accommodations elsewhere. It was raining and cold. We inquired at hotels on both sides of the street to no avail. At one hotel, the clerk told us to return at three o'clock, when perhaps they would have a room for us. We didn't wait until three, but instead returned near two, and fortunately the room was available. Needless to say, by the time we got this room, our spirits were very low. We were developing a dislike for this country.

This hotel, the Grand Europa, was a very old building, but was a rather beautiful hotel on the outside. The inside showed remnants of past beauty. Our room was nothing special and it had no bath. After the ordeal of trying to find a room, we didn't complain. We had no choice.

The weather was so nasty, we stayed in our room and read. In a few hours, the weather improved enough so that we could go for a walk; after all, this was the very famous Wenceslaus Square. After walking a few blocks, there in the center of the street, in the parkway, was a huge statue of King Wenceslaus on his horse. This was a very impressive statue of a famous man in Czech history, celebrated in Christmas songs. We always get a thrilling and a stirring feeling when we are at some historical place or see something of great historical significance. This is the way we felt standing before this overpowering statue of King Wenceslaus.

The walk in this cool damp weather and the lateness of the hour stimulated our appetites, so we searched for a restaurant, which we soon found. It was fairly decrepit-looking from the outside, but so many of the old buildings we'd seen in Czechoslovakia appeared that way. Nevertheless we entered. The restaurant was upstairs; the interior was nicer. After we were seated and checked the menu, we realized that this restaurant served only chicken. We ordered chicken in a peppery sauce. It was different, not too peppery, and very good, though we got meager portions. As usual, we had a glass of wine, coffee, and dessert. We discovered that the cost of the main meal was often less than the cost for wine, coffee, and dessert.

We went back to our room after dinner. In our experience, we found that Czech hotels are like those in Russia. There was no real charm, distinction, or elegance about them, but they were better than the ones in Poland. This applies only to those we selected; the ones that fit our budget.

We encountered many tourists, almost entirely from other socialist countries. Almost invariably, they got boozed up and went carousing up and down the halls most of the night. Apparently the culture of these countries, probably all countries in northern climes, including our Alaska, creates heavy drinkers. Come what may, we took such things in stride and made the best of it.

Breakfast was included in this hotel, and it was a farce. We got just a couple of small rolls, a bit of butter, some jelly, and a small cup of cold, weak, coffee that we sent back to be heated. I'm afraid we were spoiled after spending so much time in the Western countries. We then took off to see the sights.

First we went to Cedak, the Czech tourist office, and purchased tickets for a city tour for the following day. All our transactions became hassles. Everything was done so inefficiently, and no one seemed the least bit courteous. This done, we walked to Staromestski Square in Old Town Prague. We came to the Jewish quarters and discovered a kosher Jewish restaurant in the Jewish Old Town Hall. The dining room was gloomy and comfortless and practically empty. There was no menu. An elderly lady served us. Our meal consisted of a large bowl of chicken soup with heavy *knadelach* (dumplings), a small piece of meat, and bread. It wasn't bad, and the price was certainly right. The entire meal, for both of us, cost $2.22!

Next we bought a ticket to visit the two synagogues, the old and the new; a small museum; the old Jewish cemetery; and the rather modern Spanish Synagogue. The old synagogue dates back to the thirteenth century and it was really something to see. It was half-submerged in the ground. We felt as though we were entering a cave. Inside, it was dank, gloomy, and austere. It emanated an eerie feeling. We were relieved to get out. The years had taken their toll.

Adjacent to this ancient synagogue was an equally ancient Jewish cemetery. During a period in Czech history, anti-Semitism was rife, and the Jews were ghettoized to the extent that they could only bury their dead in their own cemetery. This was a very small plot of ground. As a result, over hundreds of years, there was no longer room for the bodies to be buried in individual plots, so they were literally stacked one body atop of another, as many as three deep!

The tombstones were so close together you could hardly walk between them. Many of them had already tumbled to the ground and many were in various stages of tumbling over. Moss covered many of them and weeds grew everywhere. You can imagine the somber feelings we had after visiting these two unusual places.

The newer synagogue was built in the sixteenth century and it too was ascetic and unadorned. Both of these synagogues had small museums that were of some interest to us.

The Spanish Synagogue (we didn't learn why it was called "Spanish") was much larger and much more modern. The two outstanding characteristics of this one were the large clock on the outside of the building, with the numerals depicted in Hebrew; and the many handmade Torah covers on display. The exquisite needlework on them was done by hand, and was extremely intricate.

We'd had enough for one day, so we walked back to our room, rested a bit, had our deli dinner, went for another walk, and then went back to our room to rest, read, and finally go to bed.

The next day started sunny, but soon clouded over and remained so all day. Again we walked to Old Town. Like Old Town in Warsaw, it was a fascinating place, except that there was much more to see here. In order to get to Old Town, we had to cross a bridge over the Moldau (Vltava) River. There are thirteen bridges in Prague, the most beautiful being the Charles Bridge, built in the fourteenth century by Charles IV.

Once in the square, we wandered around and even climbed the tower of the Old Town Hall. We got an excellent view from the tower of all of Old Town and several of the old palaces, one of which, the Castle of Prague, dates back to the ninth century.

Prague is an old city and at one time was the cultural seat of Central Europe. Because of its age and the importance of its heritage, there are many very old structures, such as castles, palaces, and churches.

By this time, we had to meet the other tourists for the guided tour of Old Town and other areas of Prague. While waiting for the bus, we met a younger couple from New York. Naturally we talked about our trip and mentioned that we'd been on the go for nearly five months.

The bus arrived, and Dorothy and I climbed aboard and started to seat ourselves alongside each other. The man from New York turned to me and said, "Hey, why don't you sit with me? You two have been traveling together for so long you are probably bored to death with each other!" Little did he know how true his statement was, to some degree.

Our tour guide was a tall, agile woman who appeared to be in her late fifties or early sixties. When we would have to do any walking, she would take off like a deer. She walked so rapidly that Dorothy and I almost ran to keep up with her. However, she was very well informed and had a great sense of humor. In addition, she was outspokenly anti-Soviet.

In the course of the tour, by foot and by bus, we saw much that was interesting, but we saw some outstanding highlights that need mentioning. One was our visit to an old building that formerly was a monastery. The monks who lived there collected books by the thousands, mostly books on religion, philosophy, and some on medicine. They dated back hundred of years, and I believe most were printed in Latin. The real eye-opener was a display of tiny books. One was less than a quarter inch square—a real book!

Then we were taken to the Old Town Hall. On the outside of the tower was a large, very old mechanical clock. It was similar to the one we'd seen in Rothenburg, West Germany, but much larger, more elaborate, and more intricate. It, too, was handmade. Within the clock were many religious figures. There were the Twelve Apostles, the Devil, several angels, and more. Every hour, on the hour, the figures automatically became animated, and passed in view. The sight was a wonder to behold. It was absolutely astonishing.

Lastly, we were taken to a street called the Golden Lane. Here were the remains of the old walled fortifications. The wall appeared to be about eight feet high and probably eight feet thick. Strangely, we noticed that built into this wall were cave-like openings that formerly had been used as dwellings. In one of them, Franz Kafka, the famous Czech writer, once lived. His former "home" is now a tiny book store. There is barely enough room in it for the books, the clerk, and at most four customers.

The tour was over at five o'clock. Our New York acquaintances were staying at the new posh Intercontinental Hotel, where our tour ended. They invited us in for cake and coffee. We chatted a bit, then parted. Before we went back to our hotel, we stopped at the tourist office and arranged for a tour for the next day to one of Europe's most renowned health spas, Karlovy Vary (Carlsbad). Carlsbad has a population of fifty thousand. It was founded in the fourteenth century. Its waters are reputed to be very curative, particularly for digestive ailments. For many years this spa was a favorite place of the aristocracy, writers, and musicians of Europe.

When we got back to our hotel, we were pleased to learn that a room with a shower was available to us. We got up early the next morning and showered. I bent over to pick up a towel off the floor, not knowing that Dorothy was standing on a corner of it. Suddenly, because of the pull, the muscles in my lower back gave out and I was in real pain. I had injured my back many years ago and had a couple recurrences of this injury, so I never leave home without my girdle. I put on the girdle and took a couple of aspirin. We dressed and went to the Hotel Intercontinental to catch the bus to Carlsbad. I could hardly walk because of my back pain. Nevertheless, I made it and we were on our way.

The trip to Carlsbad was a two-hour, unexciting trip. As we piled off the bus, the darndest sight met our eyes: people everywhere walked up and down the streets; nearly all of them were sipping from mugs—

not directly from the mug, but from the handle of the mug. It was weird. They walked, talked, and sipped the healing waters of the spa.

In the town, we walked along the banks of a small stream that flowed from the springs, the source of the healing waters. What was very unusual about the stream was that the water was warm, yet it was teeming with trout, some quite large. We never dreamed we'd see trout existing in warm water. To our knowledge, trout live only in cold water. We also saw fairly large goldfish (really carp) in the stream. We went into a large building that had several water fountains, from which people would drink. We noticed they would sip from several of the fountains and wondered why. We did the same and discovered that the temperature of the water of each fountain was slightly different.

Seeing all the people sipping from their cups, we felt the desire to buy one. We passed a souvenir shop; there on the wall hung a rack with several mugs hanging from pegs. We sought to purchase one, but the clerk explained to us that each of these cups belonged to someone and that the owners rented a peg to check his/her cup when not sipping! Pretty clever.

We had lunch at a hotel and it was one of the best meals we'd had in days—good Czech cooking. Soon we had to leave and head back to Prague. We took a different route on our return trip. We stopped at the new Lidice, which is now a memorial to the old Lidice.

Lidice was a peaceful village of about seven hundred people. When the Nazis occupied Czechoslovakia, they razed this entire village in retaliation for the assassination of Reinhard Heydrich. All the men were killed, and the women and children were deported to Auschwitz, where many died. The grounds are well kept, and white markers indicate where dwellings once stood. The town is now a national park and memorial. After the war, the Czech government built an entire new Lidice. Splendid rose gardens grow between the two towns. It is said that people from all over the world sent roses to be planted there. Ten thousand rose bushes have been planted. This was quite a sight, and it stands as a tragic reminder of mankind's past barbarism.

With sadness in our hearts, we left Lidice and returned to the Old Town Square. We arrived just in time for a delightful free concert, with Czech boys and girls performing songs and dances. It was a wonderful way to end our day, especially after just returning from Lidice.

Before breakfast the next morning, we went to the desk to see if we could stay for another night. I explained my back condition. The response was negative. I pleaded, but to no avail. What irritated us was not only that the lady clerk treated us disrespectfully, but also that she exhibited no concern or sympathy. We were so annoyed that we decided to leave Czechoslovakia and return to Vienna, not the least bit unhappy about our departure.

Decidedly, we would have liked to have seen more of Prague. It is a beautiful city with so much to see, and the city sort of grows on you as you see more of it. However, the people were the least friendly of any country we'd visited. We guessed it was a reflection of the people's smoldering dislike for the Russians. The Czechs were still angry about the invasion by the Russians in 1968. The Russian army, with the assistance of other Warsaw Pact countries, invaded Czechoslovakia in order to put down huge demonstrations by the Czech people, who were demanding democracy and less control over their lives by the USSR. Perhaps this anger carries over to their relations with foreigners. It's just a guess.

So we headed for Vienna. We had little trouble crossing the border. The landscape from there to Vienna was very much like the countryside of Czechoslovakia. The entire outlook was drab. The buildings were dusty and unattractive, except we noticed more flower gardens and more flower boxes at the windows of the dwellings. This part of Austria is certainly a far cry from the beauty of the Austria we had recently driven through.

It was mid-afternoon when we arrived on the outskirts of Vienna, a very large city of approximately 1,750,000 people. As in all the large cities we'd been to, it was very difficult for us to know how to get around, especially when the street signs were in a foreign language. There was also the problem of not knowing where to go to find accommodations.

We saw no *zimmers* in the nearby outskirts of the city and the *gasthauses* were full. We wound up in what appeared to be a seedy neighborhood within the city. We spotted a small hotel that didn't look too bad. Standing by the hotel, three plainly-clad, middle-aged women were conversing. I stopped the car, and Dorothy got out to inquire from these ladies about a place to stay and indicating this hotel. All three of the women emphatically shook their heads "No!" This hotel evidently was a house of ill repute, and by, looking at us, the women knew we didn't belong there.

They did indicate there was a small hotel a couple of blocks away. We thanked them and drove off to this other hotel. It was in a nicer-appearing section. It was more expensive than we had figured to pay (this was, after all, Vienna), but we took a room nevertheless. The room was nothing to rave about. My back was still hurting a bit, so after we settled in, we went for only a short walk and then returned to our room to rest and read.

When it came time for dinner, we decided to eat out and take a break from our deli dinners. There was a Chinese restaurant nearby. We felt that Chinese food would be a pleasant change. The restaurant was nice and clean; it was obviously a family operation. There were only two other customers, but the place was jumping with cute little Chinese kids. The dinner was very good and not too expensive.

We packed the car the next morning and left it at the hotel. After a light breakfast, we boarded the tram to take us to the subway station. After asking for directions, we got the right car to Centrum, the center of Vienna. It's difficult to describe even a portion of what there is to see in this grand, thousand-year-old city, but I will describe a few of the things that we experienced while we were there.

Upon arriving at the Centrum, we found the Tourist Office. They located a place for us at a *zimmer* just off the Ring. The Ring is a world-famous boulevard that, with the Danube Canal on one side, completely encircles the Inner City. We retrieved our car and proceeded to drive to our *zimmer*. The Ring is a bit confusing to follow, as it changes names. However, with little difficulty, we found our *zimmer*. A young woman greeted us. She lived there with her elderly mother.

The young woman took us two flights up to our room. It was very modest, somewhat overly furnished, dim, and very large. The cost for the night was fifteen dollars, not including breakfast. We carried our luggage up those two flights and soon made ready to "do Vienna."

My back felt much better and it was a lovely summer day (31 August). We felt like walking. We had gone only a block, and what a revelation! We were on the Ring, having crossed over the bridge of the Danube Canal, and there before our eyes was a sight to warm the cockles of our hearts and the cravings of our stomachs! We walked into a three-block-long open and covered market. This market contained every fruit and vegetable known to man or beast, plus all kinds of delicatessen food, bakery goods, smoked and pickled fish, barbecued foods—you name it, it was there. Talk about heaven! As much as we love fruit and vegetables, we had been limited to very little the past several days, so we gazed upon all this with stars in our eyes. I was especially enamored by the strings of plaited garlic. They were so beautiful and uniform in size and shape, I thought they were artificial. And the brilliant red radishes were nearly the size of golf balls!

We walked up and down the market taking in everything, and reveling in the variety of sights and smells. Then we walked back to the Hungarian tourist office in Centrum and arranged for a trip down the Danube River. This would be a three day, two night, visit to Budapest on September 8-10.

On the way back to our *zimmer*, we witnessed a large protest rally. The people, mostly young, gathered to protest the ban on street musicians. These musicians earn their livelihood by performing in the street square. From here we went back to the market and bought fruits and deli foods for our lunch and breakfast.

Once again we opted to eat out for dinner, and went to a small Greek restaurant, where we had a nice dinner of assorted grilled meats and French fries. (We had been served French fries with our meals surprisingly often.) Thus ended our first full day in Vienna.

The next morning we enjoyed breakfast in our room. We paid $3.75 extra for a standard, simple, breakfast. However, we also had some delicious cantaloupe and some very expensive, strong, soft cheese we had bought at the market the day before. Ooh la la, that was a real treat for us.

In most restaurants of the Western European countries, you pay for each cup of coffee you order. In Bed and Breakfasts this was not true. We've had Europeans tell us that one of the most memorable experiences of their visit to the US was that, when they ordered coffee in almost any restaurant in America, they were served as much as they desired, at no extra cost.

We walked to Centrum and purchased tickets for a city bus tour. The tour started at mid-afternoon and lasted until six o'clock. In the course of the tour, we visited the Capuchin Crypts that hold more than seventy imperial coffins. Next we went to the Schonbrunn Castle. This castle is surrounded by a beautiful park, as well as botanical gardens, which emulate the famous Versailles Palace. We walked through 40 of the 1440 rooms in the castle. This included servants' rooms. It took thirty servants daily just to mind the candles. As is true in all royal families, this castle was lavishly furnished. We saw a fantastic display of opulence and extravagance, some objects nearly priceless. All this was at the expense of the masses, who contributed their blood, sweat, and tears to provide all this wealth for the royalty.

During the drive, our lady guide pointed out a rather bizarre sight. There, in a small square in the center of the city, stood a tall statue of a Soviet soldier. In front of this statue was a long, narrow water fountain. (Remember, Austria was threatened by Hitler, and in 1938 was occupied by Nazi troops. In 1940, it was fully incorporated in Germany—*anschluss*. Many Austrians supported Nazism.) When the Russian army liberated Vienna, the Russian government erected this statue and made the Austrian Government agree never to remove it, nor cover it. The pro-Nazi Austrians, because of their hatred for the Russians, installed this fountain in front of the memorial. The result was that, when the fountain was turned on, a screen of water would rise above the statue, thus removing it from view!

Next we went to the Belvedere Palace, another ornate residence of Prince Eugene. In between these walking tours, we drove by and saw many churches, monuments, and palaces, all of which were part of Austrian history.

We had seen enough for one day. At the end of the tour, we walked to our *zimmer* and stopped again at the Acropolis restaurant for a good dinner, before going to our room. This had been another full day.

The next morning was again sunny, and it stayed sunny all day. We walked to the Stadtpark (State Park), a lovely small park on the Ring not far from the Opera House. We strolled leisurely through the park, captivated by the statues of some of the world's most famous classical music composers, including Johann Strauss, Franz Schubert, Anton Bruckner, and others. This was thrilling, for we love classical music. Also in this park was a small, nicely-landscaped lake, which was the domain of many ducks, geese, and large white swans. The park also included charming gardens with stately peacocks strutting about, and hundreds of pigeons and other birds fluttering all around us.

We then strolled to the Pensioners Platz, a section of the park for pensioners. We selected a park bench and ate our lunch in peace and quiet, except for the old-timers playing cards and banging their cards on the tables, and the *kibitzers* laughing and, occasionally, raising their voices. Their carrying-on seemed to enhance the quietude we were enjoying.

We also walked to the Kursalon, an area in the park where free concerts are given by a small orchestra. We found a couple of chairs a trifle far from the musicians. This was too far from the orchestra to really enjoy the music, so we moved onto the bleachers. The bleachers were part of a patio cafe. It wasn't mandatory that we pay to sit in the bleachers, but we felt obligated to purchase something: a small bottle of beer for me and a smaller bottle of mineral water for Dorothy. Our bill came to $4.50! The orchestra was not the best, but we enjoyed it, the relaxation, and the entire atmosphere.

On the way home, we stopped at an Italian restaurant for pizza. We also stopped at a bakery to purchase Vienna's famous baked goodie, *sachertorte*. This is a kind of small twisted cake with chocolate. We found that it was overrated and didn't compare with Danish pastry. The night was balmy, and we walked down Kartnerplatz (the main street of Centrum) and through the market to our *zimmer*. This was the end of a very pleasant, easy day. We saw much of interest, strolling in this leisurely fashion.

We had made no plans for the next day, so we just had a late breakfast and took it easy. We did shop for food at our marvelous market. This was fun for us. Later we bought our tickets for the Budapest trip. We ate our lunch on a bench in Centrum and then walked on the Ring to gaze with awe at the statue of Beethoven. We went, once again, to the Stadpark and had ice cream cones; purchased a British Sunday paper, and parked ourselves on a bench to read.

At late afternoon, the free concert began. This time, we had come early enough to get good seats so we could better hear the music. It soon clouded over and threatened rain and, since the music wasn't all that great, we decided to call it a day.

I must mention the experience of crossing the Ring. The Ring is very wide; there are secondary roads, tram lines, cross streets, angled streets, and lots of pedestrian and automobile traffic. You must be extremely alert to avoid all this and get to where you want to go without getting hit or getting lost.

We got home quite early and spent the rest of the day and night, before bedtime, reading. We bought used English books wherever we could. As I mentioned earlier, we rarely went out at night and we both enjoy reading.

The next day, sun, clouds, wind, and rain were on the weather menu. Undaunted, we decided to "do" Vienna more thoroughly this day. Fortunately for us, our *zimmer* was conveniently located so that much of what was interesting and important to see was within easy walking distance.

First we went to the Hofburg Palace, the summer palace of the Hapsburg Dynasty, the ruling family of Austria from 1282 to 1918! We walked in the elaborate gardens. The Volksgarten was gorgeous. It appeared as though they had planted rose bushes of every variety known: rose bushes by the hundreds. Unfortunately for us, hardly any were in bloom. We went to St. Michael Church, which was absolutely fantastic, and to several other interesting buildings in the palace complex.

The quarters of the emperor and empress were our next stop. Their quarters were but a few of the over two thousand rooms in the palace. As we expected, these quarters were very ornate and lavish. Finally, we visited the main dining room. The huge table was all set and ready to accommodate the royal guests. It was fabulous, unreal!

After all this, we visited just one room in the Fine Arts Museum, still in the palace complex. No matter how many museums of this nature we explored, we still were sure to see many amazing and astounding things. Such was the case here. There is no limit to people's creativity; the items displayed here merely confirmed that. Some of the items, such as clocks, tapestries, jewelry, china, glassware, intricate safety boxes, and statuary, were of such fantastic, creative artistry that we both choked up with emotion. What a display of enormous wealth! It was beyond comprehension, and almost impossible to believe that many of these items had been made by mere mortals. In our travels thus far, having visited so many palaces, castles, churches, museums, and so on, one runs out of superlatives in trying to describe them all. I can only repeat what I've been saying all along: there is no limit to man's ability to create. There is no end to our ingenuity and imagination.

Culturally satiated, we started for home just as a few drops of rain fell. We did stop at "our" market and purchase fruit, vegetables, bakery goods, and some dairy products for our dinner.

The next day, we again walked to the Hofburg Palace complex. This time, we went to the building that houses the Spanish Riding School. At this school, members of the royal family came to learn to train and ride the famous Lippizaner horses. These handsome white horses are bred in Lippice, Yugoslavia and are famous for the way they have been trained to perform very intricate foot movements. The guide books call this a "must see" for the tourists to Vienna. There was a large crowd waiting to get in, and by time we got in, it was standing room only and much of the performance had already been done. We saw just a smattering of the show, and this part wasn't very exciting.

Next we went to the second of the two museums on the grounds. This, the Museum of Natural History, had a fabulous display of rocks, stones, and semi-precious and precious gem stones. The display was exceptionally well done, and captivating. There was also a display of wild and domestic animals, mainly for children. None of them were alive. Some of the animals were stuffed and mounted, others were painted. It was a remarkable scene.

This museum closed at one o'clock, so we went back again to the Fine Arts Museum we had visited the day before. We particularly wanted to see the paintings. We saw many, but the paintings by Rubens, Van Dyke, Rembrandt, Vermeer, and other illustrious masters were, no doubt, priceless. For museum buffs, there is a pass available to six museums, good for one week, at a very nominal price. We took advantage of this pass.

The museum closed at three o'clock. We took it easy walking home and stopped at "our" market to shop for dinner food. We bought half a barbecued chicken and other items and headed home after another fulfilling day.

The next day was a nice summer day, all day, for a change. A slight problem arose that morning. Our landlady informed us that she and her mother would be gone for the weekend; they planned to go to Budapest, which meant that we would have to find other quarters. This saddened us because we were so comfortable here. Each day, when we brought food for our dinner, "mama" was cognizant of the fact that our table service was a bit lacking, so she would put extra dishes on our table. One evening, we bought a small watermelon at "our" market to have for dinner. Unbeknownst to us, mama (noticing that we had only small sized plates) placed two large plates on the table. Her daughter told us about this, later. We thought this to be a very sweet gesture, and very considerate.

After this bit of sad news, we went on a search for other accommodations. We had to do laundry, so while at the Laundromat, Dorothy and I went looking for a hotel. We found one close by. Across the street from it was a garage where we could store our car while we were gone. So all was settled for our trip, though it cost us double what we paid at "mama's."

This taken care of, we both went to a *frisseur* (beauty parlor) for men and women to get "beautified." This ordinary beauty treatment for us both cost twenty-four dollars! It was a far cry from the same treatment we got in Poland for one dollar and eighty cents. Since the day was about shot, we spent most of the afternoon in the park and gardens of the Hofburg Palace. Later we walked to Kartenerstrasse to go window shopping. Then we went food shopping at the market, and then home.

The next day, we were lucky enough to have good weather. We walked to Vienna's splendid Opera House, where we were to board the bus to the renowned sulphur springs spa in Baden. This health spa dates back to Roman times, and has been very popular ever since. It is similar to Carlsbad in Czechoslovakia, but smaller and not nearly as interesting.

We walked in and around Baden's Centrum and enjoyed gawking at people and things. It intrigued us to see the many little streets going off in all directions, just at random, it seemed. We rested a bit on a park bench and ate our picnic lunch. After lunch, we headed for the fabulous, world-renowned Vienna Woods. The Vienna Woods stretch along a bank of the Danube River. On the edge of the woods are gorgeous gardens, and a beautiful water fountain.

Many trails wound through the woods, all meticulously maintained and a delight on which to stroll. Every tree seemed to get individual care! As we strolled for over a mile, the strains of Strauss' "Tales of Vienna Woods" ran through my head. The peace, quietude, and luxuriousness of this spectacular place were not in the least exaggerated.

We not only loved it here, but were thrilled to be in such a famous place.

We hiked back to Baden. En route, we visited one of the health spas, and walked along a lovely stream, through an open market, down several of the charming little streets window shopping, and then back to the bus.

Back in Vienna, we once again shopped in "our" market, and bought some fried fish and potato salad for dinner, and a box of candy for mama and daughter. It had been another great day!

The next day, 8 September, was my sixty-ninth birthday. It had been quite some time since we had eggs for breakfast, so for my birthday Dorothy prevailed upon mama to lend us some eggs. She was going to scramble some for me, as this is my favorite way to eat them.

Dorothy asked mama for a frying pan, but just couldn't get her to understand what a frying pan was. Dorothy searched through all the cupboards and drawers with no luck. She did find a small shallow sauce pan and proceeded to scramble the eggs and fry them in this pan. When mama saw this, she let out a shriek of laughter, pulled out a drawer that Dorothy had missed, and there lay at least a half-dozen fry pans of all sizes. We all had a good laugh. The eggs were delicious, regardless. Happy Birthday!

We fondly bade mama and daughter *auf wiedersehen* and expressed our gratitude for their hospitality and kindness. We packed, drove our car to the garage where we had arranged to store it, and took the train to Mexico Platz to board the boat to Budapest. At a half past noon, we boarded the hydrofoil. Thirty of us boarded this long, low, and sleek boat.

Dorothy and I both felt excited about the trip down the "beautiful blue Danau (Danube)." The trip, however, was over five hours long and very disappointing. The Danube was neither blue nor beautiful! The water was murky. It is 1750 miles long and the section we were sailing through was supposed to be the prettiest. It was nice, but really didn't impress us overly much.

It was seven-thirty by the time we docked, went through customs, and checked into the Astoria Hotel, located right in downtown Budapest. By the time we got settled, it was dinner time. We dined in the hotel and had a nice dinner. To celebrate my birthday, we ordered a bottle of white Hungarian wine. It was very good and very expensive. A seven-tenths liter bottle cost four dollars. A young Austrian girl on our tour gave me her dish of ice cream as a birthday present. While we dined, a band played delightful, stimulating gypsy music. We literally jumped with joy. It was such a treat to hear this native music.

It was still light when we finished dining, so we took a walk. We couldn't walk for long, however, as my Russian shoes were killing me. I failed to mention that when we were in Moscow I tried to buy a pair of shoes. This minor event was something else. If I saw a pair of shoes I liked, they would have maybe a dozen pair of those shoes, but all in one size only! If that wasn't my size, I was out of luck. Then I'd find a pair my size, but only in one color—not the color I wanted. I eventually bought a pair, the color I wanted, but a wee bit tight. I settled for these, hoping that before long they would stretch. As of 8 September they were still too tight and uncomfortable. I had little choice but to wear them and hope for ultimate relief.

Before retiring, I wrote in my log and we both wrote picture post cards to family and friends. We had a bad night with little sleep because the hotel was in the center of town, and all night long we heard noisy street cars, trucks, buses, squealing autos, sirens, etc. We always sleep with windows open, so not only did we hear all this noise, but we also were victims of nasty fumes.

At mid-morning, our group boarded a bus, which took us for a tour of the city. Budapest is really two cities divided by the Danube. Buda is on the hills and Pest on the flat land. Even though our Hungarian lady guide was very good, we saw so many things in such a short space of time that it was difficult to remember much of what we saw. Like most of the big city tours we had taken, this tour consisted of the many churches, cathedrals, palaces, castles, and ancient buildings. Every city is different. They each have their own beauty, history, style of architecture, and culture. Budapest has its own unique style as well.

Hungary was founded over a thousand years ago by the Magyars and was invaded by so many tribes and other countries that this mix of cultures is more evident in Budapest than in the other cities we had visited. Especially unique is the architecture. We saw buildings of Italian, Roman, Gothic, Turkish, baroque and neo-renaissance styles all through the city. The colorful tile roofs were very different and built in unusual designs. One item of great interest was that recently archaeologists had uncovered the remains of some ancient Roman buildings— an amphitheater, an aqueduct, and others. It was exciting to view.

On the tour, we got acquainted with two young men, Art and Bill, both from New York City and both just graduated from Yale Law School. We sort of palled around together. Despite the age difference, we hit it off quite well. We stopped at a restaurant for a big lunch. Much of Hungarian food is seasoned with their most popular condiment, paprika, which we enjoy.

The tour was over at two o'clock, and the four of us went to an historical museum. The displays, not very well done, left little to see. We then strolled along the streets. We stopped at a sidewalk cafe and had some wine, and continued on to our hotel to rest for a big night.

We boarded the bus at seven-thirty and drove quite some distance out of town. Our destination was a special restaurant for a real ethnic Hungarian goulash dinner. Dorothy and I got excited at this prospect. After we arrived at the restaurant and before they seated us at the table, they gave us a small glass of some kind of drink. Someone said it was apricot brandy. It was fiery.

We all sat at one long wooden table, with no fancy linens or stylish table service, but lots of pitchers of white and red wine—good Hungarian wine. And, once again, we felt like gypsies. We were being entertained by a five-piece band playing authentic gypsy folk music! It was great. You can be sure it stirred our (adopted) gypsy blood. We loved it.

The goulash was very good. The rest of the food was so-so. The portions were small, but they poured the wine in copious quantities. It seemed that every time the pitchers would get below half full the waiters would fill them up again. And these weren't small pitchers. You can well imagine that most all of us "felt no pain." After the dinner, the master of ceremonies got us all involved in audience participation games. I was one of three chosen for a wine drinking contest. Of course, a Russian won, and I was last.

The gypsy music was excellent—wild, spirited, and very melodic. Later, the band played dance music and Dorothy and I danced a few dances. This was a most enjoyable experience for us. Towards the end of the evening, though, one thing bothered us. One of the violinists came up to each of us soliciting tips. He did this by securing a US dollar bill on the very tip of his violin bow and poking the bow in our faces while playing. This gesture didn't sit well with us. It was far too obvious, and very distracting.

The party broke up about eleven o'clock, and since we all felt good, several of us went to the cabaret in the basement of our hotel. What a let down. It was like being in a "class C" Las Vegas casino. The place was crowded and smoke-filled. The music was loud and raunchy rock. The dancing girls were scantily clad and mediocre dancers at best. Only the singing was a bit better than fair. There we were, thousands of miles from home, in a foreign land, and we were being entertained by second-rate American imitation. Anyway, we danced a couple dances, consumed more wine, and by 12:45 A.M. we grew tired. So we left and retired for the night. The day's events were a mixed bag, but a full one, lasting all day and half the night.

Upon awakening early the next morning, I had a slight hangover. After a meager breakfast, we packed and rushed out to shop in order to spend our leftover florins. We managed to get rid of them.

We boarded the bus and headed for Pomaz. This is a small town noted for a government horse training and riding school. The Hungarians are renowned for their horsemanship. There was to be a performance for our benefit, but before it commenced we went to a dining room where they served us a small fruit brandy, followed by slices of bread. The bread was covered with lard, topped with chopped onions, and seasoned with paprika—not bad. We washed this down with a weak orange drink.

Now we took our seats for the entertainment. The riders, with their horses, put on a real show. They did hurdle jumps, fancy trick riding, a stunt they called "fox and hounds," and other clever maneuvers. Best of all was the drive of a huge herd of wild horses. Without our knowing it, the drive started from behind some hills about a half mile away. All at once we heard this thundering noise of hundreds of horses' hooves pounding the ground in full gallop and we saw huge clouds of dust swirling around and over both the horses and the drivers. The riders were driving them towards us. It was a fantastic sight, a real thriller, just like in a good "B" Hollywood cowboy movie. And did we love it!

After this incredible event, they treated us to a ride in a cute little buggy, pulled by either a large pony or a small horse. There were just three of us and we were taken to a tiny hamlet nearby, and then brought back. It was fun, and a nice change of pace.

Now it was time to return to Vienna. En route, we stopped at a restaurant where we were served mineral water with wine, and then an ethnic meal. This consisted of a bowl of soup, a platter of potatoes, kraut, liver and pork cutlets, dessert, and coffee. It was not the best we had eaten.

Our three days in Budapest were well worth the cost. Although it wasn't the most exciting three days, we did see some very interesting things and indulged in some unusual experiences which will certainly find a place in our book of memories. Dorothy and I both agreed we enjoyed this trip, but didn't list it as one of the places we'd like to return to.

We returned to Vienna by bus; it was an uninteresting two-hour drive. It was quite warm. We crossed the border at 7:45 P.M., bade good-bye to all, and walked to our hotel. Our room was only fair, not the pleasant *zimmer* of Mama K. and her daughter. We planned to spend one night in this small, 2-star hotel.

The next day, the weather continued to be nice and warm. We were up fairly early for breakfast and then took off to see more sights. We walked to Centrum to the historical museum and then to the Ephosos Museum, which depicts an ancient Greek city. The displays of armor and musical instruments impressed us very much. But what really impressed us, actually overwhelmed us, was the Museum of Clocks. We gasped at the sight of hundreds of clocks of every description, from ancient to modern, simple to elaborate; many were unique and nearly priceless. The museums in Vienna are outstanding.

Time was running out, so back to Kartenerstrasse we went to buy snack food and goodies, and to take our last stroll on this fascinating street.

Vienna is a city we miss. We had been very comfortable in our *zimmer*, which was ideally located. We could walk to points of interest, and were fortunate to be so close to the fabulous market. The large marketplaces are really where a tourist should spend time. It was there that we got the "feel" of the native folks, mainly the working class, who, of course, are the vast majority. We've never failed to enjoy being in these peoples' markets.

The next morning, we bade Vienna *auf wiedersehen*. We came, we saw, and we were conquered! We were up and away shortly after

7:30 A.M., bound for Salzburg, Austria again. We were on the auto-bahn all the way, and it was easy driving.

As we neared Salzburg, we decided to go back to Hallein to the same *zimmer* we stayed at previously. We arrived in Hallein at a half past one. When we approached the *zimmer*, we noticed the *Zimmer Frei* sign was not hanging on the fence. Regardless, we knocked on the door and the same sweet lady greeted us with a look of surprise. She told us they had closed for the season, but she and her husband warm-ly welcomed us anyway. So we unpacked and settled in the same cozy and friendly room.

Since we'd eaten lunch earlier, we took off immediately for the Hellbrunn Castle and the *Wasserspeil* (literally, "Waterplay") not too far distant. We didn't expect much from these places, after our disap-pointment with the salt mine, but we were in for a pleasant surprise. The Hellbrunn Pleasure Castle was built in the early seventeenth cen-tury for Bishop Marcus Sitticus. Either the bishop had an unusual sense of humor, or (it was said) the fountains were built by a mad designer!

One of the first things we saw in the area of the fountains was a long concrete table with concrete benches on all sides. It was nothing spectacular to see. But, all of a sudden, a stream of water squirted from a hole in each bench, except the one at the head of the table. The legend goes that when the bishop's guests got drunk from drink-ing too much wine, he would turn on the water. I guess this sobered the boys up—all but the bishop, as he sat at the head of the table.

There were unique fountains all around, some balancing balls on water jets, some that just spray from anywhere, and if you were a hap-less victim, you'd get a shower. But the most fantastic sight of all was the miniature city peopled with many tiny figures representing every-day life in this old city. The most incredible thing was that all these fig-ures are set in motion strictly by water power! Every one of the fig-ures performed what he or she would have been doing in real life. It was extraordinary; so ingenious. It was craftsmanship beyond com-pare.

We then walked through the castle gardens, which were very attrac-tively set alongside sparkling ponds teeming with fish. We loved every minute of our stroll. Our walk took us up a hill to the Little Castle. It was allegedly built, on a wager, in one month. This was quite a feat, if true. We also went through the small museum in this castle, where we saw several interesting and unique works of art. Finally, we visited a very unusual grotto theater that was also uniquely designed.

When we got back to our house, the landlady presented us with several prune plums she'd picked from her tree. Thus ended another fulfilling day. It was especially gratifying because we had seen so much that was different and quite out of the ordinary.

The next day we took it easy, going back to the Hellbrunn Castle and its surroundings to see what we missed the day before. Our first stop was the zoo. This unusual zoo was constructed alongside and under a high rock wall; it was long and narrow. It did not house very many animals, primarily because most of the animals had been listed as endangered species. What the zoo lacked in quantity it made up for in quality, as we saw so many animals we had never seen before. Observing the animals in the zoo didn't take us more than two hours. We then drove back to the castle, which was close by, and again took the tour through the Wasserspiel.

The second time around was equally interesting, except that this time there was a much larger crowd. This detracted a bit from the thrills of the day before. We again strolled through the charming flower gardens and alongside the pleasant, idyllic ponds, lingering a while to watch the fish swim about.

This day had been very relaxing and most enjoyable. We made ready to trek back to our quarters. En route, we shopped for dinner. We bought some dairy products, garden veggies, and the like. When we got ready to dine in our room, Dorothy prepared some "farmer's chop suey" (sour cream, cottage cheese, chopped green onions, radishes, and cucumbers) and we opened our last can of Russian sprats that we had purchased in Russia. We topped this off with some fresh fruit and a sweet. We enjoyed an inexpensive, simple, healthful, and delicious meal.

And again the rains came! When we awakened the next day, it was pouring. We packed, had our light *frushtuck*, took a picture of our *zimmer* lady with Dorothy, said farewell, and went on our way. By the time we had left Hallein, the rain stopped and the sky cleared a little. We were headed back to Switzerland, returning by the same route we had taken when we first came to Austria. Again we drove through the ten-mile-long Arlesberg Tunnel, but this time we didn't have to pay the toll, as we had purchased a round-trip ticket.

We drove through the town of Bludenz. Not finding a *zimmer*, we continued on to Feldkirch. Before we got there, we spotted a nice house with a *Zimmer Frei* sign on it. We stopped and Dorothy checked it out to see if it was OK for one night. It was, and we were welcomed in. Our room was very nice; it had no sink or toilet, but both were close by.

At about six o'clock, we went out for dinner. It was raining a bit, but we walked anyway to a nice restaurant nearby. Because it had been an inexpensive day for us, we splurged and ordered pepper steaks, loaded with peppercorns and the works. The meal was excellent. It set us back $21.35, but what the heck. Even gypsies are entitled to "live it up" occasionally! Before retiring, our landlady gave us three nice pears from her tree.

The next morning, it was raining again. We probably would have been disappointed if it didn't rain, since we'd had so much rain on the trip. On the road again, we followed the highway along the Tirol mountains, which made the trip more pleasant. Our plan was to drive to Lucerne, Switzerland. The weather turned nasty, with rain and dense fog as we climbed the mountains and went through a high pass. This kind of driving is nerve-racking. We got lost several times and quarreled about it, which wasn't unusual, and soon got to the Austrian-Liechtenstein border, where we exchanged money.

Dorothy wanted to go by way of Interlaken, which we did. The rain had stopped, but the weather was gray and gloomy. However, it felt good to be back in familiar territory. We couldn't find a *zimmer* in Interlaken, so we drove on to Spiez. Before we got there, Dorothy called Luci "S." She told us to come on over. When we arrived, she invited us in for coffee. She told us that she had a lady guest, but the lady was leaving the next day, so she could accommodate us for a couple of nights.

Our room was too cold to sit up and read, so we undressed and climbed into bed underneath the wonderful thick, light and fluffy *pereneh* and read in bed. Now that we had finally turned around on our trip and were headed for the US, we began to count the days. We both welcomed the thought that before too long we'd be back to our home sweet home.

The gods must have been smiling on us, for the day greeted us with most welcome sunshine. Luci served us breakfast. This time, she also served us sliced cheese. She made excellent coffee and gave us a full pot. We had no plans for the day, so we took our favorite drive along Lake Thun to just past Interlaken. For the entire drive, we could see our most favorite sight, the triad of the magnificent mountain peaks: the Monch, the Eiger, and our most cherished, the Jungfrau.

We parked the car, then walked along a small side road until we spotted a path that took us beside a small stream. We reveled in all the beauty that abounded everywhere we looked. The grandiose vistas of the mountains before us was sheer ecstasy. Oh, would we ever miss this wondrous beauty!

We drove into Interlaken. It became sunny and warm. We parked and leisurely walked down the main street. It was Sunday, so many of the shops were closed. We strolled along window shopping. Interlaken reeks of wealth and is therefore no place for gypsies like us. It obviously caters to the wealthier tourists. The store windows were resplendent with expensive jewelry, watches, linens, crystal, clothing—you name it. Someone could spend a fortune here. Then we strolled through the Casino grounds. The flower beds were spectacular. They were laid out in ingenious, very colorful designs. One flower bed was in the design of a large clock.

After all this glamour, we headed back to Spiez. We stopped at a nice rest stop beside the Thunersee. Dorothy had lunch for us and for lots of seagulls. Then, on to our room to bathe, rest, and later go to the hotel for dinner. After a good meal, we stopped at a bakery and bought a pie for Luci, Ernst, and Roland. Luci made coffee and we enjoyed the pie, coffee, and conversation—in German/Yiddish, of course—till nearly ten o'clock, when we retired.

Dorothy and I both felt a bit sad thinking about how much we would miss this remarkable area, our comfortable, pleasant *zimmer*, and, above all, these wonderful people. We certainly had struck it rich when we were directed to this Bed and Breakfast home.

The next day we were up early. We ate, packed, and again sorrowfully said good-bye to them all. We are putting Switzerland on page one in our book of memories!

Vive la France!

Before we left Spiez, we shopped for groceries and other needed items. We also bought a genuine Swiss pocket knife for my birthday, then drove towards the French border by way of Lac Lemon, bypassing Geneva.

This was the scenic route that would soon put us on the highway known as the Road of Napoleon. It is on the east side of the Rhone Valley along the Rhone River. We would continue south almost to Marseille. This is a very picturesque part of France, and great wine country. It was astonishing to see the vineyards, hanging from ropes. The road took us through the towns of Aix le Bains and Annecy, which are nice resort towns. We finally stopped near Chambrey, where we wound up in a two-star hotel. We got a nice room with a shower and bidet, but didn't know how to use it!

After getting our room, we walked around the town, which was rather seedy. We noticed that many of the small towns we drove through looked shoddy and run-down. I believe we were spoiled after Switzerland. While walking, we stopped at a sidewalk bar for a small beer for me and lemonade for Dorothy.

Later, we went to another hotel for dinner. There was hardly anyone else in the dining room. The French eat their evening meals quite late. For an appetizer we were served very tasty pate. our entree was a tough, nearly raw steak with French fried potatoes. It seemed we'd been eating French fries nearly every time we ate dinner out. Oh, for some good old-fashioned mashed potatoes and gravy! The service wasn't the best, either. Our waitress snapped at me because I asked for the check. I guess one doesn't do that in France. We were miffed over her behavior, so we didn't leave a tip. Breakfast in French is called *petit dejeuner*, and instead of rolls, we were served croissants and big hunks of French bread—both delicious and a pleasant change. Soon after breakfast, we packed up and left.

Our diet was changing since entering France. When we shopped for lunch food, instead of wurst and other kinds of lunch meat, we bought pate. We also bought French bread and Roquefort cheese. The bread was always fresh and out of this world. On this day, we traveled near the French Alps. The country around us was more open, and we saw lots of farms. They appeared well kept and flourishing. It looked like it was near harvest time. We stopped several times just to admire these pleasant sights. We ate our lunch near a lake, an historic spot where Napoleon once bivouacked his army. Our lunch was super. Besides the pate, Roquefort, and French bread, we drank wine. This was especially appropriate, since we were in wine country and eating typical French fare.

In the late afternoon, just outside of the small town of Sisteron, we noticed a pleasant-looking small hotel and got a nice room with everything in it that we would need, sans toilet. This hotel had a very nice outside patio with tables and chairs. It was surrounded by a tall hedge, and lots of privacy.

Since the French eat dinner late, Dorothy and I sat out on the patio, ordered a beer, and relaxed. We also wrote letters and postcards. At seven-thirty, we went into the dining room and had a dinner similar to the previous night's, but with a bit better quality and much better service. However, we noticed something that, in a small way, troubled us. Nobody smiled, or they just barely smiled. Was this a characteristic of the French? We thought not, or rather, we hoped not. We reasoned that this judgment regarding the unfriendly French could be because we had been staying in hotels and eating in restaurants. Our only contact with the French people had been with waiters and waitresses, hotel clerks, and so on. Too many demands may have been made upon them by tourists, and this might have had a tendency to turn them sour. Aside from the above, which we could live with, this was a nice place to stay. Also, it was unfair to make this negative judgment so soon.

Our journey the next morning took us again through farm country. We could see the fruit trees, grape vines, melon patches, and corn fields, all around us. The highway was not bad, but diesel fuel was more expensive, at $2.50 per gallon. At Aix-en-Provence we stopped to shop. This was an interesting town and it was open market day. We would have loved to go to the market and see more of the town, but decided against it. This was an old town and the streets were so narrow, crooked, and poorly marked that we got lost several times trying to find our way to the highway. Finally, we found our way out of town, and my panic subsided as we headed for Arles.

Arles is the town where Van Gogh lived for a short time before he died. Some of his most famous paintings are of the town. It is also a tourist attraction because it was once occupied by the Romans. For a small fee, you can see some ancient Roman ruins. We spent some time looking at these ruins: the Roman baths, aqueducts, and statuary. The city was founded by Julius Caesar in 46 B.C., so it had a lot of history. We also visited a museum containing many works by Van Gogh. His life was interesting, but short and tragic. He painted for only ten years, committing suicide at the age of thirty-seven.

Before long, it was time to go. When it neared four o'clock, we began to look for a place to stay for the night. The small hotel we selected was in the village of Pont De Esprit. It was properly categorized as a class two hotel. Our room was just fair, yet the same price as we paid for the somewhat better class two hotel we had stayed in the night before. This hotel also had a patio, so once again we had a beer and relaxed there until dinner time. For dinner, Dorothy had a steak and I ordered a ham omelet. We also ordered a half-liter of wine. We couldn't make our waitress understand that we only wanted a half-liter; she brought us a full liter. We gave up and took the path of least resistance: we polished off the liter! As it turned out, this was the best meal we'd had since being in France.

Neither of us slept well that night because the bed was uncomfortable: the pillows were too thick and hard, like sleeping on a log, and the sheets kept crumpling up all night. Just another instance of the gypsy life.

We traveled on the west side of the Rhone River the next day, going north in the Rhone Valley. We drove through more wine country, often seeing ruins of castles and fortresses along the terraces of the steep hills. The terraces were held in place by rock walls. These ruins represented structures evidently built by the early Romans. We found them interesting to look at, and they broke up the monotony of driving. Rain hounded us nearly all that day, but we did get a break long enough to have lunch on the banks of the Rhone River.

At our usual time in the late afternoon, we started to look for a place to bed down for the night. We stopped in the tiny hamlet of Fleurville. The first hotel we came to was closed. The second one was too expensive, but the third one was OK. I should explain that in France there are no B&Bs or *zimmers*. Sometimes we found a *pension*, which is like a small hotel, but also serves meals. However, in nearly every village, hamlet, or town, we could find at least one hotel. This particular hotel looked weathered from the outside, but our room was clean and tidy, and that's what really mattered to us, considering what our wallet would allow.

There was very little to see in Fleurville, but we sauntered through this hamlet since we enjoyed walking. It was especially relaxing after a day of driving. Soon it was dinnertime, French-style—late.

The dining room was quite full for a change. Our dinner was rather elaborate that night. For starters, we each had six escargot. This was a rare treat for us. Dorothy then had a steak while I had braised short-ribs. We had a large salad, and for a pleasant change we had lyonnaise potatoes. This being Beaujolais country, we ordered a liter of Beaujolais wine. Dorothy's steak, like all the steaks we'd had thus far in France, was on the tough side, so we switched entrees. We topped off this savory meal with sherbet for dessert. The food was very good and plentiful; we were stuffed. The service was excellent also. This meal put a dent in our budget. The total cost, with tip, was twenty-five dollars. Big deal! Big meal!

Our bed was very comfortable. We both slept like babies. Our breakfast of croissants and French bread was mouth watering, but the coffee was mediocre, so we drank tea and hot chocolate. Paris was only one hundred kilometers away, so we took it easy. I didn't want to attempt driving into Paris to try to find reasonable accommodations in such a huge city. We decided to find a town near Paris to stay that night.

While driving through a small village, we noticed an open market, much to our delight. It was necessary to replenish our food supply, so

we purchased what were now our favorite deli foods: a couple of varieties of pate, Roquefort cheese, and a baguette of fresh French bread.
How we relished this simple selection of food. The scenery had
changed considerably, now that we were out of the Rhone Valley.
Instead of seeing picturesque vineyards on steep hillsides, and attractive small farms, we saw open hay fields.

After lunch, we drove just a short distance to the town of Esternay
and found a small hotel. The room was ordinary, but clean and adequate. Although it was early afternoon, our room was cold and there
was no heat. We had been noticing a definite change in the weather
the last few days. Fall was near. Actually, the date was 21 September,
the first day of autumn.

Dinner that night was simple and just fair. Dorothy had boiled chick-
en. I had a meat dish that was unfamiliar to me. Had I known what it
consisted of, I probably would have barfed. We did have smoked herring filets for hors d'oeuvres (which tasted very good), caramel pud-
ding for dessert, and a carafe of wine.

Barking dogs (the French have lots of dogs) kept us partially awake
that night. Therefore, we slept later. The coffee, that morning, was
much better. Over breakfast, we decided that we would drive to some
suburban town just outside Paris, spend the night there, and then go
into Paris by public transportation. Once in Paris, we could more carefully select a place to stay. We planned to stay at least a week in Paris.

With this plan in mind, we checked our maps and decided on the
suburban town of Lagny. Trying to find it was something else again.
We followed the signs carefully and still got lost more than once.
Finally we found it and began looking for hotels or *pensions*. We found
a very pretty *pension*, but the landlady said she was full. She was very
nice, and recommended another place. It was unattractive. We scout-
ed around and found a small hotel that was also unattractive, but an
improvement over the last one. The host said he had just one room
available and we took it, sight unseen, probably because this gentleman was so amiable. The room was very small and quite plain. The bed
was only a three-quarter-sized bed! There was a sink, no bath, and a
roll-away bidet. The lighting was so poor that we could just barely read.
The price was unbelievable, though, at just $13.75 per night.

When we got settled in this room, we went through our guide
books and maps and decided on a small hotel on the Left Bank of the

Seine River in "Gay Paree." I then settled down to write letters. I wrote a letter to our son and his wife on toilet paper, just as a gag! While touring the USSR, Poland, Czechoslovakia and even France, I had been collecting toilet paper samples, which I named. One sample I called "True Grit," another "Sandy." A few were named after two Russian newspapers, called "*Pravda*" and "*Izvetsia*." I named others "Thin Skin," and "Fingerfold." I was having fun and was going to give them to our grandkids as souvenirs.

We indulged in vodka and tonics before dinner, which was quite a switch. Then, shortly thereafter, we went to the dining room. I mentioned that this hotel, in appearance, was nothing to rave about, both inside and out.

The dining room, however, was a real eye-opener. It was rather large for such a small hotel. The tables were covered with pure white linen cloths, with matching napkins.

The table service was elegant. Each place setting had three fancy sparkling glasses and extra pieces of silverware. All this certainly seemed overly ostentatious for this place. We almost felt out of place, it was so elegant. We were the only diners, and the waiter seated us to a small table near the back. The menu showed two different price categories, one for thirty-one francs ($7.75) and the other for sixty-five francs ($16.25). I don't have to tell you which price we selected. By the time we added the 15 percent service charge and the tip, our dinners eased up to the budget-busting bracket. The dinner wasn't very high up on the "top ten" list. We were open to trying ethnic foods, but this meal was a bit too ethnic for our tastes. We had a platter of liver and kidney flambeau. Dorothy doesn't mind eating organs, but I'm squeamish. What we had eaten thus far of French cuisine didn't strike us as something special. Perhaps if we had dined in upscale restaurants, we'd have been more satisfied.

The next morning, we had a simple *petite dejeuner* (breakfast) with small portions, except that we got lots of butter and jelly. And yet our breakfasts cost nearly as much as our room. This small hotel was certainly an interesting establishment.

We took a bus from our hotel to the underground station and took the subway to the Paris Opera House. We had to pay to go into the Opera House, just to look around, but it was worth it. It's a splendid edifice. Nearby, we purchased a booklet, "Walking Tour of Paris in Three Days." With this booklet in hand, we were ready to "do" Paris.

Before we got walking, however, we went to a basement floor of the Opera House to telephone a small hotel we had picked out in one of our guide books. This hotel, the Grand Hotel de Lima, was on the Left Bank in the Latin Quarter, on the Seine River. It was right near the Cathedral Notre Dame and within walking distance of many of the places we wanted to see. Besides this, Frommer described the hotel as serving excellent coffee. This further induced us to stay there, but we had to call first to see if a room was available.

The toilets were on the same floor as the telephones. Knowing full well that we would have difficulty using the phone, we prevailed upon a young woman seated nearby, eating her lunch. She was selling toilet paper to the "needy." She consented to help us. However, it took her three times before we got connected. The first two times, I fouled things up, but she was a nice lady, and after she gave me the "My but you're stupid" look, she tried again. The third time was the charm. "Yes," I was told, "a room is available." So we reserved it for the next day.

This settled, we began walking. Although it may seem like it at times, this book is not really a guide book, so I am not going to attempt to describe all that we saw in this fabulous city. We visited the Church of Madeleine. We went to the Place de la Concorde to view the Egyptian Obelisk and the lovely fountains; then into the lovely Tuileries Gardens with its nice ponds, in which many children were having a ball sailing toy boats. From there, we went to the Jardins du Louvrie and into the world famous museum, the Louvre.

The Louvre is free on Sundays so there was quite a crowd. As at the Hermitage in Leningrad, it would take months to even begin to see all that was there. I'll name only a very few of the wonders.

As we entered the Louvre, we saw the statue of the Winged Victory. We also saw the marble statue of Venus de Milo, and then Leonardo da Vinci's "Mona Lisa." These priceless pieces of art are just three of hundreds upon hundreds of paintings, sculptures, and statues on exhibit here. Like the other tourists, we went from room to room, merely glancing at all these incredible, fabulous, exquisite works of art! We had been in Paris for just a few hours, and we could easily understand why many call this city the "crown jewel" of cities.

We'd seen plenty for one day, so we headed back to our hotel in Lagny. After resting up a bit, we went to the dining room for dinner. After the previous night's experience, we intended to play it safe.

Somewhere we had read that, according to the French, the test of a good cook is how well he or she makes mayonnaise and an omelet, so that night we ordered an omelet. Most everyone knows that drinking wine with every meal except breakfast is part of French culture. In fact, Dorothy and I had almost been doing so ever since we left England. But tonight, with omelets, we had no desire for wine, so we ordered hot chocolate. Our jovial host reacted as though we had just insulted all of France—in a jocular manner, of course! Dorothy insisted on chocolate, but in order to assuage our host, I settled for beer. It was not really the best choice with an omelet, but the omelets were delicious, and with French bread and sweet butter, it was a treat.

At this point I want to mention something regarding eating out in Paris. Although we didn't notice it until we got to Paris, a 15 percent service charge is added to your bill, which takes care of the tip.

I also don't want to forget to describe driving in Paris. Although we hadn't taken our car with us into Paris that day, it was clear that driving in the city is a cardiologist's delight. Just thinking of driving into Paris was giving me the heebie jeebies.

After breakfast, our nice landlord pointed out the way to get to the Left Bank: right through the center of Paris! Now I was really spooked. But we had no choice, so I gritted my teeth, battened down the hatches, and away we went. It's hard to believe that we didn't get lost once. I had to ask directions twice, merely to confirm I was on the right road.

There is one rule when driving in Paris: "Hurrah for me and the hell with you!" This goes for pedestrians also. Everyone is strictly on his or her own. And parking? It's preposterous! People park their cars anywhere they can find a space. They park on the curbs, on the sidewalks, in the alleys; they probably would park on someone's front porch if they thought they could get away with it. As I mentioned, we drove right to the hotel with no trouble at all. When we got there, it didn't surprise us that there was absolutely no place to park. I made a left turn and was going to double park, at least until I could unload our luggage, when, lo and behold, right in front of me was the only vacant space in all of Paris!

We unloaded our luggage, carried it up one flight of stairs to the desk, and were given our room. It was a fair room with a sink and bidet; showers cost extra. We got settled, and then made for the subway station nearby. As we went out the door of the hotel, we saw a *Complet* sign on the door, which meant "no vacancies." This was indeed our lucky day.

We took the subway to the American Express Office to arrange to have our car shipped to New Jersey and to arrange our flight to New York. We were told it would be cheaper to take the boat and train to London, and then fly to New York from there. This we did. It pleased us to know that the arrangements for shipping the car had been taken care of. They told us that a man would pick up our car—great!

While at this office, we also wanted to get tickets to the Opera for Wednesday, 26 September, Dorothy's birthday. The only seats available were the $37.50 or the $2.50. Even for Dorothy's birthday, we couldn't see spending $75, so we took the cheapies.

We took the subway back to our hotel. The Paris subway system is much simpler to figure out than the London underground. The trains are cleaner, smoother, and perhaps faster. There was also much less graffiti in the metro stations. We stopped for a snack at a sidewalk cafe, and had two small pizzas and two small beers. This had been a non-sightseeing day, but we did accomplish some important business. Feeling weary, we hit the sack early.

We got out of bed, dressed and ready for breakfast at eight o'clock, looking forward to that great coffee noted in our guide book. What a farce. We got the same warm, weak coffee we'd been getting all through France.

The Cathedral of Notre Dame was our first stop. It was just a short walk away. We walked along the Left Bank in the Latin Quarter, exposing ourselves to the sights, sounds, and smells of this unusual and exciting section of Paris. For several blocks, kiosks and their owners stood right next to each other along the river, vending and hustling prints, paintings, newspapers, magazines, maps, books, and photos of every description, size, and price. We were fascinated by all this, the poor people's Louvre. We had to cross a bridge over the Seine to get to the cathedral. We walked all around it and then went into it. It was very impressive. It was a massive, somber architectural masterpiece and it was jammed with tour groups.

From there we went to see the Monument to the Deportee, nearby on the Seine, where the Nazis, aided and abetted by the French Fascists, shipped the victims, mostly Jews, to various concentration camps by boat. This is a terrible testimony to man's depravity.

We visited the interesting Saint Jacques Tower, which is all that remains of the Church of Saint Jacques de la Boucherie. The church itself was demolished in 1797. It had been the church of the tripe seller's, knacker's, and tanner's guilds—a working man's church.

Then we sauntered to the Conciergerie Museum, but it was closed. Next, to the Palace and Gardens of Luxembourg, but we couldn't get in. Finally, we turned toward our hotel via the Rue de Bonaparte, seeing more churches and the art school. Along the way, we window shopped the art, artifact, and gift shops. We gawked at many of them.

When we got to our room, we called a French family whose son had stayed with our daughter and son-in-law, in Los Angeles, for several weeks during a past summer. The people we tried to reach weren't in, but their son said he would have them call us.

The next day was Wednesday, 26 September 1979—Dorothy's sixty-eighth birthday. We bought our own cheese to go with our breakfast of croissants, French bread, butter, jelly, and crummy coffee, the standard *petite dejeuner* we'd been having all along. Then we prepared to do more sightseeing.

Before we got away, a man came to pick up our car to be shipped. We went with him. After a couple of miles, he turned into a narrow street that had a big truck parked right in the middle. We waited and waited. Finally our man got out of our car to find out what was going on. He found out that the truck was there for the day. Only in Paris!

Our driver maneuvered our car, and by going quite a distance out of the way, got to his destination. We filled out all the necessary papers, paid for the shipping, and went on our way. We happened to be near the renowned Arc de Triomphe on the Place de L'Etoile. It was built in the early nineteenth century to commemorate the victories of Napoleon. We took the elevator to the roof, and there was a fantastic view of the twelve broad, tree-lined streets radiating from the Place de L'Etoile.

From there, we meandered down the world-famous Avenue des Champs Elysees. We stared open-mouthed at some of the fabulous jewelry, expensive clothing, and gifts we saw. Some of the shops had worldwide reputations. The same goes for Maxims Restaurant, made famous in song, dance, and literature. It's a wonder the city didn't charge for walking down this avenue!

We bought two small pastries at twenty cents each. On the street Rond Point we sat on a bench surrounded by lovely gardens, shrubs, and fountains, and ate our goodies. Next we went to the Grand Palais and the Petit Palais, where we took in the museum. It displayed mostly paintings, and was quite interesting. Last, we strolled to the Place de la Concorde to look it over. From there, we took the metro to our hotel.

It felt good to get off our feet and rest a bit before we showered, got dressed in our finery, and took off to the Opera House via the metro. The opera started at 7:30 P.M., and we thought we'd have plenty of time to eat before it started. We walked up and down the street; although we found several restaurants, none were open.

It was apparently too early for French diners. We had started to panic when, at last, we saw a fish restaurant that was open. A fish dinner wasn't quite what we had in mind, but we had no choice. We both decided on a fish platter. This meal was a disaster. It wasn't at all like a fish platter we would get in the US. This platter had all kinds of squiggly, ugly, gelatinous, smelly things on it. There were little tiny shrimp, tiny crabs, ugly little things in a shell, like sea snails, which you had to pick out with a thin nail-like pick. It had every kind of repulsive thing we'd ever seen. We're not big fish eaters, especially crustaceans, bivalves, and bivalve mollusks. We tried to peel the tiny shrimp and crabs, when a gentleman sitting at a table next to us shook his head no, no. He had seen what was happening and demonstrated to us that you ate these "goodies" whole and unpeeled!

The only saving grace to this meal was the wine, the French bread and butter, and the strawberry tarts for dessert. We both agreed, unequivocally, that this was the most unpleasant and most expensive meal we had ever eaten. The cost? Sixty-two dollars and fifty cents! Boy, did this meal ever leave a bad taste in our mouths, in more ways than one.

We had about fifteen minutes to get to the Opera, so we dashed over to it and then had to climb six flights of stairs to get to our seats. When we reached the seating area, an elderly lady greeted us. She was very plainly dressed in what looked like a uniform. She checked our tickets, then led us to a series of closed doors. She stopped at one, pulled out a large key like a jailer, and unlocked the door. She ushered us into a tiny cubicle that held four seats, and held out her hand for a tip. We were stunned. We had climbed six flights of stairs to a lousy $2.50 seat and she wanted a tip. Still, I didn't have the heart to refuse her.

To add insult to injury, the location of our box was such that we could see only the left-hand side of the stage. When the singers performed on the right-hand side, we could hear their voices, but couldn't see them. Worse yet, people stood below us, and they partially blocked what view we did have. The opera was Faust. As far as we were concerned, it should have been named "Farce-d."

What an evening it had been. On the way home, we said, "This has certainly been one hell of an experience!" Then we added, "We'll soon get over it and we'll have many laughs recalling it." That turned out to be true, whenever we would relate this incident to anyone. After all this, we certainly appreciated the thought of getting "home" and crawling into bed, as we were exhausted by the night's events. It wasn't a very happy birthday for Dorothy.

The next morning, after breakfast, we donned our walking shoes and took the metro to the Palace de Chaillot. We looked around, but found nothing special there to see. We took an hour-long boat ride down the Seine and back. it was a nice relaxing trip, but not exciting. From there, we went to the Eiffel Tower, a fascinating structure. We took the elevator to the top to observe the spectacular view of Paris. Then we walked along the Champs de Mars, with its pretty gardens, and next to the Military Academy, which was nothing much to see. On we went to the U.N.E.S.C.O. building, another impressive structure, but we didn't go in. Next, we went again to the Paris Opera House (this time for lunch), by way of the metro. We each had an elongated ham sandwich. Dorothy had coffee and I had a beer. this cost us ten dollars. It was a good thing we weren't going to stay in Paris much longer. At the American Express office, we got our tickets to go to London via Hovercraft and train. By this time, we were tired, so we went back to our room to rest.

At the proper French dining time of 7:15 P.M., we went out to eat. Near our hotel on the Boulevard St. Germain was a popular North African restaurant that specialized in couscous. We had heard it was very good. Never having eaten this type of food, we didn't know how to order. But, being hungry, we ordered the "Super Couscous." Don't ask—we had food coming out of our ears! We could have easily shared one order and still have had a lot left over. We were stuffed. It was so good, we both over-ate. Of course, we had to have our wine and dessert, peach melba, and a cup of African Orange tea. 'Twas a great meal and a delightful eating experience. We waddled back to the hotel and could barely make it up the stairs. We went to bed right away, just past eleven o'clock.

We woke the next morning to fall weather, but since we were walking, it was invigorating. Our first object of interest was to go into the Concierge. It is a rather infamous place. It was built in the Middle Ages as a government building. Later it became a prison. During the Reign of Terror, those destined for decapitation were imprisoned there. At the time of the French Revolution, many nobles and members of the royal family, including Marie Antoinette and some leaders of the Revolution, were executed there.

Next we went to the Pantheon to see the crypts that hold the bodies of such famous men as Voltaire, Zola, Victor Hugo, Braille, and many other important personalities. From there, we went to the Zoological Botanical Gardens of the Jardin des Plantes on the Seine. It was a charming place. We didn't see too much, because we didn't linger too long.

We went on to view the Colonne de Juliet, by way of the Austerlitz Bridge, located on Bastille Square. It was erected in 1840 to commemorate those who died in the 1830 Revolution. We continued on to the Place of Vasges, an area of many early seventeenth-century houses. It was quite interesting; Victor Hugo and Richelieu lived there.

Our footsies were smoking by this time, so we hopped on the metro. We enjoyed the Paris metro very much, and we pretty much got the hang of the system. The parents of the young man I referred to earlier had called back, and we made arrangements to go out for dinner that night. So when we got back from our walk, we rested a bit and then dressed in our best.

They picked us up at a quarter before eight. I judged their age to be in the early forties. They drove to a nice restaurant. It was now eight o'clock, and the restaurant was just opening. We asked them to order for us, as we wanted a real French meal. The menu was in French only, so we had no choice. They perused the menu carefully, and finally Paulette, the wife, suggested something which, she explained, was fried rabbit. I nearly went into shock!

Not that eating rabbit was repugnant to me, but, under the circumstances at that time, I just couldn't do it. What were the circumstances that created such a reaction? I had just finished reading the book *Watership Down*, a story all about the lives, loves, and habits of rabbits. No way could I eat rabbit.

I didn't explain my reluctance for this dish. We politely said we didn't prefer it. Paulette then ordered for us roast lamb shoulder chops. Our meal was pretty elaborate. For an appetizer, we had pate and eggs cooked in what we thought was chard. Next we had our just-fair chops, wine, I ate an apple tart and coffee. It was a very substantial meal. In all truthfulness, neither one of us had found French cuisine anything to rave about.

After this robust repast, Daniel and Paulette took us sightseeing. First, we went into a portion of the Halles Place. It was a shopping mall, not yet completed at that time, which descended five stories underground. You could buy anything there, from a "baby rattle to a clap of thunder!" There was even a public library. It was an astonishing place. Then we drove to the Montmarte section, parked, and walked around. This place was crowded with cars, buses, tourists, artists drawing pictures on the sidewalk for contributions, and musicians, also playing for contributions. Montmarte is a prominent tourist attraction. We saw the Moulin Rouge and the Follies Bregere, both from the outside. Lastly, we saw the Pigale section, or rather sex-tion! There was a thriving porno businesses in Pigale, of every description and category.

It was midnight when they took us back to our hotel. This had been a very full and satisfying day and night. Daniel and Paulette treated us especially nice and had shown us places in Paris that we would have never seen without them. We were also exposed to a tiny taste of Parisian night life.

We crawled out of bed a bit later the next morning. Our destination was Versailles, and the world famous Chateau de Versailles, the most beautiful of all palaces. We had to go by metro and train to get there. This palace was built for Louis XV at an enormous cost. It's a museum in itself. Surrounding the palace are magnificent gardens, fountains, and statuary. Almost every room on the first floor is a museum containing priceless paintings, unusual mirrors, historical works of art, and much more. Again we saw evidence of the opulent lifestyle of royalty. It is now a national monument.

The Chateau de Versailles was a remarkable and very impressive palace. It pleased us to have been able to see it. By this time, however, we were satiated with palaces, castles, museums, and churches, ad infinitum. We had reached the point where we desperately longed for a week or so in our club's mountain cabin, enveloped in peace and quiet. Nothing but birds, squirrels, and other wildlife to communicate with, and perhaps some close friends, too. We looked forward to savoring the taste of the clear, cold mountain water and the pungent air, redolent of pine trees.

Back in Paris, we went to bed early after dining, as Dorothy had a full-blown cold. The end of daylight savings time had caught us by surprise. We had forgotten about it, so when we went downstairs for breakfast, it was nearly ten o'clock. Later, we walked to the metro station and rode to the Place de la Concorde and started walking to the Louvre. We lingered on the way in the Tuileries and the Louvre Gardens, before going into the Louvre to see some of what we missed the previous Sunday. We took it easy, despite the rushing crowds. Then we meandered to the Opera, window shopping en route, to look at the expensive clothes, furs, and jewelry.

Dorothy's cold was worse, so we took the metro back to our room to rest. After a while, we went strolling again, this time along the Seine. I enjoyed looking over the block after block of stalls that I mentioned earlier. It was almost like going through another museum.

During this six month's trip, we'd probably walked more in Paris than in all the other cities combined. We had been walking for eight days and didn't begin to see much of what our Walking Tour of Paris promised. However, there was much more to see in this fabulous city, the cultural capital of the world, than was recorded in the tour books, especially when you do so much walking. One feature not listed was the people. They came in every size, shape, age, color, and from every part of the world. They dressed in every imaginable combination of clothes you could think of. Some attire was pretty weird. Every indication was that they enjoyed "Gay Paree" as much as we did. There were also the artists who drew rather interesting pictures in colored chalk. There were musicians everywhere, even riding the metro. Similar to the "sidewalk Cezannes," they were trying to scare up a few francs for their livelihood.

Walking the streets of Paris can be a harrowing experience. Pedestrians have less chance to stay alive there than they do in Moscow. There are many more vehicles in Paris than in Moscow. Not only did we have to be extremely careful crossing the streets, but we even had to dodge cars on the sidewalk! They drive crazily in Paris.

One other distraction is trying to avoid dog droppings. We saw a young woman holding a full grown dog in the palm of her hand. I took a picture of this, it was so astonishing. Paris is literally crawling with dogs. Between being careful to avoid this hazard and the automobiles, one is hardly able to see the sights!

After our walk along the Seine, it was dinner time. This time, we found a bistro, which is a small restaurant that specializes in wine. This bistro was jumping with tourists, mostly young people, eating and especially drinking. It was raucous, but everyone was having a good time. Our meal was pretty good and pretty cheap—just $13.75. For Paris, this is a bargain. If we got by for less than $25 for dinner for two, we felt we got a bargain.

We would imagine all these tourists, including ourselves, going back home and telling about how thrilling and exciting it was to eat and drink in a genuine Paris, Left Bank, Latin Quarter Bistro.

Monday, 1 October, was our last full day in Paris. We took our last sightseeing jaunt. By metro, we visited the statue of Joan of Arc, commemorating her effort to save Paris. She was wounded in the battle for this city. Then we walked some more, mostly killing time. We bought our son-in-law a Christian Dior necktie for $27.50—at 1979 prices! We also bought our landlady a pretty potted plant. Before we left the hotel, we had offered to sell our landlady the two sleeping bags we'd purchased in Poland. She, however, wasn't sure she wanted them. When we got back from our walk and went to the desk to pay our bill, she said she would take the sleeping bags. This was a break for us, as we didn't need them, now that we would soon be back in the US. They would be an extra burden. We paid our bill and presented her the plant. She was very pleased.

Meanwhile, as we stood at the desk, we encountered a couple from Vancouver, Canada, whom we had met previously. We chatted with this couple, named Norma and Jack. They invited us to their room, where we continued our conversation. Jack broke out a bottle of wine and the four of us proceeded to polish it off. It was getting near dinner time, so we decided to dine together. They knew of a small restaurant nearby that was in the correct financial category: real cheap.

When Dorothy and I first proposed that we all dine together, they were a bit reluctant to do so. Norma finally confessed that the both of them were suffering from a mild case of diarrhea! Upon hearing this, I told them about my problems in Lvov, USSR, and the incident with Maria, the doctor in Warsaw, Poland. I then went to our room, returned with the "Polish" pills, and gave them to Norma and Jack.

With this gesture, they decided to join us for dinner. It turned out to be a very pleasant evening: good food, good conversation, and good company. After this congenial get-together, we returned to their room, chatted some more, exchanged addresses, and then parted company near eleven o'clock. This was certainly a very gratifying way to spend our last night in Paris.

As an addendum to the incident with Norma and Jack, regarding the pills we gave them, we received a Christmas card from them, in which they thanked us for the pills. They said that those little pills were the ugliest pills they had ever taken in their lives, but they worked like magic!

Before retiring, we packed our suitcases. The next day, we would be in London. For all practical purposes, our trip to Europe, which began on 2 April, ended that last day in Paris.

Paris—the city that so many people dream of visiting someday. This was certainly true of us. And, as I have previously written about large European cities, there is just much too much to see, do, and indulge in, in such a short period of time as we had spent here. Paris is probably the most exciting city in Europe. It's a city of two thousand years of history, art, culture, and romance unequaled, perhaps, by any other major center. In our eight days here, with our limited funds, by boat, by train, by metro, and mostly by foot, we tried to see as much as we possibly could, experience whatever we could, and thereby capture the magic of "Gay Paree." We, like most all others, fell in love with her!

The only negative factors we can record are the high prices (especially for eating out); the French cuisine, which was disappointing for our tastes; and the driving conditions in the city—a nightmare! I might add that generally speaking, the people were not as outgoing or as warm as in other countries. Maybe they have too many tourists; maybe tourists expect too much of the French. Who knows? So we bid a final *au revoir* to Paris. We enjoyed our stay and we will miss you. We shall return!

We woke early, and breakfasted on our customary *petite dejeuner* of croissants and French bread. We said *au revoir* to the hotel staff, tipped the maids, and then took a taxi to the Gare du Nord train station. We were to leave on the ten-thirty train to the English Channel and go via Hovercraft to Folkestone, England. However, we had too much luggage for the Hovercraft, so we had to wait two hours for a regular ferry boat.

At eight o'clock on 2 October, we were back in the Victoria Station in London. There, we got a hotel close by through the hotel reservation desk, got settled, and then went out for dinner. We located a small restaurant and had fish and chips (what else in England?), a salad, and beer. It certainly felt good to once again hear English spoken, even if it was a bit difficult for us to understand.

Much to our dismay, the US dollar had shrunk in value by thirty-five cents on the pound since we were in England, six months previously. We purchased our plane tickets on Freddy Laker's airline, but on the flight two days away. Then we turned in.

Well, what a treat it was to once again sit down to an English breakfast. We got the works! Orange juice, corn flakes, bacon, one egg, toast (English toast that borders on cardboard), butter, jelly, and fair, but hot, coffee. When we left England five months before, we swore we would never be able to eat another English breakfast again. But that morning, it was most welcome and most delicious—almost.

Again we went walking after our big breakfast. We wandered to Buckingham Palace, but didn't see the changing of the guards. Then we strolled a while in St. James Park, and went back to the hotel.

Near the hotel, in Charing Cross, we noticed an acceptable restaurant which had a fairly nice dinner for thirty-five dollars. This being our last night in Europe, we splurged. We had previously purchased tickets to a play for thirty-seven dollars and ten cents for the both of us. This kind of entertainment in London is not cheap. After our dinner, we went to the theater. The play was *Once a Catholic*, a parody of a teen-aged girls class in a Catholic school. It was pretty raunchy! There was considerable emphasis on sexual behavior. We weren't overly impressed with the play. Maybe we're too prudish?

The next day, Thursday, 4 October 1979, was our very last day. it was not the "last supper," but the last breakfast we had in Europe before we were finally on our way to the USA!

We walked "the last mile" to Victoria Station; took the train to Gatwick Airport, suddenly realizing that this was where it all began six months ago. This was where we began the gypsy life. It was right here where we first entered "fairy tale" land. What fairy tales we now have to tell. What memories will live in our hearts and minds forever. What a trip!

To sum up our remarkable trip, and keep it brief, is somewhat of a task. But before I start, I must impart to you a confession Dorothy made to me right after we set foot on US soil. She said, "Honey, I don't know why, but I never expected we would come home from this trip alive!" She was that fearful of this overwhelming undertaking. I must admit that I, too, was a bit apprehensive, but not nearly to that extreme. We both had quite a chuckle over this.

The trip taught us many things. Foremost was what we learned about the people everywhere we went. I guess most all of us have a latent fear of the unknown, and this applies to people of a different color, country, culture, and tongue. Because of these differences, we tend to feel, subliminally, that they are different from us in many respects, even inferior! What we discovered on this trip, and on many others since, is that people are people, all over the world. We're convinced that people everywhere have the same hopes, the same dreams, and the same aspirations, especially their yearning for peace! This last is particularly true in the former USSR. We found that people want good health, security, a decent education, a good and secure job, etc. These are the same things that we desire for ourselves here in the US. With this knowledge, we became aware that no matter where you are and whom you meet, to paraphrase the Golden Rule: you must not do unto others as you would not have them do unto you! By practicing this common decency, the pleasure of our trip was greatly enhanced. In the final analysis, it is mainly the people you meet, not the places you see, that make your trip and leave you with the fondest memories.

In my introduction, I mentioned the advice given to us by a very dear friend, who said; "Wherever possible, find accommodations in Bed and Breakfast places or in private homes." Bed and Breakfast homes are quite different in Europe than here in America, excepting Hawaii. In the states, B&Bs are more like businesses and the fees are much higher. In Europe and in Hawaii, they are private homes, owned by working class families who need the extra money to supplement their income. As a result, the atmosphere is more friendly and warm. If you stay more than one night with a family, you are often accepted almost as a family member. In our case, whenever we stayed more than a couple of days with a family, we would always give the lady of the house a small gift. If there were children, we would give them something, also. The gifts didn't have to be expensive. It was just a nice gesture and was greatly appreciated by the recipient.

One other positive experience in the B&Bs had to do with eating. We often ate a lot of delicatessen dinners in our room in order to stay within our budget. In the B&Bs, we had many more conveniences than would be available in hotels. For example, if we needed any utensils, we never hesitated to ask for them, and they would always be provided willingly. In many instances, tea or coffee, fruit, etc., was served to us. Furthermore, we almost always would socialize with our host and hostess. This is truly how to get to know people. Despite the language barrier, we found that we could communicate, although sometimes inadequately.

I used the expression that we traveled like gypsies. Except for our stay in the USSR, in a sense we did. We had no strict itinerary that we had to adhere to. We would go where we chose and stay as long as we wanted. And, also like gypsies, our means of existing were somewhat austere. Perhaps we didn't see or do as much as we would have liked to, since money, or the lack of it, was a factor. Nevertheless, we felt we had gotten a great deal out of our trip. Aside from all the sights we saw and the things we did, we had such unbelievably great experiences that there is no way we could have put a price on them. You can't buy precious memories, you must experience them.

Finally, we left Europe with so many good impressions. Never did we have really bad one experiences. We learned so much about the history, geography, art, and culture of the countries we visited. Best of all was our involvement with the many people we met, in a variety of situations. This aspect was the richest and most rewarding of all our experiences. Our book of memories is replete with our encounters with these beautiful people.

Yes, the gypsy life is footloose and fancy free. That's just the way it ought to be—for us, the greatest experience in our lifetime.

Afterword

What you have just read is a journal of the six-month trip we took in 1979. In 1984, we returned to Europe for another six months. On this second trip we did pretty much as we did in 1979.

We purchased another Volkswagen (we had sold the first one), only this time we picked it up directly at the factory in Wolfsburg, West Germany. Again we spent five months driving on the continent and one month in Great Britain without a car.

On this second trip, we skipped some countries we visited in 1979, and instead visited some other ones: Italy, Greece, and Yugoslavia. This second trip was prompted primarily by several of the people who worked for Intourist, the Soviet State Tourist Department. When we had the occasion to be critical of some of the conditions we experienced in the campgrounds, dining places, etc., they, in almost every instance, urged us to return in five years. They claimed that the next Five Year Plan of the government was to concentrate on the production of more consumer goods and to increase the quality of production. This would then translate into an improvement in the standard of living. That, in turn, would reflect favorably on all aspects of life in the USSR, both for their people and for tourists. So return we did.

During this second trip, we stayed a week longer in the USSR than we did in 1979, drove two thousand miles more and visited other parts of the country. However, because we stayed in motels rather than campgrounds, we didn't have many opportunities to duplicate the unusual experiences we had on our first trip. We had much less contact with the natives, other than hotel, restaurant, and Intourist employees.

In several instances, we stayed with people we had met on our previous trip, and who had invited us to stay with them. In some countries, we stayed in the same B&Bs as we did on our 1979 trip. As a result, we spent many more nights in hotels, pensions, and *gasthouses*. These conditions restricted our opportunities to meet new people and experience new and exciting adventures. Our gypsy way of traveling was, to a degree, inhibited.

During our 1984 trip to the USSR, we stayed in motels, which are similar to hotels except that they are much cheaper, a bit poorer in quality, and generally located away from the center of town. We weren't aware of this last fact when we planned our itinerary. As a result, we either had to use public transportation if we wished to go into town, or else drive, which we tried to avoid doing.

In Leningrad we stayed in the Hotel Olgino; it was about nine miles from the center of Leningrad. One day, we arranged to take a bus tour of the city. On the bus with us was a younger couple from Holland and their son, Hans, a recent college graduate. We introduced ourselves. Their names were Gerta and Teakle. They lived in the city of Hoogeveen. As in several other instances, Teakle and Hans spoke English quite well, but Gerta didn't, even though she understood pretty much of what we had to say. The tour was very good. We saw many things that we hadn't seen in 1979.

When we got back to the Leningrad Hotel, our starting point, it started to rain very hard. Our new Dutch friends said to us, "We are going to the Hermitage Museum. Would you care to join us?" We answered, "Of course." So the five of us piled into their small car and off we went.

Since they were Hollanders, they were interested in going to the room that displayed many paintings of famous Dutch painters. This display consisted of paintings by some of Holland's great painters and covered several centuries of Dutch art. Among these priceless paintings, we gazed in awe at those by the greatest of the great: Lucas van Leaden, Jan Vermeer, Rembrandt, Vincent van Gogh, and others.

When we finished with the museum, we went to the Europa Hotel for coffee and cake. Later we visited several shops. Gerta wanted to buy an umbrella, but the cheapest one was twenty-eight dollars. She didn't buy it. Hans wanted some particular maps. He located a store, and it was stacked to the rafters with posters and cards. He bought maps, and we bought cards. All this time, it was raining hard, so we decided to go back to our hotel. Our friends were camping, and we felt sorry that they had to put up with the nasty weather, so we invited them to join us for dinner.

Before we went to the main dining room of the hotel, Dorothy and I went to a *Beriozkya* store and purchased a half-liter of vodka and some soft drinks. Then we all went to our room for a "happy hour." Oh yes—the vodka cost us nearly five times what we paid in 1979!

Now that we all felt warm, dry, and relaxed, we went to dinner. While dining, the band arrived; as on our previous trip, it played loud and lousy rock. We wanted to pay for the meal, but Teakle insisted on paying part of it.

Despite everything, it was very pleasant being with these folks. We enjoyed their company very much. As in the past on similar occasions, we exchanged addresses. They insisted that we visit them in Holland before we went back to the US. It was highly improbable we could do so. However, in 1986, Gerta and Teakle came to visit us. We arranged to meet them in Salem, Oregon, where they had friends, and drive from there to Vancouver, B.C. for the 1986 World Exposition. Afterwards, we drove back to our home. We spent time together for about three weeks and had a marvelous time. They are our kind of folks: modest, unassuming, and down-to-earth. Teakle is a retired school principal. We have been corresponding with each other ever since we first met.

During our trip in 1979, I told of several unusual experiences we had with people we unexpectedly encountered. We have also kept up a correspondence with many of them. So, when we informed them in our letters that we might revisit Europe, they all insisted we visit them.

One of these exceptional visits began while on a tour bus in East Germany in 1979. The following tale pertains to the couple we met on that tour, Margaret and Jack, who live in Kennington, England. I have stated that it is not often that, on a tour, you meet people with whom you establish close relationships. Margaret and Jack were the exceptions. Although we knew each other for just a very brief time, we soon discovered that we had much in common, politically and philosophically. From the time we returned to our home after the 1979 trip, we corresponded with each other. Consequently, when we planned to visit Europe in 1984, they invited us to visit them. We did.

We spent four unforgettable days with them. They are a very cultured, refined, and educated couple. They are immersed in music and art, and very active in the peace movement and other areas relating to social concerns. As the four of us were so compatible, we got along nicely.

While there, they drove us to the beautiful Cotswold country, to small historic villages whose names are so fascinating. They took us to Greenham Commons, where the Women's Peace Movement was camping and picketing the US cruise missiles placed on a British military base. We talked with some of the women campers, many of whom had been protesting for weeks. They lived in tents and other makeshift accommodations. The stories they liked to tell would tear at your heart. They honestly lived like gypsies; dedicating themselves, body and soul, to the cause of peace. We contributed to their cause, generously.

In the course of these four days with Margaret and Jack, we met their son, Mike, and other folks. One gentleman was a publisher of a magazine devoted to country living and environmental issues. On the last night of our visit, they invited several of their friends of like-minded interests to meet us. We felt quite honored by this warm gesture.

We had a fabulous time with this lovely couple. Only in the farthest stretch of our imagination could we have predicted such a remarkable happening, all through a chance meeting.

When we got to Yugoslavia, we made it a point to visit Sarajevo. It was a beautiful drive along the Adriatic Coast, then northeast into the equally beautiful mountains.

Upon arriving in Sarajevo, we had some difficulty finding accommodations. The reason for this was because the 1984 Winter Olympics had been held there the previous winter. Due to all the worldwide publicity the city got because of this event, it subsequently became a tourist attraction.

We drove to the center of the city and noticed a small hotel, but there were no vacancies. While standing on the corner, a young girl, passing by, stared at us so intently that Dorothy asked if she could speak English. She quickly replied, "Yes. Can I help you?" We explained our dilemma. She then took us to two other hotels, but we had no luck. She led us to the Tourist Office. There the lady clerk checked around and told us that the only available accommodations would be at a new motel, out of town a ways. We knew where it was, since we had passed it coming in.

This problem solved, our young guide, Aida, said, "Tomorrow is Saturday, so I have no school. Would you like me to take you around and show you Sarajevo?" Naturally, we jumped at the opportunity and made arrangements to meet at noon at a selected place. We then parted and drove to the motel.

That night, it poured, and was still raining pretty hard when we got up for breakfast. Shortly after breakfast, we got a phone call in our room. It was Aida. She was clever enough to locate us though she didn't know our name. She called to see about our planned get-together later. She said, "You know it's raining now. Do you still want to go out?" I replied, "If you are willing, we are too." Then she asked, "Do you have rain clothes?" I said, "Yes we do. We also have umbrellas." With that, she said, "OK, I'll meet you when and where we had previously arranged to meet." By the time we met, the skies had cleared and the weather was delightful. We had come by tram, and met Aida at the appointed time and place.

Let me describe Aida. She was small in stature, cute as a doll, with bright eyes and a look of self-confidence and self-assurance. In the few moments we spoke with her, we could plainly see that she was as bright as a new penny. She spoke very good English. But more important than anything else, we felt completely at ease with her.

By the time we met, it was lunch time and we asked Aida to take us to a restaurant. She said, "If you wish I will take you where the students eat." This was fine with us. We had a nice lunch of ethnic food. The main dish was a dough-covered meatball with potatoes. In the course of our conversation, we learned that Aida was sixteen years old. I asked how she learned to speak English so well. She said, "I study it in school," and she told us, "When the Olympics were held here last winter, I volunteered to help out. I was assigned to the American team." She said she fell in love with the American athletes.

I then asked her, "Aida, would you like to visit America?" "Oh yes," she replied. Then I asked, "Would you like to live in America?" "I don't think so," she said. "Why not?" I asked. "Well," she replied, "in America you can say anything you want to," she hesitated a moment, "but nobody listens! In my country, often times, somebody does listen!" Dorothy and I were speechless. "Out of the mouths of babes," we thought. She was very sharp and well informed.

Aida then led us through Old Town, the old Turkish section of the city, and into an old Turkish mosque, where people prayed. While in Old Town, we went to a section where local artisans created a whole variety of gadgets from metal, mostly copper and brass: utensils, souvenirs, gift items, and the like. They did this exquisite work with simple tools. It was exceptional workmanship. Then we went to an historical museum and to the spot where Franz Joseph Ferdinand, Crown Prince of Austria, was assassinated—an event which touched off World War I. Later we went to a supermarket where we shopped for food, and also bought Aida a small bottle of perfume. By this time, Dorothy and I felt tired. Like the old gray mare, we ain't what we used to be!

Earlier, when we had arranged for Aida to show us around, she had said, "After our walk, I'll take you to my house for some Turkish coffee." The walk to her house was quite lengthy, for a couple of tired oldies. As it turned out, her "house" was an apartment house and her apartment was four flights up, with no lift. We barely made it.

Apparently, she had told her parents that she was bringing company, for as we entered this large apartment, we were greeted by a "welcoming committee" of her parents, grandmother, aunt, and some neighbors. This was certainly a pleasant surprise—with all this unexpected attention. Only Aida could speak English, but the others, with big, friendly smiles and gestures, made us feel very comfortable. Aida's mother escorted us to chairs. The apartment was not only large, but also spotless and well furnished. They pampered us with pillows to insure our comfort. When we were seated, Aida's father brought out wine plus the Yugoslavian traditional drink: homemade *slivovitz* (plum brandy—dynamite!) The drinks further warmed an already warm atmosphere.

I called Aida over and told her to tell her parents that we intended to take her to California with us. Of course everyone laughed over this. Then Grandma brought us her homemade goodies, a platter of *sitnicas* (like our cheese knishes) with a platter of sliced cucumbers, a platter of *ruzicas* (somewhat like honey-less honey cake), and Turkish coffee. Mother served the coffee in beautiful tiny cups and saucers.

Everything was so delicious, especially Grandma's contributions, that I was prompted to tell Aida to tell everyone that we had decided that, rather than take her to California, we would take her grandmother! Needless to say, we thought the roof was going to fall in with all the laughter and shouting after Aida told them this. It was hilarious.

Grandma was so pleased with us that, with vigorous gesticulations and Aida's interpretations, she insisted we stay with them! Aida knew we couldn't, and explained it to her.

It was soon time to leave, and we presented Aida with the bottle of perfume. She was so elated she dashed out of the room and returned to give us an official book of the Winter Olympics, in English; an Olympic key chain; and three lapel buttons, replicas of the first, second, and third place medals given at the Olympic event. It was our turn to be overwhelmed.

Meanwhile, Mama and Grandma were still plying us with food. We both seemed ready to *platz*! Papa had to leave, and about an hour later, we bade them all the fondest of farewells.

Again Dorothy and I looked at each other and shook our heads in amazement over this rare, totally unexpected, and pleasurable event. We felt especially pleased by our relations with Aida. For total strangers, with an age gap of more than two generations, it was amazing how at ease we felt with each other.

At one time, we got on the subject of politics. She knew more about the US than most American kids her age know about America! I would guess that very few American kids know much about Yugoslavia. She was, in every respect, a gem. This event was truly a fairy tale experience for us.

I chose to close this "Gypsy Journal" with this final event to once more illustrate what remarkable adventures we experienced during our trips to Europe. Like our friend, who advised us how to travel, we advise you to do likewise. Stay in B&Bs where possible. Seek private homes, if available. In Europe, travel like the not-so-rich Europeans.

We feel safe in saying that what you'll remember most from your trip will be your experiences and involvement with the people you meet, if it is more than a casual meeting.

Enjoy! Enjoy!